·新体验商务英语系列教材·

现代商务英语写作

Modern Business English Writing

主编 束光辉
编者 束光辉 东 刚

清华大学出版社
北京交通大学出版社
·北京·

内容简介

本书共17个单元,主要内容包括商务信函的构成、商务信函的语言风格与文化认知、商务信函的语气、询购函、回复函、拒绝函、友好与社交信函、办公室日常信函、备忘录、电子邮件、通告、销售信函、广告、商务报告、合同、调查问卷、商务概要、就业写作等。

本书所涵盖的内容较为全面,涉及商务环境中主要信函及文本的写作。本书中所有信函、文本的范文均来自各种商务实践工作,同时文本的选择还兼顾了商务写作的得体性和功能性,表现了文本作者的写作目的和期望所达到的效果,能够让读者学到真实的写作技巧并体验到商务信函的写作风格。

本书可供英语专业学生、商务英语专业学生及具有较好英语基础的其他经贸专业学生作为教材使用,同时也可用作外企白领阶层和其他商务英语写作爱好者的自学用书。

本书封面贴有清华大学出版社防伪标签,无标签者不得销售。
版权所有,侵权必究。侵权举报电话:010-62782989　13501256678　13801310933

图书在版编目(CIP)数据

现代商务英语写作/束光辉主编. —北京:北京交通大学出版社:清华大学出版社,2016.4(2018.7重印)
ISBN 978-7-5121-1826-3

Ⅰ. ①现… Ⅱ. ①束… Ⅲ. ①商务-英语-写作 Ⅳ. ①H315

中国版本图书馆CIP数据核字(2014)020396号

现代商务英语写作
XIANDAI SHANGWU YINGYU XIEZUO

责任编辑:张利军	
出版发行:清华大学出版社　　邮编:100084　　电话:010-62776969	
北京交通大学出版社　邮编:100044　　电话:010-51686414	
印　刷　者:北京时代华都印刷有限公司	
经　　销:全国新华书店	
开　　本:185 mm×260 mm　　印张:20.25　　字数:505千字	
版　　次:2016年4月第1版　2018年7月第2次印刷	
书　　号:ISBN 978-7-5121-1826-3/H·392	
印　　数:2 001~3 500册　　定价:39.00元	

本书如有质量问题,请向北京交通大学出版社质监组反映。对您的意见和批评,我们表示欢迎和感谢。
投诉电话:010-51686043,51686008;传真:010-62225406;E-mail:press@bjtu.edu.cn。

　　进入 21 世纪，随着全球经济一体化进程的加快，我国与世界的经贸联系更加紧密，贸易形式更趋多元化。与此相伴的是，中国的商务英语教学与研究也发生了巨大的变化。这至少表现在以下几个方面：第一，如今，商务英语已是一个相当大的概念，它已从最早的一门单一的"外贸英语函电"课程发展到了涉及金融、保险、国际企业管理、国际经济法、海外投资与企业合作等多领域的学科；第二，人们对商务英语学习的需求持续旺盛，不仅几乎全国所有的高校都开设了商务英语专业或课程，而且越来越多的企业在职人员也迫切需要学习商务英语；第三，外语界对商务英语的研究也提高到了一个新的层次。

　　为了适应新的形势，许多高校都正在对一些传统的经贸英语类课程进行调整、改革和扩充，以培养新型的国际商务专业人才。这就向教材建设提出了更高的要求。教材不仅是教学内容的表现，更体现了人才培养的规格。纵观过去的一些教材，我们便不难发现，无论从内容上还是体例上，它们都已远远落后于当今国际经贸发展的形势，例如大多围绕语法、词汇和翻译等来展开，缺乏商务英语专业的实践性和语言的真实性，难以满足工作的需要。而另一些教材则又过于突出"专业"的内容，把商务英语教材混同于国际商务专业教材。因此，编写能够适应时代要求的国际商务英语教材显得尤为重要。正是在这样的背景下，由束光辉老师主编的"新体验商务英语系列教材"面世了，它体现了"贴近时代，融合语言与专业"的编写理念，是一次积极而大胆的尝试。

　　该系列包括《进出口贸易实务》《现代商务英语写作》《商务英语函电与合同》《商务报刊选读》《商务英语汉英翻译教程》《跨文化商务沟通》等教材。它们在内容设计和编写形式上具有以下特点。

1. 融专业性与语言技能于一体

　　该系列教材在编写上突出了以培养学生的实际工作能力为目标的思路，所选材料涉及了商务环境的各个方面，均能反映出商务工作实践性的特点，同时也体现了语言技能系统化培养的理念。该系列教材通过拟定各种商务环境，将商务知识和语言技能融合在一起，使学生的语言应用能力在更接近于真实的商务实践中得以提高。

I

2. 选材新，贴近时代

该系列教材在材料选择上参考了国内外最近几年出版的教材和其他相关材料，充分吸收了国内外最新的教学科研成果，体现了国际商务活动不断变化的特点和商务领域专业性的特点，具有鲜明的时代特征。同时，该系列教材的许多文本、范例和研究材料均来自于近年来各类商务实践，体现了商务英语的真实性和实践性。

3. 练习形式多样，针对性强

该系列教材的练习将语言技能训练与商务环境较好地结合在一起，通过各种题型，对所涉及的商务环节和领域，有针对性地对学生进行训练。这不仅能够巩固学生所学的专业知识，而且还将提高他们的语言技能。

21世纪的中国更加开放，更加开放的中国在诸多方面都在与世界接轨。作为国际商务沟通的一个重要工具，商务英语的教学和研究理应跟上时代的发展和社会的需求。我们要更加重视并加强对商务英语教学的研究。该系列教材的编写是一次很好的探索，希望借此能进一步提高我国高校商务英语的教学和科研水平，为培养我国新型国际商务专业人才做出贡献。

中国国际贸易学会
国际商务英语研究委员会
原副主任
2016年3月

前言

商务英语写作是国际商务人员必须具备的业务技能之一,也是商务英语学生的必修课。在国际商务活动中,如何进行有效的对外沟通是决定业务成败极为重要的一个因素。因此,帮助学生学会各种商务英语写作技巧,培养较好的写作能力,是目前商务英语教学的重要任务之一。正是本着这样的认识,我们编写了这本教材。

本书几乎全部用英文编写,所涵盖的内容较为全面,涉及商务环境中主要信函及文本的写作。本书中所有信函、文本的范文均来自各种商务实践工作,同时文本的选择还兼顾了商务写作的得体性和功能性,表现了文本作者的写作目的和期望所达到的效果,能够让学生学到真实的写作技巧并体验到商务信函的写作风格。

本书共17个单元,主要内容包括:商务信函的构成、商务信函的语言风格与文化认知、商务信函的语气、询购函、回复函、拒绝函、友好与社交信函、办公室日常信函、备忘录、电子邮件、通告、销售信函、广告、商务报告、合同、调查问卷、商务概要、就业写作等。

本书有以下特点。

(1) 本书所收录的信样十分详尽。每一单元所涉及的信函样本多达近十封,而且写作风格也不尽相同。每单元均配有详细的注释译文和生词表,以便于读者更好地掌握和理解。

(2) 本书对各种写作技巧进行了全面的介绍,不但采用了国外较新的商务写作材料,而且结合国内的商务写作惯例来进行编写。同时,本书还吸收了国外商务沟通的最新成果,从交际学的原则出发,突出读者的心理需求在交际过程中的作用。此外,本书对这些信函及文本的典型句型进行了提炼和归纳,有利于学生更好地掌握和应用商务写作的常见句式。

(3) 本书的练习注重语言能力的培养,内容逼真,形式多样,贴近实际。本书克服了国内同类教材重语言形式、轻语言运用能力之弊端,将练习的重点放在语言的运用能力上,即突出学生篇章、文本写作交际能力的培养,通过拟定各种商务环境,让学生有针对性地进行写作训练，使他们的商务写作更接近真实的商务实践。同时，练习中还提供了一些写得欠妥的信样让学生去分析、改正，以培养学生的创造能力和分析能力，而不是简单地模仿。

　　本书的主要读者对象为英语专业学生、商务英语专业学生及具有较好英语基础的其他经贸专业学生，同时也可用作外企白领阶层和其他商务英语写作爱好者的自学用书。

　　本书由束光辉担任主编，东刚参加编写。其中，束光辉编写了前 10 个单元的课文和练习，以及后 7 个单元的部分练习；东刚编写了后 7 个单元的课文和部分练习。

　　本书的编写与出版得到了北京交通大学语言与传播学院领导的大力支持及北京交通大学出版社张利军编辑的热情帮助，在此一并表示衷心的感谢。

编　者

2016 年 3 月

Contents

Unit 1　The Components of Business Letters
　　商务信函的构成 ……………………………………………………………… (1)
　1.1　The Essential Parts of a Business Letter ……………………………… (1)
　1.2　The Optional Parts of a Business Letter ……………………………… (3)
　1.3　The Formats of a Business Letter ……………………………………… (5)
　1.4　The Overall Appearance of a Business Letter ………………………… (9)

Unit 2　Language Style and Cultural Awareness of Business Letters
　　商务信函的语言风格与文化认知 ………………………………………… (13)
　2.1　Concise ……………………………………………………………………… (13)
　2.2　Intercultural Awareness …………………………………………………… (16)

Unit 3　The Tone of a Business Letter
　　商务信函的语气 …………………………………………………………… (21)
　3.1　Writing for Your Audience ……………………………………………… (21)
　3.2　Three Approaches in Dealing with Messages ………………………… (26)

Unit 4　Inquiries
　　询购函 ………………………………………………………………………… (36)
　4.1　Introduction ………………………………………………………………… (36)
　4.2　Sample Letters …………………………………………………………… (36)

Unit 5　Replies
　　回复函 ………………………………………………………………………… (47)
　5.1　Introduction ………………………………………………………………… (47)
　5.2　Sample Letters …………………………………………………………… (48)

I

Unit 6　Letters of Declining
拒绝函 ··· (60)
- 6.1　Introduction ··· (60)
- 6.2　Sample Letters ··· (61)

Unit 7　Goodwill and Social Letters
友好与社交信函 ··· (70)
- 7.1　Invitation Letter ·· (70)
- 7.2　Letter of Thanks ·· (80)
- 7.3　Letter of Congratulations ······································ (84)
- 7.4　Letter of Sympathy and Condolence ··················· (89)
- 7.5　Letter of Complaints and Claims ·························· (93)

Unit 8　Interoffice Routine Letters
办公室日常信函 ··· (111)
- 8.1　Letter of Appointment ··· (111)
- 8.2　Letter of Introduction ·· (118)
- 8.3　Letter of Recommendation ·································· (122)
- 8.4　Letter of Notification ··· (127)

Unit 9　Memos, E-mails and Notices
备忘录、电子邮件及通告 ··· (143)
- 9.1　Memos ·· (143)
- 9.2　E-mails ·· (151)
- 9.3　Notices ··· (153)

Unit 10　Sales Letters and Advertisement
销售信函与广告 ··· (163)
- 10.1　Introduction ·· (163)
- 10.2　Sales Letters ··· (165)
- 10.3　Advertisement ··· (175)

Unit 11　Business Reports（Ⅰ）
商务报告（一）·· (187)
- 11.1　The Introduction to Reports ······························· (187)
- 11.2　Components of a Business Report ··················· (194)

Unit 12　Business Reports (II)
　　商务报告（二） ……………………………………………………… (200)
12.1　Informational Reports ………………………………………………… (200)
12.2　Analytical Reports and Feasibility Reports ………………………… (210)

Unit 13　Business Reports (III)
　　商务报告（三） ……………………………………………………… (217)
13.1　Proposal Reports ………………………………………………………… (217)
13.2　Annual Report …………………………………………………………… (224)

Unit 14　Contracts
　　合同 …………………………………………………………………… (239)
14.1　Types of Business Contracts ………………………………………… (239)
14.2　Components of a Business Contract ………………………………… (241)
14.3　Language and Stylistics Features …………………………………… (241)
14.4　Layout …………………………………………………………………… (244)
14.5　Writing Steps …………………………………………………………… (245)
14.6　Samples ………………………………………………………………… (247)

Unit 15　Questionnaires
　　调查问卷 ……………………………………………………………… (265)
15.1　Introduction …………………………………………………………… (265)
15.2　Types of Questionnaire ……………………………………………… (265)
15.3　Layout of a Questionnaire …………………………………………… (266)
15.4　Preparing a Questionnaire …………………………………………… (268)
15.5　Interpreting the Findings …………………………………………… (269)
15.6　Samples ………………………………………………………………… (270)

Unit 16　Business Summary
　　商务概要 ……………………………………………………………… (279)
16.1　Introduction …………………………………………………………… (279)
16.2　Features of a Well-written Summary ……………………………… (279)
16.3　Writing a Summary …………………………………………………… (280)
16.4　Checklist and List for Speech ……………………………………… (283)

Unit 17　Employment Writing
　　就业写作 ……………………………………………………………… (291)
17.1　Job Description ………………………………………………………… (291)
17.2　Job Application Letter ………………………………………………… (293)

17.3 Curriculum Vitae ·· (296)
17.4 Job Offer and Acceptance ·· (301)
17.5 Reference Check ·· (304)

References ·· (312)
参考文献

Unit 1

The Components of Business Letters
商务信函的构成

1.1 The Essential Parts of a Business Letter

Business letters are the main means of written communication to establish business relations with the outside world. Business letters are sent out to convey the image of a business organization, therefore they must be presented on quality letterhead paper, with suitable layout, well-structured message, correct use of English and appropriate tone. A typical business letter consists of seven parts: the letterhead, the date, the inside address, the salutation, the body of the letter, the complimentary close, and the signature.

1. The Letterhead

The letterhead occupies the top most part of the paper. It usually consists of the name, address, telephone number and fax number of a company. The letterhead can be typed out but is usually printed on the company's stationery. Sometimes it also includes other items like the company logo, website, e-mail address, etc.

2. The Date

The date consists of the date, the month, and the year. The common ones are M/D/Y (widely used in US), D/M/Y (typical in the Great Britain). Do not use all figures in the writing of the date, i. e. 12/6/15, because not all English-speaking people agree about whether the month or the date appears first. Some people have the habit of abbreviating the date, but this is not recommended for business letters, for this will create confusion.

3. The Inside Address

The inside address is the recipient's address, the same as the delivery address on the envelope. The inside address should include the reader's name, title, and address. The inside address is placed at the left margin both with the block and modified block styles. Depending on the length of the letter, place the inside address two or four-line spaces below the date line. The full name of the recipient is required with a courtesy title before it, e.g. Mr., Mrs., Miss, etc. The address is typed as it will appear on the envelope.

4. Salutation

For most letter styles, place the letter greeting or salutation two lines below the last line of the inside address or the attention line (if used). If the letter is addressed to an individual, use that person's courtesy title and last name, e.g. Dear Miss Helen. The salutation varies according to the writer-recipient relations and the formality level of the letter. "Dear Sir", "Dear Sir or Madam" or "Dear Sirs" and "Ladies and Gentlemen" can be used to address a person of whom you know neither the name nor the sex.

Sometimes some special titles may be used as the salutation. They are preceded by Dear and followed by the surname only, e.g. Dear Dr. Watson, or Dear Prof. Young. Be sure to add a colon or a comma, (not a semicolon) after the salutation.

Examples of typical salutations are:

Dear Mr. ×××

Dear Mrs. ×××

Dear Miss ×××

Dear Ms. ×××

Dear Dr. ×××

Dear Prof. ×××

Dear Sir(s)

Gentlemen

Ladies and Gentlemen

To Whom It May Concern

5. The Letter Body

It is the central part of the letter, usually following a subject line. If there is no subject line between, the message begins two lines below the salutation. Double spacing is used to separate paragraphs in the letter body.

The closing sentence

At the end of the body, the sender wants to express a certain courtesy or a wish to further contact the recipient, he or she may usually start with:

- We are expecting your immediate reply.
- Looking forward to your detailed reply soon.
- I am looking forward to your reply soon.

Or just to show a kind of consideration or trying to be considerate by simply saying:

- If you have any questions, please let me know, etc.
- If you have any questions, please feel free to contact me.

6. The Complimentary Close

The complimentary close provides the writer of a business letter with an opportunity to say "Goodbye" at the end of his written "conversation". In this way it is the same as the salutation saying "Hello" at the beginning at the message.

There are a number of standards and accepted forms which may be used for the complimentary close. However, whatever they are, they should be chosen carefully to agree in tone and manner with the salutation used at the beginning.[1] The most commonly used forms for the complimentary close of a letter are listed below.

"Yours faithfully" is used in letters beginning with "Dear Sirs", "Dear Sir or Madam" or "Dear Sirs" and "Yours sincerely" is used to match "Dear (name)" letters, or rather formal "Yours truly" and the most formal, "Yours respectfully" or "Respectfully yours" or simply "Respectfully".

7. Signature

Every business letter must be signed. The signature indicates the approval of the responsibility for the content of the letter.

Type your full name on the fourth or the fifth line below and align with the complimentary close. Sign your name in the triple space between the two.

In most business letters the type-written signature and the title of the writer are needed to help the reader decipher illegible signature. The type-written signature and the title are typed below the hand-written signature, for example:

> Yours faithfully
> (Your signature)
> Ma Qiang
> Personnel Director

1.2 The Optional Parts of a Business Letter

For one reason or another, you may need more parts to be included in a business letter, say to direct the letter to a specific person without your knowing the name of that person. Any one or all the parts listed in this section can be added to the letter.

1. The Return Address

In most cases, the return address is printed on the letterhead. It is necessary only when you are using a blank sheet of paper.

2. The Attention Line

If you want your letter attended by or directed to a specific person or department, add an attention line. This will speed up the sorting process within a company. For instance, it can indicate by "attention: Mr. Zhao" or "attn: Mr. Zhao".

3. The Subject Line

It is written to indicate the subject and purpose of the letter so that recipients can easily identify the contents of the letter. There are a few ways to write the subject line.

- American Cars
- Re: Your order No. 453 for electric drills
- Subject: Insurance policy No. 234

4. The Enclosure Notation[2]

When something else is sent together with the letter, you add the enclosure notation to inform the reader of what is enclosed. The notation may be spelled out (Enclosure/Attachment), or it may be abbreviated (Enc./At.). It may indicate the number of enclosures or attachments, and it may also identify an enclosure specifically (Enclosure: Copy of Invoice 3505).

5. The Postscript Notation[3]

The postscript is used to add an afterthought. In sales letters, it is used mainly as added punch. If copies of a business letter have been made for other individuals, a copy notation is typed one or two lines below the enclosure notation. A colon following is optional. Most people prefer to use notations like CC, cc, Cc, which all means carbon copy. Since most copies are now photocopied, some people use the notation XC (Xerox copy), PC (photo copy), or C (copy). However, if you do not want the addressee to know that someone else is receiving a copy, do not include this notation on the original copy.

Sample Letter

◆◆ Star Bank ◆◆
45 River Road Stirling Scotland ST 3341
Tel: 123498   Fax: 197663   Web Site: http://www.sss.com

September 5, 2015
Universal Software, Inc.
468 Oak Street
San Francisco CA 94105
U.S.A.

Attention: Sales Manager

Ladies/Gentleman:

Subject: Inquiry about your product

Sincerely Yours

SHEN John (Mr.)
Client Manager

Encl: Catalogue
CC: Previous Woods Amazon, Hong Kong Office
PS: Please visit our web site: http://www.sss.com

1.3 The Formats of a Business Letter

The often used formats are explained as follows:

1. Indented Format

Almost all elements of the letter should have an indentation, for instance, letterhead, inside address, letter body.

There is a rule for indentation. Each line of the "Inside Name and Address" should be indented 2-3 spaces, while in the body of the letter, the first line of each paragraph should need 4-5 space indentation on the left-hand side of the sheet, while the complimentary close and the signature are centered or on the right-hand side of the sheet.

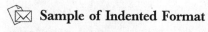 **Sample of Indented Format**

□□ _____
□□ _____

Salutation

Body

□□□□ _____
_____

□□□□ _____
_____

Complimentary Close
Signature
_____
_____

2. Semi-block Format

It's a combination of indented format and modified block format. It is very similar to the indented format with the only difference that the inside address should start neatly from the left-hand side of the sheet.

Sample of Semi-block Format

Letter Head

Date

Inside Address
_____
_____

Salutation

Body

☐☐☐☐ _____
_____

☐☐☐☐ _____
_____

Complimentary Close

Signature

_____
_____

3. Modified Block Format

In this format, the first line of each paragraph in the letter body is not indented, while the letterhead, date line, complimentary close, and signature are aligned slightly past the center of the sheet.

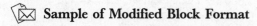 **Sample of Modified Block Format**

Letter Head

Date

Inside Address
_____
_____
_____

Salutation

Body

_____

_____

_____

                                              Complimentary Close

                                              Signature

                                              _____

                                              _____

4. Full Block Format

    Letterhead is laid out in the center of the letter, while the rest elements of a business letter start from the left-hand side of the sheet neatly. Open punctuation is adopted for the inside address, which means that both sender's address and recipients' address must avoid using more punctuations.

    The body of the letter has double spacing between the paragraphs. Typists generally prefer the full block format, for it has a simple appearance, and is quicker to type.

✉ Sample of Full Block Format

                                              Letter Head

Date

Inside Address

_____

_____

_____

Salutation

                                              Body

_____

_____

Unit 1 The Components of Business Letters

_____

_____

Complimentary Close

Signature

_____

_____

1.4 The Overall Appearance of a Business Letter

The appearance of a letter is very important to projecting the right image of your company or yourself, you need to ask the following questions about the presentation of your letter:

(1) Do you use the good quality stationery?

(2) What format do you prefer to use? Is the spacing right or the paragraph balanced in terms of length?

(3) How do you highlight your points, use fond and/or size variations, underlining, or italics?

(4) How do you present a number of parallel ideas, using numbers, or bullets?

(5) Have you proofread your letter and eliminated any spelling mistakes?

The appearance of a message is an important nonverbal message. The appearance of a letter builds up the first image of yourself and your company. A neat, carefully prepared message suggests that the writer or the company is well-organized and also has concerns for the reader. Therefore, whether you merely stick to the standard parts of a business letter or pick up one or more specialized parts to construct a letter, be sure to make your letter appear neat and effective by using a correct format and clear writing organization.

New Words and Expressions

| appropriate | a. | 合适的，恰当的 |
| logo | n. | 公司标志 |

abbreviate	a.	省略
recipient	n.	收信人，接受者
precede	v.	在……之前，领先（于）
approval	n.	同意，批准
decipher	v.	解读，辨认
illegible	a.	看不清的
optional	a.	可供选择的
project	v.	展示，显示
highlight	v.	突出重点，强调
italics	n.	斜体字
bullets	n.	子弹头形状
proofread	v.	校对
nonverbal	a.	非语言的
complimentary close		结束语
modified block style		改良齐头式
courtesy title		尊称，头衔
align with		与……成一行
the subject line		事由
the enclosure notation		附件标注
the postscript notation		附笔标注
indented format		缩进式
semi-block format		半齐头式
modified block format		改良齐头式
full block format		完全齐头式

1. ... they should be chosen carefully to agree in tone and manner with the salutation used at the beginning.　……我们应该非常谨慎，使结束语在语气和形式上与开头的称呼相一致。
2. the enclosure notation 附件标注
   它写在签名人的下方，用来提醒收件人信封里还附有别的材料。如果材料过多，可以一一注明。
3. the postscript notion 附笔标注
   它位于附件标注之下，可缩写为 P. S. 或 PS，用以补充信写完后又想要说的话。

Exercises

I Review questions.

1. What are the necessary components of a business letter?
2. What are the optional elements of a business letter?
3. Can you detail the four different formats of a business letter?

II Fill in special notation in the following letter.

1. Indicate the letter is signed by the sales manager Li Ming, and typed by his assistant Liu Yan.
2. Two copies of the letter are sent to President Wang Xin and General Manager Zhang Xing.
3. Indicate that a tentative schedule is enclosed in the letter.
4. Indicate that the letter is to be registered.
5. You want to add to the letter a statement: "We will arrange for you to visit Mount Tai after you have paid a visit to our corporation."

International Trading Corporation

65 Shengli Road, Ji Nan City, 245000 Shandong Province

Tel: ×××××××, Fax: ×××××××

May 3, 2015

Bertoit Schmidt
Purchasing Director
Rhein Biscuit Ltd.
Gaerstransse 5, D-84524
Neuotting, Germany

Dear Mr. Schmidt,

We are pleased to receive the news that you are going to visit our company in May.

According to our work schedule, the best time for us to receive you is from May 15 to May 22. During this period, both the President and the General Manager will be able to meet you and have a discussion with you for our future cooperation. Now we are making a tentative schedule for your consideration, and this is enclosed. We hope that such a schedule will not bring you too much inconvenience.

> We are looking forward to seeing you.
>
> Best wishes!
>
> Li Ming
> Sales Manager
>
> ------------------------------
> ------------------------------
> ------------------------------
> ------------------------------

III Writing practice.

You are requested to write a letter in which you give a brief account of how to lay out a full block format and its advantages in its typing and letter composing.

Unit 2

Language Style and Cultural Awareness of Business Letters
商务信函的语言风格与文化认知

Despite the traditional conventions putting much emphasis on formality, business letters have become more and more informal and relaxed today. There will be occasions which call for more formal language, for example, disciplinary letters, complaints, letters requesting payment, etc. However, these occasions should not be excuses for the long-winded, old fashioned, jargon-filled language, which was used several decades ago. Effective letter language today should be concise, businesslike, and polite.

2.1 Concise

Concise messages are essential. Learning to write concisely — to say in three words rather than ten — will mark you as a highly effective communicator. They will help save time and money for both the writer and the receiver. The receiver's attention is directed towards the important details and is not distracted by excessive words and details.[1] To prepare a concise message, include only those details that the receiver need, and avoid any vague words that might give rise to misunderstanding.

1. Use Specific Words

Normally, specific words serve business writers better than general words. Specific words are not only more vivid but also helpful in avoiding misunderstanding.

The difference between general words and specific words is shown as Table 2-1.

Table 2-1 General words and specific words

General	Specific
Congratulations on your recent honor.	Congratulations on being named the employee of the month.
Please submit the completed report as soon as possible.	Please submit the completed report by March 15.
Sales skyrocketed this month.	Sales increased by 10 percent this month.

2. Eliminate Clichés

Phrases that have become overused are called clichés. In writing, cliché can make reading monotonous and can make the writer or speaker seem like a copier. Being worn out, a cliché usually keeps from having no originality, although some of the phrases are convenient and can be used easily and quickly.[2] The following list contains many other expressions that have become clichés.

(1) Pursuant to your request, the physical inventory was scheduled for May 3.
(2) Please send a reply at your earliest convenience.
(3) Enclosed please find a copy of my transcript.
(4) Reference is made herewith ...

They can be revised respectively as follows:

(1) As you requested, the physical inventory was scheduled for May 3.
(2) Please send a reply by Friday, November 5.
(3) The enclosed transcript should answer most of your questions.
(4) I am referring to ...

3. Avoid Wordy Sentences

Wordy sentences convey the same meaning with unnecessary words or details. They will delay the major purpose of the message.

Notice how the following sentences are improved when implied ideas are reorganized.

(1a) She went to the bank and made the daily deposit.
(1b) She made the daily bank deposit.
(2a) She took the executive grammar course and passed it.
(2b) She passed the executive grammar course.

Sometimes, wordy sentences can be shortened by using suffixes or prefixes, making changes in word form, or substituting precise words for phrases. Note the following differences in the following examples.

(1a) She was a manager who was courteous to others.
(1b) She was a courteous manager.
(2a) He walked in an impatient manner.
(2b) He walked impatiently.
(3a) ... the solution that we could debate about the longest.
(3b) ... the most debatable solution.

4. Emphasize Courtesy

A courteous message takes its reader's feelings and points of view into consideration. A

Unit 2 Language Style and Cultural Awareness of Business Letters

courteous message, like a courteous person, is polite, considerate, and emphatic. Courtesy is extended primarily through the feeling content of your message, though the subject content may well be influenced by your consideration for your reader. Courtesy depends on the writer's understanding of the reader's viewpoint and the assumption that the writer and the reader can cooperate on an equal basis.³

1) Be polite

Whenever you ask your reader to do something for you, don't forget to say "please", "thank you", "I would appreciate it".

2) Be equal to each other

Any letter you write should demonstrate your feeling that the reader is doing business with you because he or she has chosen the right person he or she trusts. Any word or sentence that interferes with the one-to-one relationship of equals is usually detrimental to the success of a message. Compare the following messages:

Poor — This letter is to inform you of an important change in our policy concerning insurance.
Good — Since you are our regular customer, we are writing to let you know about our important policy change in insurance.

Poor — You obviously made a mistake by sending me the wrong goods.
Good — Thank you for your prompt delivery. However, the goods that reached us were not the one that we had ordered.

Poor — We have received your letter in which you claimed that ten teasets were damaged in shipment.
Good — We have noticed in your letter that one damage to ten teasets in shipment was found.

5. Choose the Simple, Informal Words

The degree of formality in writing is dictated by the nature of the message and the backgrounds of the receivers. The writing in dissertation, theses, legal documents, and high-level government documents is expected to be formal. Business memorandum, e-mail messages, letters, and reports are expected to be informal. Business writers prefer the informal words from the right column rather than the formal words from the left column:

Formal Words	Informal Words
terminate	end
procure	get
renumerate	pay
corroborate	support
utilize	use
elucidate	explain

Simple, informal words, compared with formal words, are readily understood, easier to spell, require less time in keyboarding and less space on a page, and are less likely to draw attention away from the idea being expressed.[4] If a receiver stops to question the writer's motive for using words similar to those in the left column, the impact of the message may be seriously diminished. Just remember the purpose of business messages is not to advertise the knowledge of infrequently used words but to transmit a clear and tactful message.[5] For the informal writing practiced in business, use simple words instead of more complicated words that have the same meaning.

6. Avoid Slangs

Although business letters have become more and more informal and relaxed today, written language should always be more formal than that for oral communication, and they cannot be so informal as to resort to slang or overly casual expressions.

The following examples in Table 2-2 show incorrect style of language for business letters.

Table 2-2 Incorrect and correct style of language in business letter

Incorrect	Correct
We'll contact you when it's OK.	We shall contact you when it is ready.
How cool your latest series of Benz are!	Your latest series of Benz are very attractive.
We have got your letter of 11 Oct.	Thank you for your letter of 11 October.

Business writing differs from other types of writing in that it tends to be informal and simple, concise and polite. Its purpose is to convey the message clearly and appropriately so as to build up business relationship. Therefore, we will strive to make our writing effective by emphasizing clarity, politeness and appropriateness so that we can get our message across to the audience successfully.

2.2 Intercultural Awareness

With the globalization of world economy, it is imperative for managers, both present and future, to be sensitive to differences in intercultural business communication. Therefore, understanding how to communicate effectively with people from other cultures is becoming more integral to the work environment as many companies increasingly conduct business with international companies or become multinational.

Culture can be described as "the way of life" of a people and includes a vast array of behaviors and beliefs. These patterns affect how people perceive the world, what they value, and how they act. These patterns can create barriers to communication if you are interacting with a person who behaves according to different cultural patterns. It is thus important for us to overcome cultural obstacles by improving our intercultural awareness and competence when conducting international business.

Unit 2 Language Style and Cultural Awareness of Business Letters

In order to minimize the cultural impact on communication, we should train ourselves as effective international communicators. The following may help us achieve that goal.

(1) Improve English writing skills. You should follow closely the principles guiding business English writing and observe basic English writing conventions. For example, avoid abbreviations, slang, acronyms, technical jargon, and other devices, all of which are possibly culturally bound.

(2) Be aware of your contacts' culture and traditions and study how it differs from your own culture.

(3) Be careful with metaphors and idioms, and other culture-related expressions. For instance, the expression of "sharp as brass tacks" will mean nothing to someone who has no idea of that specific meaning of the slang in a particular culture.

(4) Use graphics, visual aids, and forms whenever possible, because they simplify the message.

(5) Don't translate culturally bound idioms or slang from your own language into English. If you are to do so, please do not seek the exact equivalents to them in the target language unless you know them thoroughly. You can resort to the device of making more explanation to get the approximate meaning of these idioms or slang in your translation.

(6) Develop your cultural sensitivity and bear it in mind that business writing not only involves grammatical and structural correctness, but also is related with the cultural appropriateness in receiver's business environment. Learn to acquire the knowledge of cultural differences concerning your trading partners will always be one of your jobs in business dealings.

New Words and Expressions

disciplinary	a.	处分的，惩罚的
long-winded	a.	冗长的
jargon-filled	a.	行话连篇的
distract	v.	分散注意力，打扰
cliché	n.	陈词滥调
emphatic	a.	强调的，显著的
detrimental	a.	对……有伤害
dictate	v.	决定，命令
dissertation	n.	论文
memorandum	n.	备忘录
tactful	a.	有策略的，讲究方法的
slang	n.	俚语
imperative	a.	必要的，重要的

integral	a.	不可分的，完整的
array	n.	展列，(排列整齐的) 一批
minimize	v.	减少为最低点
graphics	n.	图示，图表
equivalent	n.	对等词，对等物
approximate	a.	大约
get ... across to		使……被理解
interact with		与……交流，互动
visual aids		直观教具 (如图片、电影等)
culturally bound		充满文化意蕴的

1. The receiver's attention is directed towards the important details and is not distracted by excessive words and details.　读者可以对重要内容予以关注，而不是被多余的语言和细节所干扰。
2. Being worn out, cliché usually keeps from having no originality, although some of the phrases are convenient and can be used easily and quickly.　虽然这些陈词滥调使用起来方便快捷，但是由于使用过多，往往缺少新意。
3. Courtesy depends on the writer's understanding of the reader's viewpoint and the assumption that writer and the reader can cooperate on an equal basis.　行文谦恭需要作者理解读者的观点，并基于这样的一种认识，即作者与读者可以在平等的基础上进行合作。
4. ... and are less likely to draw attention away from the idea being expressed.
　　……而往往不会影响读者对被表述内容的注意。
5. Just remember the purpose of business messages is not to advertise a knowledge of infrequently used words but to transmit a clear and tactful message.　请记住：商务信函的目的不是炫耀你究竟掌握了多少生僻的词汇，而是明确而富有技巧地表达一种信息。

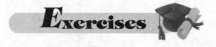

I Rewrite the following sentences and tell why you think it necessary to revise so.

1. In the event of your wishing me to do so, I will call on you next week.
2. The surrounding circumstances do not justify an advance of more than US$ 2,000.
3. The manager who is most experienced and with the greatest efficiency, it seems obvious, should be

Unit 2 Language Style and Cultural Awareness of Business Letters

given consideration for being promoted first.

4. Upon examination of our records, it seems that you have forgotten to file the personal data form which is required.
5. All applicants who are interested in the job are obligated to provide the names of three references whom we can write to for evaluation of your job performance.
6. The vice president was a woman who had graduated from law school and with long experience in the business world.
7. The salesperson told us that we should write to the main office directly for whatever information we were in need of.
8. It goes without saying that we are acquainted with your policy on filing tax returns, and we have every intention of complying with the regulation, which you have stated.
9. American business has a goal, which is to try to raise the standard of living.
10. It is true that often great affluence is accompanied by another problem, unrest socially.

II Fill in the blanks of the following letter with the words given below, and change the form when necessary.

item, expect, mail, market, remit, sample, reach, advise

Dear Sirs,

Your catalog and price list of the captioned product have _____ us. Some of the _____ appear to be attractive and are probably _____ in our area.

In order to have a better knowledge of your product, we would like to have some of your _____ for inspection and testing. Please _____ us of the cost of these samples including postal charges so that we could _____ it to you.

Meanwhile, please _____ us more catalogs for distribution to our customers. If catalogs are not available, can you send us copies of color photos?

We _____ your samples and catalogues.

Faithfully yours

III Please compare the following passages and account for your justification for such revisions.

1. Part One

Passage A

Details of our new price structure are enclosed, and you will find that they have had to rise by 15% to cover inflation but we shall honor the old price list until the end of this month, when we shall be forced to introduce the new prices, so if you order before the end of this month, you can make some splendid savings!

Passage B

Details of our new price structure are enclosed. Although you will find that our prices have had to increase by 15% to cover inflation. We shall honor the old price list until the end of this month, when we shall be forced to introduce the new prices. So, if you order before the end of this month, you can make some splendid savings!

2. Part Two

Passage A

We were pleased to receive your enquiry regarding our Omega range of T-shirts, which are our top range and are made of a strong blend of natural and man-made fibers, which makes them both rugged and good looking and suitable for casual and heavy sports wear, and which come in a wide range of colors and sizes which are suitable for both men and women.

Passage B

We were pleased to receive your enquiry regarding our Omega range of T-shirts. These are our top range and feature a strong blend of natural and man-made fibers which makes them both rugged and good looking. It also means that they are suitable for both casual and heavy sports wear. They come in a wide range of colors and sizes, and are suitable for both men and women.

VI Writing practice.

Write a business letter in the format you prefer, and keep your letter until you have finished this course to see what needs to be improved.

Unit 3

The Tone of a Business Letter
商务信函的语气

3.1 Writing for Your Audience

You should adapt your message to fit the specific needs of your audience. A good writer has a strong mental picture of the audience. To help you envision the audience, first focus on relevant information you know about the receiver. The more familiar you are with the receiver, the easier this task will be. When communicating with an individual, you immediately bring to mind a clear picture of the receiver — his or her physical appearance, background (education, occupation, religion, culture), values, opinions, preferences, and so on. Most important, your knowledge of the receiver's reaction in similar, previous experiences will aid you in anticipating how this receiver is likely to react in the current situation. Add to your mental picture by thoughtfully considering all you know about the receiver and how this information might affect the content and style of your final message. After you have envisioned your audience, you are ready to adapt your message to fit the specific needs of your audience. Adaptation includes assuming an empathetic attitude, focusing on the receiver's point of view, using bias-free language, avoiding statements that destroy goodwill, and projecting a positive, tactful tone.[1]

1. Assume an Empathetic Attitude

Empathy is an attitude that enables a person to identify another's frame of reference (knowledge, feelings, and emotions) and to project or communicate understanding back to the person. The phrase "putting myself in your shoes" implies that empathy requires you to experience another person's situation firsthand. But relying on firsthand experience is not necessary to be able to provide genuine empathy. In situations when you cannot "walk in another's shoes", you can empathize by mentally projecting how you believe you would feel if that situation had happened to you. That is, first, trying to understand the situation from another's point of view. Your receivers will appreciate your attempting to understand their feelings. The outcome may be mutual trust, which can greatly improve communication and people's feelings about you, your ideas, and themselves; second, seeing a situation or problem from the receiver's perspective not only will permit you to address the receiver's needs and concerns but will also enable you to anticipate the receiver's possible reaction to the message. Therefore, empathy is an excellent way to establish rapport and credibility and to build long-lasting personal and business relationships. [2]

2. Focus on the Receiver's Point of View

Ideas are more interesting and appealing if they are expressed from the receiver's viewpoint. Thus, develop a "you attitude", which involves thinking in terms of the other person's interests and trying to see a problem from the other's point of view. A letter or memo reflecting a "you attitude" sends a direct signal of sincere concern for the receiver's needs and interest.

"You" (appropriately used) conveys to receivers a feeling that messages are specifically for them. However, if the first-person pronoun "I" is used frequently, the sender may impress others as being self-centered — always talking about self. "I" used as the subject receives significant emphasis. Compare the following examples in Table 3-1 of I- or writer-centered and receiver-centered statements.

Table 3-1 Examples of I- or writer-centered and receiver-centered statements

I- or writer-centered	Receiver-centered
We have two laser printers compatible with your software.	Your software is compatible with two of our high-quality laser printers.
I am interested in ordering ...	Please send me ...
We allow a 2-percent discount to customers who pay their total invoices within ten days.	Customers who pay within ten days deduct 2 percent from their total invoice.

In composing a business letter, the writer will have to concentrate on such questions as: Are ideas expressed clearly and concisely and does the message serve as a vehicle for developing positive business relationships — even when the message is negative? Or is the message sent to indicate courtesy? Having these points in mind will boost the receiver's confidence in the writer's competence and will communicate nonverbally that receiver is valued enough to merit the writer's best effort. [3]

3. Use Bias-free Language

In today's competitive workplace, a writer or a speaker cannot afford the risk of sending an insensitive message. In addition, managers in today's highly competitive diverse workforce cannot afford to alienate employees and customers. Therefore, carefully selecting words free of any bias to alienate employees and customers is very important to writers.

Please avoid use of gender-bias language. Pay special attention to the pronouns "him" and "his". When the gender of a noun has not been revealed, do not use a masculine pronoun. Although this usage was once standard and accepted, it can be considered offensive today. The receiver's attention may be diverted from the message to the writer's stereotypical attitudes and insensitivity. [4]

Let us look at the following examples:

(1) When your accountant completes year-end financial statements, ask <u>him</u> to send a copy to the loan officer.
(2) The human resources manager must evaluate <u>his</u> employee's performance at least twice a year.

The writers of these sentences are communicating an insensitive message between the lines that only males serve in certain professions. Avoid referring to males and females in stereotyped roles and occupations. So in writing, learning to use the style of being gender-neutral is helpful to avoid any misunderstanding arising from the gender-biased language. There are many ways to correct gender-biased language.

1) Avoid using a pronoun
When your auditor arrives, <u>he</u> is to go ...
Instead: Upon arrival, <u>your auditor</u> is to go ...

2) Repeat the noun
... the courtesy of your guide, ask <u>him</u> to ...
Instead: the courtesy of your guide, ask <u>the guide</u> to ...

3) Use a plural noun
If a supervisor needs assistance, <u>he</u> can ...
Instead: if supervisors need assistance, <u>they</u> can ...

4) Use pronouns from both genders
Just call the manager. <u>He</u> will in turn ...
Instead: Just call the manager. <u>He or she</u> will in turn ...

Occasional use of "he or she" may not be particularly distracting, but repeated use can take attention away from the message.

4. Avoid Statements that Destroy Goodwill

Tone is the way a statement sounds. The tone of a message conveys a writer's or speaker's attitude towards the message and the receiver. Chances for achieving good human relations are diminished when the tone of a message is condescending, flattering.

1) Eliminate condescension
Condescending words seems to connote that the communicator is temporarily coming down from a level of superiority to join the receiver on a level of inferiority.[5] Note the following examples:

(1) As a retired editor of best sellers, I could assist you in editing your PTA newsletter.
(2) With my PhD and your GED, we should be able to work out a suitable set of bylaws for the new club.

Such reminders of inequality seriously hamper communication.

2) Deal with a flattering tone appropriately

Compliments normally elicit favorable reactions. They can increase a receiver's receptivity to subsequent statements. Yet even compliments can do more harm than good if paid at the wrong time, in the wrong setting, in the presence of the wrong people, or for a suspicious motive.[6]

Flattery (words of underserved praise) may be accepted gracefully, but the net result is almost negative. Although flattery can be accepted as a sincere compliment, the recipient is more likely to interpret underserved praise as an attempt to carry favor. Suspicion of motive makes effective communication less likely.

3) Avoid statement of surprise, doubt and judgment

Phrases that reveal a writer's surprise about a receiver's behavior can cause problems in human relations. Why are the following sentences risky?

(1) I am surprised that you did not accept.

(2) I just cannot understand your attitude.

"I am surprised" risks conveying something like "I am accustomed to normal behavior. Yours is abnormal and therefore bad or totally unjustified." "I cannot understand" takes the same risks. Such expressions are particularly offensive to receivers because they seem to place them in a position of recognized inferiority.

Similarly, expressions that reveal judgment of recipients' emotional state are very risky. "I am so sorry you are upset" may be intended as a heart-felt apology, but the "I am sorry" can be completely overshadowed by "you are upset". This statement could mean "Your conduct is such that I recognize your lack of self-control. Because of your condition, you could not be thinking rationally." Avoid expressions of surprise, doubt, and judgment when they would be interpreted as insults.

5. Project a Positive, Tactful Tone

Being adept at communicating negative information will give you the confidence you need to handle sensitive situations in a positive, constructive manner. You will find that stating unpleasant ideas tactfully and positively preserves the receiver's self-worth and builds future relationships.[7] To reduce the sting of an unpleasant thought, you should follow some rules.

1) State ideas by using positive language

Be cheerful and optimistic. In the following pairs of sentences in Table 3-2, note the difference in tone between the first and second example.

Table 3-2　Negative tone and positive tone

Negative Tone	Positive Tone
Don't forget to submit your time and expense report by noon on Friday.	Remember to submit your time and expense report by noon on Friday.
We cannot ship your order until you send us full specifications.	You will receive your order as soon as you send us full specifications.

Unit 3 The Tone of a Business Letter

(continued)

Negative Tone	Positive Tone
You neglect to indicate the specifications for 332-3.	Please send the complete specifications for 332-3, so we can complete your order quickly.

Each sentence in the left column contains a negative word or phrase—"don't", "cannot", "neglected". In each pair, both sentences are sufficiently clear, but the positive words in the sentence in the right column make the message more diplomatic. The sentences in the right column sound more pleasing and do a better job of promoting human relations. For good human relations, rely mainly on positive words — words that speak of what can be done instead of what cannot be done, of the pleasant instead of the unpleasant.

2) Avoid using second person when stating negative ideas

The following sentences use the second-person pronoun. In which sentence is "you" less advisable?

(1) You keyed a perfect copy.

(2) You made numerous mistakes on this page.

The first sentence contains a positive idea. The person to whom the sentence is addressed can hardly resent being associated with perfection. The second sentence contains a negative idea. The person will likely become sensitive about the mistake when he or she is directly associated with it. If the speaker's desire is to be diplomatic (at least to be no more negative than necessary), the second sentence could be revised to avoid the use of second person: "This page contains numerous mistakes." For better human relations, avoid second person for presenting negative ideas. Use second person for presenting pleasant ideas. However, use of second person with negative ideas is an acceptable technique on the rare occasions when the purpose is to jolt the receiver by emphasizing a negative.[8]

3) Use passive voice to convey negative ideas

Presenting an unpleasant thought emphatically makes human relations difficult. Compare the tone of the following negative thoughts written in active and passive voices in Table 3-3.

Table 3-3 Active voice and passive voice

Active Voice	Passive Voice
Armando failed to proofread this bid proposal carefully.	The bid proposal was not proofread carefully.
Armando completed the job two months behind schedule.	The job was completed two months behind schedule.

Because the subject of each active sentence is the doer, the sentences are emphatic. Because the idea is negative, Armando probably would appreciate being taken out of the picture. The passive voice sentences place more emphasis on the job than on who failed to complete it. When passive voice is used, the sentences retain the essential ideas, but the ideas seem less irritating. For negative ideas, use passive voice.

4) Use the subjunctive mood

Sometimes, the tone of a message can be improved if the writer switches to the subjunctive mood. Subjunctive sentences employ such conditional expressions as I wish, as if, could, might, and wish. Subjunctive sentences speak of a wish, necessity, doubt, or conditions contrary to fact. Let us look at Table 3-4.

Table 3-4   Negative tone and positive tone

Negative Tone	Positive Tone
I cannot approve your transfer to overseas operation.	If positions were available in our overseas operation, I would approve your transfer.
I am unable to accept your invitation to speak at the November meeting.	I could accept your invitation to speak at the November meeting if I were to miss the annual stockholders' meeting.
I cannot accept the recommendation of the site-selection committee.	I wish I could accept the recommendation of the site-selection committee.

In all three pairs, a negative idea is involved; but the sentence in the right column transmits the negative idea in positive language. Positive language is more diplomatic. The revised sentences also include a reason. Because a reason is included, the negative idea seems less objectionable; and tone is thus improved.

Tone is important, but clarity is even more important. The revised sentence in each of the preceding pairs sufficiently implies the unpleasant idea without stating it directly. If for any reason a writer suspects the implication is not sufficiently strong, a direct statement in negative terms is preferable. For tactful presentation of an unpleasant thought, consider stating it in the subjunctive mood.

3.2 Three Approaches in Dealing with Messages

In business communications there are roughly three approaches in dealing with messages, that is, direct approach, indirect approach and very polite approach. Which approach to adopt is usually determined by the interrelationship between the two communicators or business entities. The closer relationship both maintains, the more informal they might be in conveying the messages. Therefore, an old customer will tend to make inquiries in a direct manner in its letter of inquiry, while a potential customer will approach the seller with the message sent in a polite form, and the reply to a potential customer also keeps the same formal and polite style as that in the letter of inquiry sent out by a potential customer.

1. Direct Approach in Dealing with Good-news and Routine Messages

The direct approach means arranging ideas in a direct order, usually by beginning with the most important point and working downward. This approach is good for all good-news and routine messages. The direct approach gives the reader the sense of immediacy. It is often adopted by two familiar partners or by two companies with good relations. In addition, in modern life people live a faster tempo of life. By taking your reader directly to the issue in question, you save his time.

In the direct approach, the message is organized as follows:

- Present the most important information in a positive way;
- Give the necessary explanations;
- Cover the remaining part of the objective;
- End with goodwill.

Routine inquiries and replies, favorable response to claims and adjustment requests, recommendation letters, good news about employment, congratulations, messages of appreciation, condolences, announcements, and greetings, all falls under this category.

 Sample Letter 3-1

Dear Mr. Johnson,

May we have a copy of your brochures concerning the meeting, which was held on July 10, 2015, for announcing projects on industrial development in the Northwest China.

Yesterday's China Daily includes an article about the meeting. Some thoughts and plans were presented on the electronic and water-treatment fields. We would appreciate more details than those printed in the paper.

It would be more helpful if you could send us all the necessary information. We are sure that it will be beneficial to both of us in the near future.

Yours sincerely

 Sample Letter 3-2

Dear Sirs,

We are interested in importing cars and would be grateful if you would send us a copy of your latest catalogue, your price list and export terms. Could you also let us know the name of your import agent in Egypt?

We look forward to hearing from you.

Yours faithfully

Zhang Li
Marketing Manager

2. Indirect Approach in Dealing with Bad-news Messages

The purpose of a business is to render services to the customers and meet their demands. Only by so doing can a business survive and thrive, but no business can meet all the demands of all the customers all the time. In other words, a business sometimes has to say "no" to its patrons. Nobody would like to receive a "no" answer, and the negative effect of rejection may damage business relations. So, a skillful manager will try his best to reduce the negative impact. As a matter of fact, the ability to say "no" tactfully to customers is essential to the success of a business.

When you write a negative message, you use the indirect approach. By the indirect approach we mean that we do not tell the bad news at the beginning. Instead, we begin with some good news or at least some neutral information and put off the bad news until some explanations are made. Such a writer's main effort in conveying unpleasant information will help the reader preserve a positive self-image and maintain the reader's positive attitude towards the writer and the writer's company. The following indirect organizational pattern is recommended when an unfavorable response is called for.

- Begin with a buffer.
- Explain why the refusal has to be made.
- State the refusal.
- Offer a constructive suggestion or an alternative plan.
- Close positively.

In order to obtain an effective communication in conveying negative information, let's look more closely at the five parts of a bad news message.

1) Begin with a buffer

A delayed opening is frequently called a buffer beginning because it "buffers" the negative message which follows. Begin with something to which the reader will respond positively, but be sure not to mislead the reader into thinking that you are going to meet his requirements. It is proper to find something to agree with, pay the reader an honest compliment, give a positive answer to one of the reader's questions, or thank the reader for having written to you. You may begin as follows:

(1) Congratulation on the establishment of your new marketing outlets.

(Showing positive attitude towards the reader's good news)

(2) We appreciate your writing to us about the quality of our products.

(Presenting appreciation for the reader's writing)

(3) You have every right to expect the best service when you have placed your order so often.

(Demonstrating your understanding of the reader's problem)

2) Explain why the refusal has to be made

Presenting the facts with an analysis is an effective technique for emphasizing reasons. The more clearly your reader understands the reasons, the less likely he or she will think that the decision is illogical, unfair, or arbitrary.

3) State the refusal

When your readers accept your explanation, much of the negative impact is already absorbed. You are now safe to release your bad news. But your refusal should be the logical and natural outcome of the explanation. Consequently the solution lessens the refusal's impact. The language used should be concise and clear. A tacit or implied statement is an effective way to avoid the negative conclusions.

4) Offer a constructive suggestion or an alternative plan

It is better to include an alternative rather than ending the letter immediately after the refusal presented. Do remember the goal of writing a refusal is still to keep the goodwill and recall the products or services. Therefore, if it is possible, try to offer your suggestions or ideas for improving the situation. However what you suggest should be reasonable, helpful, or obtainable. Alternative plans or ideas far beyond the fact will only strengthen the negative impact.

5) Close positively

After stating the refusal or suggesting an alternative course of action, change the subject and end the letter on a pleasant note. At least, you should not remind your readers of the negative message. So, do not apologize for your refusal but try to make your readers less unhappy.

 Sample Letter 3-3

Dear Mr. Phillips,

Thank you for sending us your reservation request. We appreciate your interest in our quality hotel accommodation.

Early reservations for two large convention groups have left us with no free rooms for the week of March 15. However, we will be happy to arrange an accommodation for you at the Golden Dragon Hotel, a fine hotel, which is directly across the street from us. May we reserve two single rooms for you at that hotel for the week of March 15? For fast service, please use our FAX number: ××-××-×××××××. Our machine will take your message at 24-hour service.

Enclosed is a copy of our newest brochure showing some modified rules in reservation. We are sure that it would help you make your best choice in future. By staying at our hotel you will continue to obtain top quality accommodation and the most convenient commercial service.

We are looking forward to your visit to Beijing.

Yours sincerely

3. Polite Approach

In business letters, as in direct dealings with others, politeness plays a great part in helping us to gain our ends. Whatever type of letter we write, complaint, thanks, recommendation, disciplinary, etc, politeness should always be put in the tone, and particularly as letters are addressed to potential customers or to those you are going to invite, polite approach will be the first priority in terms of language and tone to be considered. In an eye of modern business writer, the delaying vital information as a way to show courtesy and respect is unnecessary or a waste of time, and will divert reader's attention, but to achieve the effect of courtesy and respect in a business letter writing, slowly beginning message by saying something polite cannot be avoided and sometimes is necessary. For any business letter is intended to build up relationships with trading partners and to create a better image of a company, therefore sending courteous message will be helpful in your efforts to achieve such goals, and courtesy is usually extended primarily through the feeling content of your message, though the subject content may well be influenced by your consideration for your reader.

 Sample Letter 3-4

Dear Sir or Madam,

We are writing to you on behalf of our principals in Melbourne who are interested in importing chinaware from China.

Could you please send us your latest catalogue and price-list, quoting your most competitive prices?[9]

Our principals are a large chain store in Australia and will probably place substantial orders if the quality and prices of your products are suitable.[10]

We look forward to hearing from you soon.

Yours faithfully

 Sample Letter 3-5

Dear Mr. Li,

Thank you very much for your letter of 16 July in which you inquired about our insurance cover.[11]

I have enclosed leaflets explaining our three fully-comprehensive marine policies[12] which offer the sort of cover you require, and I think that policy 1281 would probably suit you best as it offers the widest protection at 0.0065 with full indemnification.

If you wish, I could get one of our agents to call on you to discuss any details that might not be clear.

I look forward to hearing from you soon.

Yours sincerely

Daniel Cooke
General Manager of the Great China Region

To sum up, the above mentioned three approaches in dealing with messages will guide us through our writing of business letters. Which one to use in a particular letter is usually determined by the interrelations between the two trading partners or by real purpose that the writer has for achieving the effect. Theoretically, they are expounded in the preceding sections, but how they will work in real business letters will be shown in the above-mentioned sample letters.

New Words and Expressions

envision	v.	预想，预见
anticipate	v.	预期，期望
bias-free	a.	没有偏见的
goodwill	n.	友好，善意
appreciate	v.	理解，感激
perspective	n.	视角，角度
rapport	n.	友好关系
credibility	n.	信任
appealing	a.	有吸引力的
convey	v.	传达，表达
impress	v.	给……印象
compatible	a.	与……一致的
negative	a.	否定的，负面的
boost	v.	提升
alienate	v.	与……疏离
gender-bias	a.	无性别歧视的
stereotypical	a.	固有形象的
gender-neutral	a.	中性的
condescending	a.	带着优越感表示关心的
flattering	a.	奉承的
connote	v.	意味着
hamper	v.	妨碍
compliment	n.	表扬，赞美的话
elicit	v.	引起，引发
abnormal	a.	非正常的
offensive	a.	引起……反感的
upset	v.	使……不安
overshadow	v.	给……笼罩着阴影
diplomatic	a.	有策略的
pleasing	a.	讨好人的
jolt	v.	给……以一击
irritating	a.	使人恼怒的
objectionable	a.	引起反对的

Unit 3 The Tone of a Business Letter

approach	n.	途径，手段
potential	a.	潜在的
render	v.	使……成为
buffer	n.	缓冲
arbitrary	a.	任意的，专断的
tacit	a.	保持缄默的
alternative	a.	另一个的，可供选择的
priority	n.	优先考虑的事
expound	v.	阐述
water-treatment	n.	水处理
principal	n.	委托人
chinaware	n.	瓷器
to carry favor		奉承
to place more emphasis on		强调
the subjunctive mood		虚拟语气
to make inquiries		询问
in question		有关的
marine policy		海洋险

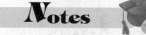

1. Adaptation includes assuming an empathetic attitude, focusing on the receiver's point of view, using bias-free language, avoiding statements that destroy goodwill, and projecting a positive, tactful tone.　迎合读者的需求包括：换位思考，明确读者的观点，使用不带偏见的语言，不说有损友谊的话，说话语气要有益于双方关系的发展，并具有策略性。
2. Therefore, empathy is an excellent way to establish rapport and credibility and to build long-lasting personal and business relationships.　因此，换位思考是发展友谊、确定信任、建立持久的个人和贸易关系的有效途径。
3. Having these points in mind will boost the receiver's confidence in the writer's competence and will communicate nonverbally that receiver is valued enough to merit the writer's best effort.　牢记这些道理将增强收信人对写信人的信任，并能让收信人感觉到他们是值得写信人重视的。
4. The receiver's attention may be diverted from the message to the writer's stereotypical attitudes and insensitivity.　收信人会将注意力从信函转移到写信人固有的偏见和漠然上。
5. Condescending words seems to connote that the communicator is temporarily coming down from a level of superiority to join the receiver on a level of inferiority.　提出要帮助别人，但语气

中带有一种优越感，似乎让人觉得讲话者从高高在上的位置暂时下来和对方处于同一的地位。

6. Yet even compliments can do more harm than good if paid at the wrong time, in the wrong setting, in the presence of the wrong people, or for a suspicious motive. 然而，即使是溢美之词，如果场合不对、时间不对、赞美的对象不对或者动机让人怀疑，均是弊大于利。

7. You will find that stating unpleasant ideas tactfully and positively preserves the receiver's self-worth and builds future relationships. 你会发现：如果在阐述令人不快的观点时采取积极而富有技巧的方式，你就能给足收信人的面子，并建立好未来的关系。

8. However, use of second person with negative ideas is an acceptable technique on the rare occasions when the purpose is to jolt the receiver by emphasizing a negative. 然而，在少数情况下用第二人称来表达负面的意思是行之有效的方式，此时的目的就是通过强调负面的东西来给收信人一个刺激。

9. ... quoting your most competitive prices? 其中的 "competitive prices" 在这里意为 "富有竞争性的价格"，即 "最为便宜的价格"。

10. ... will probably place substantial orders if the quality and prices of your products are suitable. 本句中 "substantial orders" 的意思为 "数量大的订单"。

11. ... in which you inquired about our insurance cover. 其中，"insurance cover" 为 "保险单" 的意思。

12. I have enclosed leaflets explaining our three fully-comprehensive marine policies ... 我随函附寄了一些宣传册，宣传册上介绍了我们的三种保险责任全面的海洋险……

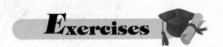

I Review questions.

1. In what way can you assume emphatic attitude when you are writing a business letter?
2. What need you pay a particular attention to if you are going to avoid any statement that might destroy goodwill?
3. What are the three approaches adopted in letter writing? Can you describe the features of each of them?
4. How will you deal with the negative messages or a refusal in your business letter? What steps can you follow in your writing?

II Rewrite the following sentences taken from letters, and pay attention to the tone.

1. Each accountant must submit his time and expense report by the 15th of each month.
2. It has been quite some time since I did the type of work, but I can help you for a while.
3. I am sure you will understand our reasons for refusal.

Unit 3　The Tone of a Business Letter

4. We realize that you are upset, but the fee is due on May 10th.
5. The corrected order cannot be sent until March 4th.
6. This innovative advertisement was designed by Mr. Smith.
7. The shoes you bought were from a faulty batch — we have sent you the replacement now, so this should be OK.
8. It's a pity your tablecloth faded, but you can't have read the washing instructions.
9. I had an interview with you ages ago, but I have not heard a word — have I got the job or not.
10. You will have to wait a while because we are out of stock now — we'll be in touch with you when more arrive.

III The following are parts of a letter mixed in an improper order. Rearrange and put them in a logical order.

1. It's a great pleasure to receive your letter of February 5, 2016.
2. You have found the right range hood manufacturer. As a leading enterprise in our industry, we constantly translate high-tech technology into satisfactory products for our customers. And our product is hugely popular in most parts of Asia and Australia.
3. Looking forward to your order soon.
4. A special offer we supply for each user is two free nets every year.
5. Enclosed is the catalogue of our products.

VI Please rewrite the following letter and point out the shortcomings.

Dear Sirs,

Your letter together with the order form has been referred to our department today.

Unfortunately, the mono-sodium glutamate makers you requested are unavailable at present. According to our file records, the Huaguang Food Processing Machinery Export Group stocks the one which meets your need. May we suggest that you place your order there.

Thank you for your interest in our merchandise.

Faithfully yours

Unit 4

Inquiries

询购函

4.1 Introduction

Inquiries for information about goods are sent and received in business all the time. A businessperson will send an inquiry whenever he or she wants some information especially about the availability or supply of goods, leaflets or catalogues, samples, quotations or prices, terms and discounts, delivery times, method of transport, insurance and terms of payment. So they consider requests for information routine, and they cooperate in exchanging information.

Because of business cooperation conducted in such situation, we can write most requests for information in a straightforward way. Such a method can save time both for the writer and the reader, for it can get down to subject matter immediately.

But it does not mean that all inquiry letters can be composed in such an order. If you believe that the reader will not consider the request routine, you need to use indirect order. Otherwise, you can adopt direct approach. For instance, if a prospective customer approaches seller for the first time, it is useful to tell the seller something about the customer's own business, the kind of goods needed and for what purpose they are required. In the case of customers of long-standing or repeat orders, the inquiry may be very simple. Often a phone call or a printed inquiry form will do.

4.2 Sample Letters

 Sample Letter 4-1

Dear Sirs,

Would you kindly send us details of your Shang Di bicycles, which you advised in latest issue *Bicycle World*?

Please quote us all the items listed in the enclosed inquiry form, giving your prices CIF Shanghai. Will you please also indicate delivery time, your terms of payment and discount details for regular purchases and large orders.

Our annual requirements for the bicycle are considerable, and we may be able to place substantial orders with you if your prices are competitive and your delivery is prompt

We are looking forward to your reply soon.

Yours faithfully

 Sample Letter 4-2

Dear Sirs,

I am writing to ask you about the cutlery as shown in your latest catalogue, which was passed to me by our office manager.

We are interested in buying new cutlery for our chain of hotels in Hong Kong. So we would like you to send us your pricelist and let us know details of any discount you could offer. Information on details of delivery and method of payment would also be appreciated.

I am looking forward to hearing from you soon.

Yours faithfully

 Sample Letter 4-3

Dear Sirs,

Subject: Chromium plated products

We should like you to send us a catalogue and price list regarding your chromium plated domestic products. You were recommended to us by colleagues at Loyan Industries in Kedah with whom you have, we understand, done business for a number of years.

This company produces a large range of domestic and office furniture, and we are interested in using a number of products from your current range in the manufacture of our goods. As we are about to expand our export operation, it is essential that our suppliers be both competitive in terms of price, and extremely reliable.[1]

We will be interested in discussing terms with you as and when the final decision has been taken, but, prior to this, can you tell me what discounts you offer on bulk purchases?

I look forward to hearing from you soon.

Yours faithfully

Mr. Liu Xinming
General Manager

 Sample Letter 4-4

Dear Sir or Madam,

We are a company that imports yachts for sale to Japanese clients and we have enclosed our company's brochure for your reference.

Your company's name is made to our attention through an article in the August issue of Ocean Magazine and we understand that you manufacture yachts of various sizes. Since we might be interested in doing business with your company, we should like to have some information about your company and your products. We would therefore appreciate your sending us your company's catalogue so that we can examine the business potential more politely.

Yours faithfully

Sample Letter 4-5

Dear Sirs,

We have learned from the Chamber of Commerce that you are a dealer of handbags in a variety of leathers.

We are now engaged in a quality retail business and despite that our sales volume is not large, we obtain high price for our goods.

Would you please send me a copy of your handbag catalogue with details of your prices and payment terms?

It is helpful if you could also supply samples of the various leathers from which the handbags are made.

Yours faithfully

Sample Letter 4-6

Dear Sir or Madam,

We are interested in your product, which we saw exhibited in the recent electronic show held in West Germany.

In recent years we have introduced various foreign brands into Hong Kong, China and have built up a considerable market for the manufacturers.

Please send us all available data on your product.² We would like to point out that we can offer your customers an excellent after-sales service with the best maintenance facilities.

We are expecting your reply with great interest.

Truly yours

Sample Letter 4-7

Dear Sirs,

We visited your stand at the London Trade Exhibition last week, and we were greatly impressed by your display of ladies' open-toed sandals. We should be grateful if you would send us your catalogue of your complete range of this type of shoes, and also your export price-list.

We are a large chain of retailers and are looking for a manufacturer who could supply us with a wide range of lady-wears for the local market.

As we usually place very large orders, we would expect a quantity discount in addition to a 20% trade discount off net list prices, and our terms of payment are normally 30-day bill of exchange, document against payment.

If these conditions interest you, we can place orders of over 5,000 pairs at one time. We hope to hear from you soon.

Yours faithfully

 Sample Letter 4-8

Dear Sirs,

Does your company manufacture a semigloss printing paper that is, paper of a very heavy weight (approximately 25 lbs.)?

Our company has developed a new skill for printing high quality booklets. It produces excellent results. However, it requires a much heavier bond paper than what we are presently able to obtain.

Please send your reply concerning the above, plus sales terms and conditions, prior to October 12th. We are sure what you may provide would be helpful for us to meet the commitments to our customers.

Thank you in advance for your kind cooperation.

Faithfully yours

Sample Letter 4-9

Dear Sirs,

Your advertisement for cotton tablecloth and embroidered beddings arouse our attention. Would you please send us details of your various selections, including sizes, colors and prices (FOB San Francisco) and also indicate the different qualities of materials used?³

When you quote, please state your terms of payments and discounts that you would allow on purchase of no less than 200 dozen of individual items. We would also like you to send us samples of each category by airmail so we can make a sound decision.

As we are a large dealer in textiles in the US and there is a promising market in our region for moderately priced beddings, your prompt attention will bring you a big business with us.⁴

Hoping to hear from you soon.

Yours faithfully

New Words and Expressions

leaflet	n.	宣传单，广告单
catalogue	n.	产品目录表
sample	n.	样品
quotation	n.	报价
cutlery	n.	餐具
pricelist	n.	价目单
discount	n.	折扣
manufacture	n.	制造，制造业，产品
yacht	n.	游艇
brochure	n.	宣传册
maintenance	n.	维修
retailer	n.	零售

lady-wear	n.	女士服装
booklet	n.	小册子
airmail	v.	航空邮寄
delivery times		发货次数
terms of payment		付款条件
inquiry form		询价表
regular purchase		经常性购买
chain of hotels		连锁饭店
chromium plated		镀铬的
export operation		出口业务
bulk purchase		大宗购买
business potential		商业机会
electronic show		电子产品展览
after-sales service		售后服务
export price-list		出口价格单
net list price		货物净价
bill of exchange		汇票
document against payment		付款交单
semigloss printing paper		半光打印纸
bond paper		装订纸

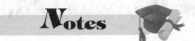

Notes

1. As we are about to expand our export operation, it is essential that our suppliers be both competitive in terms of price, and extremely reliable.   如果我们扩大出口业务，我们的供应商必须在价格上具有竞争力，并且要非常可靠。

2. Please send us all available data on your product.   请寄给我们有关你们产品的信息。
   此句中的 "data" 为 "信息" 的意思。

3. Would you please send us details of your various selections, including sizes, colors and prices (FOB San Francisco) and also indicate the different qualities of materials used?   你能否寄给我们有关你们产品的详细资料，其中包括规格、色彩及价格（FOB San Francisco），并注明所采用材料的质量情况？
   本句中 "selection" 的意思为 "产品种类"。

4. ... there is a promising market in our region for moderately priced beddings, your prompt attention will bring you a big business with us.   ……在我们地区，价格适中的床上用品市场前景良好，你方若能及时回复，则会给你们带来良好的业务。

此句中的"your prompt attention"是指"及时回复"的意思。

Sentence Menu

1. **Opening for first inquires**
   (Tell your supplier what sort of firm you are, or how you heard about the firm you are writing to, or use other references.)

   (1) We are importers in ... and would like to get in touch with suppliers of ...
   (2) Our company is ... and we specialize in the import and export of ...
   (3) We are engaged in/a dealer in ...
   (4) We have learned from ... that you are a leading manufacturer of plastic travel goods.
   (5) We were very much impressed by the quality and competitive pricing of your catering equipment shown at the recent Trade Fair in Paris, and feel that they could be marketed successfully in our country.
   (6) We are interested in your recently-developed technology.

2. **Ask for catalogues, price-lists, samples, details ...**

   (1) Would you please provide information on the types and quality of carpeting you have available, together with the prices.
   (2) I would appreciate your sending me an up-to-date price list for your electronic products.
   (3) Please let us know $\begin{cases} \text{what qualities you are able to supply from stock.} \\ \text{what quantities you are able to deliver at regular intervals, while} \end{cases}$
   quoting your best price of FOB Shanghai.

   Similarly we can adopt similar sentence patterns as follows:

   It would be helpful if you could ...
   We would be grateful if you could ...
   We would be appreciative if you could ...
   We would appreciate it if you could ...
   It would be very much appreciated if you could ...
   We would be obliged if you could send us ...
   Your information on ... will be appreciated.
   With reference to your advertisement appearing in the local press, I hope to ...
   Please inform us of what special offer you can make us.

   (4) We would like to/intend to/want to ...
   (5) We are prepared to purchase substantial quantity of ... and shall appreciate your quoting us your bottom prices and acceptable terms of payments.

3. Closing your letter

(1) Look forward to receiving your reply.

(2) Look forward to hearing from you.

(3) Look forward to your prompt reply.

(4) We appreciate your early reply.

(5) We are expecting your quotation soon.

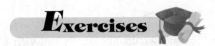

I. **The following is a sample of inquiry, please make favorable comments on this letter in terms of writing skills, tone and etc.**

ABC Building Materials Supplies Co., Ltd.
Walton Industrial Estate, Speke, Liverpool, England
Telephone: 627841   Fax: 627843

China Metal Products Corporation
The Industrial Zone
Shenzhen
China

Dear Sir or Madam,

We are interested in purchasing large quantities of Steal Cleats in all sizes. We would appreciate it if you would give us a quotation per kilogram CFR Liverpool, England. We would also be grateful if you could forward samples and your price list to us.

We used to purchase these products from other suppliers. We may prefer to buy from your company because we understand that you are able to supply larger quantities at more attractive prices. In addition, we are confident about the quality of your products.

We look forward to hearing from you by return.

Your faithfully

Robert Johns
Purchasing Manager

Unit 4 Inquiries

II Rewrite the following letter and point out where is improper for an inquiry.

We saw the selection of sweaters that were displayed on your stand at the "Men-swear Exhibition" that was held in Guangzhou, and found them very attractive.

We used to purchase sweaters from another producer; but unfortunately enough, that producer has discouraged us this year on delivery and quantities. We are hoping to see that you will not do the same; otherwise, we would not initiate a contract of long time with you.

Your immediately reply will be demanded.

III The following statements are taken from the text of a letter asking for discount. Rearrange the sentences in a correct order.

1. Should you offer a discount of 4%, we would be able to place an order of 2,000 CDQC-333 electric thermoses.
2. As you know, our company has been purchasing from your company for many years. Due to the recent economic crisis, we are in a throat-cutting competition in India.
3. I am writing to ask whether you could offer us a discount for CDQC-333 electric thermoses.
4. We are looking forward to your positive reply. Thank you very much.
5. A discount of 4% of your supply might reduce our pressure a great deal.

VI Fill in the blanks of the following letter with the words given, and change the form where necessary.

mutually, cover, inform, specialize, refer, promotion, act, regard

Dear Sir or Madam,

We would like to _____ you that we _____ on a sole agency basis for a number of manufacturers.

We _____ in finished cotton goods for the Middle Eastern market. Our activities _____ all types of household linen.

Until now, we have been working with your textile department and our collaboration has proved to be _____ beneficial. Please _____ to them for any information _____ our company.

45

> We are very interested in an exclusive arrangement with your factory for the _____ of your product in Bahrain.
>
> We look forward to your early reply.
>
>
> Yours faithfully

V Writing practice.

Suppose you were now working at Shanghai Textiles Import and Export Co., Ltd., 123 Tianshang Road, Shanghai 200300, China. Your company is going to import some textiles from a Paris-based foreign company. You are now requested to write an inquiry to the Sales Department of the foreign company, asking for data about quotation, discount, range of textile products, and if necessary, pricelist and catalogue will be enclosed.

Unit 5

Replies
回复函

5.1 Introduction

In your reply to an inquiry from a regular customer, it is important to keep your style direct and you will have to better proceed with your letter as follows:

1. Opening

Please be sure to thank the writer of the inquiry for the letter in question. It is necessary to express your appreciation for his or her interest in your goods and company. When you thank the writer for his or her inquiry, do not forget to mention the date of his or her letter and quote any references that appear.

You had better avoid opening with expressions like "We are in receipt of your inquiry" or "In reply to your inquiry", because these opening tend to sound rather cold and distant. And also you should avoid phrases or structures like "It was with the utmost pleasure that we received..." or "We deeply regret that we cannot supply you with...", you will appear at best desperate or, worse, insincere. A straightforward "Thank you for...", "I would like to thank you for..." or "I am sorry that..." is enough.

2. Confirming That You Can Help

In answering a letter of inquiry, if your company has the stock of the goods asked about, and is satisfied with the business relations existent between, and you are not ready to hesitate the deal, then you will make sure that you are positive about the inquiry, and well on the way to carry forward your contacts, so you will try to convey a positive message by confirming that you can help. Therefore you can write this way:

(1) I'm pleased to inform you that we can supply most items from the stock.

(2) We are glad to tell you that we have a wide selection of..., which I think will be to your satisfaction.

(3) As for your request, I think your requested products are obtainable from our stock.

(4) Most types can be supplied from our stock.

(5) ... is in stock and is available to you until ...

3. Answering Each Request from the Inquirer

The inquirer might have listed many a request — like catalogue, price list, samples and trade terms in his or her last letter. The writer of the letter should be patient enough to answer each of the list, even though the list goes on long.

4. Suggesting Alternatives

If you do not have what the inquirer has asked for, but have an alternative, offer it to him. But do not criticize the product he or she originally asked for.

5. If Necessary

But if your company is keen to increase sales, or is putting a new product on the market, the letter of reply must do something to get the reader to know about your new product, sustaining the reader's interest and persuade him or her to place an order. Therefore, simple answer that you have the goods in stock is not enough. Of course, you can encourage and try to initiate business relations by writing positively.

6. If Not Having Thanked Your Customer

Please thank your customer before you conclude your letter, if you have not expressed your appreciation at the beginning of your letter.

7. Concluding Your Letter Courteously and Confidently

In the concluding paragraph, you need to express your sincere expectation of further contact or even an order courteously. This is the last chance to build goodwill and induce readers to make a purchase.

To sum up, a reply to an initial inquiry is the first impression your customer will have of you, and that will be how he or she judges you. So a direct approach, telling the customer what the product is, why she or he should buy it, how much it will cost, and what concessions you are going to offer, will create an impression of an efficient company that can handle his or her order smoothly.

5.2 Sample Letters

 Sample Letter 5-1

Dear Sirs,

Thank you for your interest in our services of project management.

We provide consulting, training, contracting and other services specifically designed for the public sectors in Australia, and the Pacific and Asia.

For public sector managers, we are able to provide contractors with valuable experience, expertise and skills. We are particularly competitive in providing strong project management support. You can trust that our service will definitely enhance efficiency and reduce the costs a great deal.

Enclosed are the quotations of our service of project management. Considering that you are one of our first clients in China, we will grant a discount of 8% to you.

If you have any questions, please feel free to contact us.

Yours faithfully

Sample Letter 5-2

Dear Mr. Perkins,

We appreciate your interest in Success Supplies and are delighted to send you the information you requested.

Ruled ledger paper only costs US$40 per ream; with the purchase of six or more reams, the price is reduced to US$36 per ream, a saving of at least US$24.

As for black reinforced binders, I am sorry to inform you that they are temporarily out of stock, but now our company manufactures the binders of other colors, which are the same in size and quality. If you are interested, I will send you some of catalogues enclosed with this letter for your reference.

Because we are manufacturers of many other fine office supplies, ranging from ball-point pens to promotional novelties, we have enclosed for your consideration a copy of our current catalog. Should you decide to place an order, you could use the convenient order form in the catalog.

Please let us know if we may be of further assistance.

Sincerely yours

Sample Letter 5-3

Dear Mr. Warner,

Thank you for your letter of 31st August, 2015 inquiring about our company and our products. Enclosed are latest brochures listing all the types of yachts we manufacture as well as our financial statement for the year ending 31st December, 2014.

We did not sell our products in the Japanese market in the past, and we would be delighted to do business with your company. Please go through the enclosed material. We would be happy to answer any questions that may come from you.

We are looking forward to hearing from you soon.

Yours sincerely

 Sample Letter 5-4

Dear Sirs,

Thank you for your letter of October 6th, 2015 in which you requested about our product No. 1208

While the specifications of the product are enclosed, our commercial terms such as price and shipping and payment terms are indicated as follows:

1. Quantity: 100 units
2. Price: US$100.00 per unit, CIF New York
3. Payment Terms: L/C to be established within one week after order
4. Shipment: Within one month after receipt of L/C

We hope the above quotations are of interest to you and we are looking forward to hearing your reply soon.

Faithfully yours

Sample Letter 5-5

Dear Ms. Liu,

Thank you for your fax of 24 May requesting information on our range of electronic products. I was pleased to learn that we had been recommended to you by Hulex Industries.

I am now enclosing our renewed catalogue and price list. This company is a well-established and reliable leader in the electronic industry. What is more, you will identify on pages 4-8 of the catalogue enclosed that we offer exactly the type of goods that you are interested in.

We are to inform you that we can offer extremely competitive prices, because of our new production lines, and in addition, we could grant you a further 3% discount on sales exceeding US$6,000.[1]

I hope this information will prove useful to you.

If you have any questions, please feel free to contact me.

Yours sincerely

 Sample Letter 5-6

Dear Mr. Wilson,

We thank you for letter of 21st November and are pleased to enclose a detailed quotation for bathroom fittings.

In addition to those advertised in the Builders' Journal, our illustrated catalogue also enclosed shows various types of bathroom fittings and the sizes available. Most types can be supplied from stock. 45-60 days should be allowed of those marked with asterisk.[2]

Building contractors in Hong Kong and Taiwan have found our equipment easy to install and attractive in appearance. Naturally all parts are replaceable, and our quotation includes prices of spare parts. We can allow a 2% discount on all orders of US$5,000 and over, and a 3%c on orders exceeding US$20,000.[3]

As you can see our price is generally low, for the market at this time is somewhat dull and you are very fortunate in purchasing the goods now. American market seems to pick up in this activity, so we hope you to buy goods before the recovery reaches a peak. We can hold our offer open in 2 weeks from the date of this letter.⁴

We hope that this can accommodate your interest, and we can get your immediate approval. Any orders you place with us will be executed promptly.

Yours sincerely

Francesco Marani
Sales Manager

Encl. 2

 Sample Letter 5-7

Dear Johnson,

Thanks for your letter dated May 21st, 2015, expressing your interest in our air conditioners.

Enclosed are our latest catalogue, price list and a brochure regarding our new line of products for your consideration. You will get a special discount of 6% if you place an order over 6,000 sets.

Since we are a well-established and specialized maker and exporter in this line in China, we will be able to offer you the best quality products at low prices. Due to the increasing demand for the products in the market, we will be obliged to raise our price in the near future. We suggest you order with us before June 2015.

We hope you can offer us the chance to provide you with our best quality products.

Sincerely yours

Sample Letter 5-8

Dear Mr. Bacon,

We thank you for your letter of May 8, and are now enclosing a report from one of our users on Coal Cleaning Equipment.

We hope that the report will offer you the necessary information. If there are any questions concerning the operation and service of the equipment, just let us know. We await your response with a keen interest.

Yours sincerely

 Sample Letter 5-9

Dear Mr. Wang,

Subject: US Retailer Report No. 2-438/1

Thank you for your fax dated 15th April requesting the above-mentioned report on the retail industry in the USA. I am now enclosing the details of this report.

As you can see from our brochure, the report identifies US retail development and retail channels, and contains the relevant recommendations for China-based companies, which are going to export to the USA.

If you like to have this report, the cost is RMB¥100. The report is on sale at Shanghai headquarters or by mail order by completing the enclosed order forms.

Yours sincerely

Ms Petra Woo
Information Assistant
Media Communications Department

Encl.

New Words and Expressions

stock	n.	库存
initiate	v.	建立
expertise	n.	专业知识
enhance	v.	提高，增强
ream	n.	一令（纸）
temporarily	ad.	临时地，暂时地
renewed	a.	更新的，最新的
well-established	a.	市场地位稳定的，完备的
identify	v.	确定，找出
asterisk	n.	星状记号
replaceable	a.	可置换的，可替换的
exceed	v.	超出
dull	a.	市场萧条的
accommodate	v.	满足（需求）
execute	v.	执行（订单）
promptly	ad.	及时地
date	v.	注明……的日期
response	n.	回复，答复
recommendation	n.	推荐
China-based	a.	位于中国的
complete	v.	填写（单据等）

public sector		公共部门
out of stock		缺货
ruled ledger paper		直线账页
reinforced binder		硬面账页夹
promotional novelties		促销用的小礼品
convenient order form		现成的订单表
bathroom fittings		浴室设施
pick up		市场复苏
retail industry		零售业
retail channel		零售渠道
on sale		出售

Unit 5 Replies

1. ... in addition, we could grant you a further 3% discount on sales exceeding US$ 6,000.   ……而且，如果贵方的订单超过 6 000 美元，我们将再给予 3% 的折扣。
2. Most types can be supplied from stock. 45—60 days should be allowed of those marked with asterisk.   大多数种类的产品均可供应，那些标有星号的产品可以在 45～60 天后交货。
3. ... and a 3% c on orders exceeding US$ 20,000.   ……如果订单超过 2 万美元，将给予 3% 的佣金。
   句中的"a 3% c"为"a 3% commission"的缩写。
4. We can hold our offer open in 2 weeks from the date of this letter.   自收到本信之日起，我们将保留该发盘 2 周的时间，即在 2 周的时间内有效。

1. Opening

   (1) Thank you for your letter of, ... in which you asked about/inquired about our range of plastic goods.

   (2) We thank you for your letter of ..., and are pleased to enclose a detailed quotation for you.

   (3) We are pleased to receive your letter of ... and delighted to send you ...

   (4) It is a pleasure to receive your letter of, and we are enclosing ...

   (5) We thank you for your interest in our range of lightweight luggage.

   (6) We appreciate your interest in ...

   (7) It is a great pleasure of having your inquiry for our new HU Company Equipment. We are enclosing a copy of the pamphlets which illustrates the operating directions.

   (8) In regard to your request of May 28, we are pleased to send you by separate parcel a copy of our sample products.

2. Answering each request from the inquirer

   • Catalogues, price-lists, samples and trade terms

   (1) Enclosed is our catalogue, describing the product, the catalogue provides you with complete information on ...

   (2) Enclosed is our latest catalog in which page 14 details the unique features of our product.

55

(3) We are pleased to enclose/fax you our latest price list for the goods/catalogue you inquiry about.

(4) The pamphlet enclosed not only provides you with the message/information about the machine, but also illustrates the way of operating them.

- **Terms of payment**

(1) We are pleased to inform you that our quotation is...

(2) We can quote/submit the price/you the best price.

- **Discount**

(1) We can allow/grant you a special discount of 2% for/on orders exceeding... in value (on repeat orders, on prices quoted, off net price)...

(2) If your order is valued at..., we would allow you a special discount of...

(3) If your order is large enough, we'll be ready to reduce our price by 2 percent.

(4) The price we offer compares favorably with quotations you can get elsewhere.

- **Price terms**

(1) Our prices are quoted CIF Melbourne.

(2) Prices are quoted on CIF Eastern Coast basis.

(3) To supply you goods on FOB basis.

(4) As for your inquiry about price terms, we are now going to quote as follows:

- **Suggesting alternatives**

(1) The goods you inquired for in your letter are out of stock now, but we can offer you a substitute which I think is equal in... and...

(2) We are very regretful that we are unable to supply what you required in quality, with the same physical characteristics but we supply you the products of...

(3) This new model of machine has all the qualities of the one you asked for, and it has added advantages of being lighter, stronger and more durable.

- **If necessary**

  (**If you need to take this letter as an occasion to advertise your products**)

(1) We are sure you will find a ready sale for our products, in your... as have other relations in other countries, and we do hope that we can reach an agreement on the terms quoted.

(2) We hope that you will agree that our prices are very competitive for these good quality goods.

(3) The motto of our company is to grant our customers every satisfactory purchase which includes a money-back guarantee, free installation and immediate delivery service.

3. Closing

(1) Please contact me if you need any further information.

(2) Please reply as soon as possible $\begin{cases} \text{because we don't have sufficient stocks.} \\ \text{since suppliers are limited.} \end{cases}$

(3) We are looking forward to your order.

(4) I hope that this information will help you.

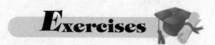

Exercises

I Please read the following letter of inquiry, and write a reply to the letter.

Dear Sirs,

We have seen your advertisement in today's *Business Weekly* and are interested in your tablecloth, especially Art No. 603 and 604.

Please quote us the lowest prices CIFc 2%, Port Sudan and indicate the respective quantities of various sizes that you can supply for prompt shipment. In the meantime, please forward us respective samples. If your prices are workable and the quality is satisfactory, we shall place regular orders for fairly large numbers.

For your information, we have dealt in tablecloths for more than 20 years and have a good connection in this country. We also have some associated firms in the neighboring countries, where a ready market can be found for your products. Therefore, we should like to make sure if you could appoint us your sole agent in Sudan, which, we think, would be helpful to your business.

Your immediate attention to our inquiry and proposal would greatly oblige us.

Yours faithfully

II Compare the following two reply letters and point out the differences in terms of tone and writing techniques.

Letter A

Dear Mr. Tangley,

We thank you for your request for information concerning our CKY metal products. You can find the necessary information on the 5th page in the enclosed pamphlet. Hoping to hear from you soon.

Sincerely yours

Letter B

Dear Mr. Tangley,

Thank you very much for your interest regarding our CKY metal products. Enclosed you will find our catalogue, describing the product. The pamphlet provides you with complete information.

Our company's policy is to offer each customer our complete service. This includes a money-back guarantee, immediate delivery, and free delivery service.

Please tick your box on the order blank if you would like additional information on any of products. Remember, we are here to serve you and are happy to answer any questions.

Sincerely yours

III **The following statements are taken from the text of a letter asking for discount. Rearrange the sentences in a correct order.**

1. Although we are interested in your products, we find your price is so high that our margin of profit would be either very little or nil.
2. We hope, therefore, you will reduce your price so as to stand up to the competition.
3. Information indicates that the socks of similar quality are available at present on the market and at a price 10%–15% lower than yours.
4. We wish to thank you for your letter of March, 2, offering us 1,000 pairs of captioned socks at RMB¥14 per pair on the usual terms.
5. We are looking forward to your reply.

Unit 5 Replies

VI Fill in the blanks of the following letter with the words given below, and change the form where necessary.

> interest, off, deal, ready, on, association, allowance, selection

We are pleased to receive your inquiry of 2 March, and to hear that you liked our range of sweaters.

There would certainly be no trouble in supplying you from our wide _____ of garments which we make for all age groups.

We can offer you the quantity discount you asked for which would be 5% _____ net prices for orders over $20,000, but the usual _____ for a trade discount in our country is 10%, and we always deal _____ payment by sight L/C. However, we would be prepared to review this once we have established a firm trading _____ with you.

We are enclosing our summer catalogue and price-list quoting prices CIF Vancouver.

We are sure you will find a _____ sale for our products in Canada as have other retailers throughout Europe and America, and we do hope we can reach an agreement _____ the terms quoted.

Thank you for your _____; we look forward to hearing from you soon.

Yours sincerely

5. Translate the following reply letter into English.

×××先生：

棉花和茶叶

兹确认贵方8月5日要求我方报棉花和茶叶实盘来电。今晨我方电告，以（净重）每公吨……美元 CIF 哥本哈根价或欧洲任何主要港口价报给你方50公吨棉花，2015年9月至10月装运。此报盘为实盘，以我方8月25日前收到回复为准。

请注意，我方所报价格为最优惠价格，不再接受任何还盘。

关于茶叶，兹告知，我方现有的存货已向其他地方发盘。不过，倘若贵方能给我们一个可接受的价格，你们有可能获得该货。

贵方熟知，上述商品近期需求量甚大，而这种需求增大定会引起价格上涨。所以，如果贵方能立即给予答复，你们会得到目前行市看涨的好处。

Unit 6

Letters of Declining
拒绝函

6.1 Introduction

It is clear that knowing how to communicate bad news or decline the request as delicately and clearly as possible is an essential business skill. A skillful manager will attempt to say "no" in such a way that the reader or listener supports the decision and is willing to continue a positive relationship with the company. To do this successfully, manager must first have empathy, she or he must try to understand how the recipient of the unpleasant news will feel. If you are sending the information in a letter, you must first think how you would approach the news if the recipient were there to receive it in person. A letter is much less likely to be "cold" if you use empathy in addition to tact and effective writing skills. To deal with such letters, you can adopt the indirect approach of handling the negative message discussed in the preceding chapter. That is, briefly stated, five steps as follows:

1. Delay Opening

It is also called buffer or sometimes called introductory paragraph. The paragraph is there to let the recipient know what the letter is about and serve as a transition into the discussion of reasons.

2. Explain the Refusal

People who are refused want to know why. To them and to the person making the refusal, the reasons are vital; they must be transmitted and received. A well-written first paragraph should put the receiver into a logical, but concise, discussion of the reason for the refusal.

3. State Your Refusal

The refusal statement should be in the same paragraph as the reasons. It should not be placed in a paragraph by itself; this arrangement should place too much emphasis on the bad news or the declining of requests. Because the preceding explanation is tactful and seems valid, the sentence that states the unpleasant news may arouse little or no resentment.

4. Offer a Constructive Suggestion or an Alternative Plan

If appropriate, you can add a suggestion or an idea to help the recipient improve the situation, which will assist in preserving future relationships with the other party. But your suggestion should be presented in a tactful, sensitive manner.

5. Close Positively

A closing paragraph will be concerned about some aspect of the topic other than the bad news itself — like showing confidence in the reader and his company and prospect of continued business relations.

6.2 Sample Letters

 Sample Letter 6-1

Dear Sirs,

Thank you very much for your letter concerning our technical training programs. Your tentative plans sound excellent and we are sure that your personnel will benefit from the training you intend to establish.

The courses we have worked out for the engineers in the research department of our East Power Industry Company are the result of several years' effort. Since some of the areas it pursues are of a classified nature both for our purposes and because of industrial regulations, you can appreciate why it is not possible for us to send you a detailed outline of the program.

We have already referred your letter to one of our extension division. They will contact you within two weeks. The program they have developed is specially established for the engineers in the atomic power application, which will prove of the same value to you. Meanwhile, for your most convenience, we are enclosing an article in the June issue of Engineering Research, which describes several corporate training programs for engineering development in the power industry of our country.

Thank you again for your interest in the cooperation of human resource development. And we are also looking forward to your success in this field.

Yours faithfully

Sample Letter 6-2

Dear Mr. Preston,

Thank you for taking the time to send us your résumé and the returned application form. We appreciate the interest you have expressed in working in our company.

It is clear that you are a motivated individual with some important skills to offer. Unfortunately, after reviewing your experiences and interests related to our current opportunities we have to conclude that we do not have a suitable position available.

This decision is certainly not a reflection on your qualifications or capabilities. We are only in a position to assess your qualifications as they relate to our present opportunities.

We do, however, keep your application on file for a period of two years. If our situation changes, we will be happy to get in touch with you within that time frame.

In the meantime, we wish you a good luck in finding a challenging position in your field of interest.

Sincerely yours

 Sample Letter 6-3

Dear Bruce,

Thank you for your letter of October 14 regarding your visit next month.

Although we would very much like to meet with you to discuss your new products, I am afraid neither I nor my deputy manager will be available between November 17 and 19 due to our business trip at that time. Therefore, we suggest that you send us a brochure listing your new products. We still study the brochure and contact you for any further information or questions.

We hope to see you next time you are in South Korea.

Sincerely yours

Sample Letter 6-4

Dear Mr. Qian,

Thank you for your interest in our company. We are always pleased to hear from a valued customer.

I am regretful to inform that we cannot agree to your request for business information regarding our sales systems and profits generated from our newly developed security software. The fact is that most of our competitors also keep such information confidential.

We do hope that this will not bring you too much inconvenience. If there is any other way in which we can help, please do not hesitate to let us know again.

Yours sincerely

 Sample Letter 6-5

Dear Mr. Ma,

Thank you for inviting me to talk about the latest development in the production of health food at next month's FMA Seminar. I would like very much to join the discussion

and offer my own views to business people and professionals.

Unfortunately, I have got to go to Mexico next month to visit some of our factories. I am afraid I won't be able to attend the seminar.

If you are planning to have other seminars in the future that will feature the same subject, I would be glad to speak, schedule permitting. Thanks you again for the invitation.

Sincerely yours

Sample Letter 6-6

Dear Ms. Stevenson,

Thank you very much for your letter dated July 15, 2015, in which you showed your interest in our products.

Unfortunately, we must let you know that for competition reasons our production line comprises only specific items. We do not produce the merchandise you request.

We have, therefore, asked BCP Corporation, with which we have close connections, to send you an appropriate offer.

We are including a brochure showing the items we manufacture. If you are interested in any of these, please let us know. We will then send you a detailed quotation including delivery, prices, terms of payment and etc.

Sincerely yours

Encl: Brochure

 Sample Letter 6-7

Dear Mr. Keen,

It is a great pleasure to receive your first order for 60 dozen Panda toys (Article No. 469). We are eager to have your name included into the list of our loyal customers.

In an effort to minimize shipping and office costs, we have established US$ 8,900 as the minimum account for every order.[1] The savings that result from this regulation are passed on to our customers. We are sending you a copy of our current catalogue under separate cover. When you go through the details we are sure that you will find many cost-saving items which sell fast in your local markets.

Provided that you supplement your original order so that the minimum figure is US$ 8,900, we will be delighted to process it immediately and ship it as required.[2]

Looking forward to your favorable reply.

Yours sincerely

Unit 6 Letters of Declining

 Sample Letter 6-8

Dear Sirs,

Thank you for your impressive sales presentation on 3rd March. It was very informative and you answered all our interested questions very professionally.

We have considered your proposal very thoroughly. Unfortunately enough, we have decided not to proceed at this time for the sake of our financial situation.

Over the next few months, we will be scaling down our operations to offset the downturn in trade. When the economy picks up, however, we will certainly be interested in talking to you again.

If it is possible, could you please contact us in five months' time, when we might be interested in taking matters further?

Yours faithfully

 Sample Letter 6-9

Dear Mr. Bayle,

Thank you for your letter of 15 May, 2015 requesting a change in our contract for 6 MT565 Drilling machines.

In your letter, you asked for the delivery date to be brought forward by two months. [3] Whenever it is possible, we will try to oblige our customers.

In this case, unfortunately, we have examined our production schedule for the next three months and find we are fully committed. [4] This makes it impossible to advance the delivery date we agreed on in our contract.

To be fair to all our customers, we must stick to our original schedule. We hope you will understand our position.

Yours sincerely

65

New Words and Expressions

empathy	n.	同感，共鸣
recipient	n.	接受者，收信人
tact	n.	策略
tactful	a.	有策略的，有技巧的
generate	v.	生成，产生
confidential	a.	秘密的，保密的
seminar	n.	研讨会
comprise	v.	包括，由……组成
impressive	a.	印象深刻的
informative	a.	提供信息的，增进知识的
offset	v.	补偿
oblige	v.	满足……的请求
extension division		分部，分支机构
health food		保健食品
favorable reply		肯定的回答，答复
scale down		减少
downturn in trade		贸易下降

Notes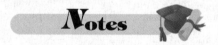

1. In an effort to minimize shipping and office costs, we have established US $ 8,900 as the minimum account for every order. 为了减少运费和行政费用，我们确定 8,900 美元作为每份订单的最低价格。
2. Provided that you supplement your original order so that the minimum figure is US$ 8,900, we will be delighted to process it immediately and ship as required. 只要你将原有的订单增加到我们所规定 8 900 美元，我们将非常愿意根据你的要求立刻处理订单。句中的"provided that"意思为"只要"，等同于英语中的"on condition that"。
3. In your letter, you asked for the delivery date to be brought forward by two months.
在信中，你要求将货物发运日期提前两个月。
4. In this case, unfortunately, we have examined our production schedule for the next three months and find we are fully committed. 在这种情况下，我们查看了未来三个月的生产计划并遗

憾地发现我们的生产计划已满。

Sentence Menu

1. Delay opening

（1）Thank you for your inquiry of 23 August. We are always pleased to hear from a valued customer.

（2）We are pleased to receive your letter of ... in which you request to ...
We appreciate this opportunity to serve your needs.

（3）We were pleased to receive your order of ... for a further supply of 500 air-conditioners. We appreciate your continuing confidence in our products.

（4）We are referring to your letter of ... in which you asked for ...

（5）In reply to your letter regarding the supply of 10 free sample units of our product No. 1080.

（6）We understand your concern about the ... you mentioned in your letter of May 6th.

2. Explain refusal

（1）As we are going to launch a new serial of products onto the market, we need to have adequate funds to facilitate this promotion.

（2）Much as I should like to attend your exposition, my schedule will be fully engaged next week.

（3）In order to minimize shipping and office costs, we have established ... as the minimum amount for every order.

（4）As you know that owing to ..., we will not be able to meet the agreed delivery date.

（5）Your plan sounds excellent and we are sure that it will bring lots of benefits to your personnel. But we will have to ...

（6）As you know that I am fully engaged with a conference out of town during that period.

3. State your refusal

（1）To our regret, we cannot participate in this occasion

（2）Much to our regret, we are unable to accommodate your request.

（3）Unfortunately, we are not in a position to accept your request.

（4）Unfortunately I have a schedule conflict and I will be unable to attend the forum.

（5）We are sorry that we are unable to comply with your request.

（6）We apologize for not being able to give you any samples.

（7）Unfortunately enough, owing to ..., and we should be glad if you would accept our apologies.

4. Offer a constructive suggestion or an alternative plan

(1) If you have any other projects, however, please let us know as we are always open to new investment proposals.

(2) We are now enclosing new brochure in which you can know about my newly issued regulations regarding this product.

(3) We have referred your letter to one of our counterparts, which specializes in this line of services.

(4) I am checking with other manufacturers in the area who are working with the materials you want. They may be able to give you the quality you desire at a fair price.

(5) But we can only offer your order on the basis of a confirmed, irrevocable letter of credit.

5. Close positively

(1) We are looking forward to receiving your favorable reply and always ready to entertain your consistent orders.

(2) We are also looking forward to your success in this field.

(3) Thank you for giving us this opportunity to explain the situation.

(4) We hope our reply will not be disappointing.

(5) We look forward to the opportunity of serving you again.

(6) We are always pleased to do business with your organization and will continue to serve you with quality industrial equipment.

Exercises

I Write a letter to G. E. Water & Co., 72 Flint Street, London E. C. 2, England, with the following particulars.

1. 确认收到3265号订单。
2. 表示遗憾不能接受所报价格，并陈述理由。
3. 报我方现价，可否接受。

II Writing practice.

Situational Writing 1

Now your company has received an order of black leather gloves today, but your company has not manufactured the required goods, due to difficulty with dye. But you can supply from the stock the gloves of other colors. You are requested to write a letter in which you state your refusal and suggest other alternatives.

Unit 6 Letters of Declining

Situational Writing 2

> You have received a fax requesting a price reduction, the reason being that the competition in that location is fierce. Now you are requested to write a letter of declining in which you will state your reasons.

III **The following explanation passage is taken from an adjustment refusal. Read it carefully and then revise it to eliminate negative and insulting language. Add missing details to make it a reasonable one.**

We find no way to grant your claim for a new water-proof watch because the scratches on the back of the little machine indicate that you tempered with it. By opening the watch, you had broken the waterproof seal. Such an action negates the guarantee, as you can see from the one enclosed.

VI **The following statements are taken from the text of a letter of refusal. Rearrange the sentences in a correct order.**

1. We have contacted the shipping company and regret to tell you that you are unable to comply with your request.
2. We are very sorry that we are unable to advance shipment.
3. Thank you for your letter of 19 January requesting earlier delivery of goods under your purchase contract No. 954.
4. We have been informed that there is no available space on ships sailing from here to your port before 5 April.
5. We will, however, do everything possible to ensure that the goods are shipped within the contracted time.

Unit 7

Goodwill and Social Letters
友好与社交信函

7.1 Invitation Letter

On many occasions business firms need to perform special functions to publicize a certain event such as the opening of a new branch office, carry out promotional activities, the celebration of the anniversary of companies, the retirement of a senior member of staff, etc. Invitation should be sent out to all guests for their presence. The invitation letter can be classified into formal and informal invitations.

7.1.1 Formal Invitations

1. Introduction

There are no hard and fast rules in laying out an invitation[1], but it is customary that formal invitations are typed on A5 or A6 good quality paper or decorative card. Often they are specially printed and enclosed in envelopes. As shown in the following specimen, formal invitations are written in the third person, stating the nature of the event, name of the host, giving the exact time and date, and the venue. If there is any dress requirement for the occasion, it is usually specified on the lower left-hand corner of the invitation.

Formal invitations often require a reply with RSVP placed at the bottom right, which is French meaning "please reply". Alternatively some invitations have the following expressions placed immediately before the address of the sender at the bottom left:

- Please reply
- Please answer
- Please send reply to
- Regrets only (It means only those who are unable to attend are required to reply.)

The tone of formal invitation should be made cordial and courteous with words carefully chosen to convey the hospitality and seriousness of the host.

2. Sample Letters

 Sample Letter 7-1

                The President of
                BDA Co., Ltd.
    request the pleasure of the company of

    ----

  at the banquet celebrating BDA's 10th Anniversary
                to be held at
                the Rotary Hall
                Westin Hotel
                2 Aston Road
                East Finchley
                London
      at 6:30 p.m. to 8:00 p.m.
      on Wednesday 29 June, 2015

Suggested dress code: informal but smart

Mr Richard Bird
The President of
BDA Co., Ltd.
23 Manor Road
London
N3ED4AX

                                                    RSVP

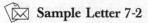 **Sample Letter 7-2**

                  Mr. Xu Ling
    request the pleasure of the company of

Mr. and Mrs. Lawrence Wentlow
at dinner
on Monday, the fourth of April
at seven o'clock

Blue Room
Hilton Hotel

Please present this card at the entrance.

R. S. V. P.

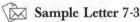 **Sample Letter 7-3**

The Winchester Co-operative Bank
Request your presence
At the formal opening ceremony
To be held in its new quarters
On Saturday 6 June, 2015 at 8 a.m.
His Royal Highness the Duke of Kent
Vice Chairman of the British Overseas Trade Board will be present
Prior to its opening for business
On the following Monday

7.1.2 Reply to the Formal Invitation

1. Introduction

An invitation is a courtesy and must be promptly acknowledged. Whether a reply is called for or not, one must advise either as an acceptance or refusal. A host should know how many guests to expect. A reply to an invitation must be a definite acceptance or refusal. An open ended or ambiguous acceptance is not satisfactory.

An acceptance requires the repetition of both the date and the hour to prevent the possibility of a misunderstanding. Invitations should be answered in kind: formal invitations should be answered formally, informal invitations informally and oral invitations orally.

Formal replies should be written in the third person. There should be no heading, no salutation, no complimentary close, no inside address, or no signature. The writer should not refer to himself as I or to the addressee as you. Avoid all abbreviations except Mr., Dr., Mrs., and Messrs. Numbers occurring in dates should preferably be spelled out. Above all, the reply needs to start with thanks and, to the close of the reply, end by clearly telling whether the invitation is acceptable or not. If it is not accepted, due to some reasons, it is essential that a cautious treatment should be given to guard against possible hurt to the respect of the other party.

2. Sample Letters

Sample Letter 7-4

Mr. Michael Jones
thanks the President of
BDA Co., Ltd.
for this kind invitation to
the banquet celebrating BDA's 10th Anniversary
to be held at
the Rotary Hall
Westin Hotel
2 Aston Road
East Finchley
London
at 6:30 p.m. to 8:00 p.m.
on Wednesday 29 June, 2015
and has much pleasure in accepting.

Mr. Michael Jones
Marketing Manager
All Seasons Co., Ltd.

Sample Letter 7-5

Mr. Michael Jones
thanks the President of
BDA Co., Ltd:
for this kind invitation to
the banquet celebrating BDA's 10th Anniversary

to be held at
the Rotary Hall
Westin Hotel
2 Aston Road
East Finchley
London
at 6:30 p.m. to 8:00 p.m.
on Wednesday 29 June, 2015
but regrets being unable to attend due to a planned business trip to Spain.

Michael Jones
Marketing Manager
All Seasons Co., Ltd.

7.1.3 Informal Invitation

1. Introduction

Informal invitations are usually presented in the form of a letter, known as a letter of invitation. The form of invitation letters varies, depending on the degree of intimacy between the writer and the person addressed. Informal invitations are more personal and intimate. They usually have a heading, an inside address, a salutation, and a signature. Should plain paper or monogrammed paper be used, it is customary for the writer to place his own address in the lower left corner of the letter, as indicated in the following sample. The writer may use the first person, referring to himself as I and to the addressee as you. Wording should be made sincere and courteous.

2. Sample Letters

 Sample Letter 7-6

Dear Mr. Smith,

We are planning a small dinner party in honor of Mr. Liao Yalin, President of this company. The dinner will be held at the Capital Plaza, Beijing from 6:30 p.m. to 8:30 p.m. on Friday, May 20 and dress will be informal business wear.

We hope that you will be able to join us in this opportunity to meet the senior directors of our company. Will you please notify us before May 15 whether we can expect you.

Best regards.

Yours sincerely

 Sample Letter 7-7

Dear Mr. Spencer,

We are pleased to inform you of the Grand Opening of our EverDeli Chinese Food Restaurant at 18 Green Avenue, Edgewood.

The ceremony begins at 10:30 a.m. on Saturday, 18 May, 2015 and a cocktail party and buffet will be held at our restaurant at 12:00 noon. We have pleasure in inviting you to attend.

We hope you will be able to join us.

Yours sincerely

Elizabeth Maze

 Sample Letter 7-8

Dear Sir/Madam,

We would like to invite you to an exclusive presentation of our new DX800s audio-visual system. The presentation will take place at the Wilson Exhibition Center, 300 King Street, Green Land, at 2:00 p.m. on Tuesday, May 15. There will also be a reception at 4:00 p.m. We hope that you and your colleagues will be able to attend. Mark Tech Inc. is a leading producer of high-quality audio-visual equipment. As you well know, recent technological advances have made audio-visual systems increasingly affordable to the public. Our new models offer superb quality and sophistication with economy, and their new features give them distinct advantages over similar products from other manufacturers.[2]

We look forward to seeing you on Tuesday. Just call our office at 123-4567 and we will be glad to secure a place for you.

Faithfully yours

Kathleen Curtis
Marketing Department Mark Tech Inc.
143 Wedgemere Avenue
Los Angeles 28, California

Sample Letter 7-9

Dear Sirs,

Annual General Meeting (AGM)

This year marks the 30th Anniversary of the Association. This is a special occasion and in order to celebrate our birthday in style, we have arranged to hold a Cocktail and Light Buffet Evening on Tuesday, 20th November at the Sheraton Hotel. This event will replace the Buffet Lunch previously scheduled for Thursday, 15th November.

We apologize for the change in dates, and sincerely hope that you will still be able to attend the celebration.

The AGM will be held immediately before the Cocktail and Buffet, at 5:30 p.m. in an adjoining room.

More information will be sent to you shortly, but in the meantime, please mark your diaries — Association AGM and Cocktails, Tuesday, 20th November.

Yours faithfully

Unit 7 Goodwill and Social Letters

 Sample Letter 7-10

Dear Sirs,

We should like to invite your Corporation to attend the 2016 International Fair which will be held from August 29 to September 4 at the above address. Full details on the Fair will be sent in a week.

We look forward to hearing from you soon, and hope that you will be able to attend.

Yours faithfully

 Sample Letter 7-11

Dear Ms. Ainsworth,

You are invited to be our guest at the Moorcliff Resort for our Annual Dealers' Convention Banquet which will be held at the River Oak Banquet Room on Saturday, July 10.

The evening will begin with a reception at seven o'clock, followed by dinner, a speaker, and the awards presentation. For the first time this year, an award will be presented to the dealer with the largest percentage of new accounts acquired during the dealer's second year with Staggers Wholesaler.[3]

Please let us at Staggers know by July 5 whether you will attend. I will be eager to see you there.

Sincerely yours

7.1.4 Reply to Informal Invitation

1. Introduction

Acknowledgements of informal invitations may likewise be more personal and informal than replies to formal invitations. Such acknowledgements may have a heading, an inside address, a salutation, a complimentary close, and a signature. The use of the pronoun "I" is permissible.

The writing guidelines are set as follows:

(1) Thank the recipient for inviting you.

(2) Say that you are delighted to accept the invitation.

(3) Confirm the date and other details about the meeting or visit.

(4) Ask for more information.

(5) Express your appreciation again at the end of the letter.

2. Sample Letters

 Sample Letter 7-12

Dear Mr. Warner,

I am very pleased to accept your kind invitation to the dinner party in honor of Mr. Liao Yalin, to be held at Capital Plaza on Friday, May 20. It will indeed be an honor to meet the senior directors of your company and I am looking forward to this opportunity.

Thank you very much for the invitation.

Sincerely yours

 Sample Letter 7-13

Dear Sirs,

I sincerely appreciate your kind invitation to a luncheon on May 12. It would be indeed a great honor if I could attend. Unfortunately, my schedule in May will not allow me to be present on this occasion. I certainly hope you will understand.

Thank you again for your invitation.

Yours faithfully

Sample Letter 7-14

Dear Mr. Simpson,

Thank you for your letter of June 28 inviting our corporation to participating in the 2016 International Fair. We are very much pleased to accept and will plan to display our electrical appliances as we did in previous years.

Mr. Li will be in your city from July 2 to 5 to make specific arrangements and would very much appreciate your assistance.

Yours sincerely

Sample Letter 7-15

Dear Sirs,

I thank you for your kind invitation occasioned by your opening celebrations to be held on the 10th April.

My wife and I are pleased to accept your invitation, and will travel by flight CAL826, arriving at New York at 6:00 p.m.

We are both looking forward to this opportunity to wish your organization continued success.

Yours faithfully

Sample Letter 7-16

Dear Mr. Scott,

I shall be pleased to accept your invitation to speak at the American Business Administrator's annual meeting on March 5 at 2:00 p.m.

What do you think of "The Corporate Development Strategy in the 21st Century"? This is simply a suggestion. You have not indicated how long you wish me to speak. Unless I hear from you, I shall limit my address to 30 minutes.

I am looking forward to meeting you and the other members of your society.

Yours cordially

 Sample Letter 7-17

Dear Mr. Abbott,

I have your kind invitation of July 4 to speak before your organization. I am pleased to accept unless something unforeseen interferes within the next 3 days. In such an event I will send you a fax. Otherwise, you may consider this letter my acceptance.

I thank you for the invitation and hope that my topic will be informative and stimulating to your group.[4]

Yours sincerely

7.2　Letter of Thanks

7.2.1　Introduction

　　Businessmen have many opportunities for writing "thank-you" letters to express appreciation and good will. They include letters to new customers for the first order, letters to established customers for a particularly large order or for regular business letters to customers who give advice or perform a service. Every gift, every favor or courtesy requires sincere and gracious acknowledgement. In most cases in business, formal acknowledgement is all that is necessary. As with all other goodwill letter situations, your message should be written deductively, and reflect your sincere feeling of gratitude. Therefore, you express your sincere thanks usually at the opening of your letter of thanks. Immediately after that, what is stated will be specific about that which is appreciated, which reflects a sincere feeling of gratitude, for instance, your pleasant feeling elicited on that occasion. Finally close your letter with a warm statement — show your wish for reciprocation and good wishes for the other party.

7.2.2 Sample Letters

 Sample Letter 7-18

Dear Mr. Dakin,

Thank you for your order No. 464 of September 20, 2015.

The models you selected from our showroom go out today under my personal supervision.

The package is being airfreighted to you on Swissair. The relevant documentation is enclosed.

I enjoyed meeting with you and hope that this order represents the beginning of a long and prosperous relationship between our companies.

The next time you visit us, please let me know in advance so that I can arrange a lunch for you with our directors.

Yours sincerely

Jack London
Sales Manager

 Sample Letter 7-19

Dear Mr. Jones,

Back now in my own country, I wish to thank you most warmly for your excellent hospitality extended to myself and my colleagues. The opportunity to meet yourself and your directors is something I had long looked forward to, and I can only hope that one day I may be able to receive a visit here from you.

I very much appreciated your kindness and that of your colleagues in showing me around the new plant and introducing to us your production line.

Thank you again on behalf of us all.

Sincerely yours

 Sample Letter 7-20

Dear Ms. Simpson,

Thank you very much for all the trouble you and your staff went to during my visit to your plant. The tour and the subsequent discussion with you and your staff are extremely informative. This trip has not only given me a better understanding of your strict quality control system, but also enhanced my confidence in cooperation with you.

I would like to ask you to convey my appreciation to every one of your staff and look forward to your coming visit to Chengdu.

Sincerely yours

 Sample Letter 7-21

Dear Mr. Graham,

Please accept my thanks for the informative and very enjoyable day you offered me when I visited the Hovan plant. I have just written to Mr. Smith to express my appreciation for the courtesies extended to me, and to tell him how impressed I was with the breadth of your knowledge. I could not have had a better guide or a more delightful host than you.

I do hope I could have an opportunity to reciprocate your kindness in the future.

Yours sincerely

Liu Hua
Product R&D Dept.

Sample Letter 7-22

Dear Mr. Karl,

I would like to write to you to say how much we appreciate the promptness with which you settled your accounts with us during the past year, especially as a number of them have been for very large sums. It has been of great help to us at a time when we ourselves have been faced with heavy commitments connected with the expansion of our business.⁵ We hope you will continue to give us the opportunity to serve you.

Sincerely yours

Sample Letter 7-23

Dear Mr. Yi,

Thank you for attending our meeting last Friday and for sharing your suggestions and experience with us. As beginners in telecommunication business, our group found your suggestions and recommendations extremely helpful.

We hope we can return the favor some time in the future. Just give us a call when we can assist in any way.

Yours sincerely

Sample Letter 7-24

Dear Mr. Thomas,

I am writing to say thank you very much for being such a wonderful visit arrangement you made for us in San Francisco. On the eve of our departure, I am pleased to get the opportunity to send you and your associates a thankful message for the cordial reception and hospitality extended to us during our stay here. We all believe that this visit is very fruitful and is also helpful to our future business cooperation.

We do hope to have an opportunity to reciprocate your hospitality by visiting us in China as our guest. My associates and I would be delighted to entertain you in the near future. By the time, both sides can meet and discuss how to work more closely for further expansion of our business.

We wish you every success.

Sincerely yours

 Sample Letter 7-25

Dear Mr. Hughes,

This is a short note to thank you very much for introducing us to EFG Corporation. We would like to report that our visit there last month resulted in an initial order from EFG, which hopefully may develop into large orders in the future.

Without your introduction we would not have been able to establish this connection with EFG, and once again we wish to thank you for your help. We look forward to expanding our relationship even further.

Yours sincerely

7.3 Letter of Congratulations

7.3.1 Introduction

The letter of congratulations indicates the writer's profound interest in the success or good luck of the recipient. Sending congratulatory messages provides an excellent way for managers to build goodwill. Because the subject matter of congratulatory letters is positive, which is easy to write. There are many occasions calling for congratulations, such as a new appointment, the award of an honor, the establishment of a new business, success in the examination, or even a marriage or a birthday. Whatever the occasion, your letter is sure to be well received. It may be either short and formal or conversational and informal, depending on the circumstances and the relationship between you and your reader. A short, straightforward letter is usually all that is necessary. The writing of such type can go as follows:

(1) Express your delight at hearing the good news and, if necessary, make favorable comments.

(2) Express your congratulations.

(3) Close with a warm, courteous statement, namely, your best wishes for the future success, or cooperation, etc.

Letter of congratulations are usually brief and prompt. Be sure to send the letter within a few days after the event; otherwise, all your efforts will be fruitless.

7.3.2 Sample Letters

 Sample Letter 7-26

Dear Mr. Braund,

I was overjoyed to learn that you were awarded Businessman of the Year. Your business record has been one of consistent success and your active involvement in civic service makes your achievement even more remarkable. You well deserve this high honor that has come to you.

Please accept my congratulations on the recognition that you have earned by your superb performance as a business executive.

Yours sincerely

 Sample Letter 7-27

Dear Mr. Wool,

I was delighted to see in yesterday's Times the story about your promotion to Chief Engineer at the Jack Chemical Company. I know that you earned the promotion through years of hard work, and the Jack Chemical certainly picked the right person for the job.

It is always a pleasure to see someone's true ability win recognition. Congratulations and best wishes for continued success.

Yours cordially

Sample Letter 7-28

Dear Mr. Stockstill,

Please accept our warmest congratulations on the opening of your Beijing Office. The expansion of your business in China is truly impressive and your commitment to Chinese market is encouraging. We at Haide International Group wish you every success in your increased involvement in this market.

If I personally or my company can be of assistance to you, please do not hesitate to let me know.

Yours sincerely

 Sample Letter 7-29

Dear Mr. Green,

We have learned from your company's May 1st announcement that you have been named President of BP Chemical Industry Co., Ltd.

Please accept our warmest congratulations on your appointment. Our thoughts and best wishes are with you as you take up your new and important position.

It is our sincere hope that the close relationship existing between our two companies will continue and perhaps even be strengthened further, and I look forward to being able to contribute to our mutual benefit. Once again, congratulations.

Yours sincerely

Sample Letter 7-30

Dear Ray,

Heartfelt congratulations on your promotion to Chief Clerk of the Glen Ridge Office. I know how very happy you and your family must be. You should consider this promotion a well-deserved reward for your many years of conscientious and untiring efforts on behalf of your company.

I rejoice with you in your good fortune. All my best wishes go with you as you begin your new duties.

Yours sincerely

 Sample Letter 7-31

Dear Charles,

On looking through the ConPad Times this morning I came across your name in the New Year Honors List and hasten to add my congratulations to the many you will be receiving.

The award will give pleasure to a wide circle of people who know you and your work. Your services to local industry and commerce over many years have been quite outstanding and it is very gratifying to know that these have now been so suitably rewarded.

Warm regards and best wishes.

Yours sincerely

Sample Letter 7-32

Dear Mr. Peon,

I am writing to convey my warm congratulations on your appointment to a Board of Telephone Engineering Ltd.

My fellow directors and I are delighted that many years of service you have given to your company should at last have been rewarded in this way, and we join in sending you our very best wishes for your future.

Yours sincerely

 Sample Letter 7-33

Dear Mr. Thomas,

Our heartiest congratulations on your promotion!

Your promotion to national marketing manager certainly came as no surprise to us in view of your brilliant record of achievements while you worked as the regional sales manager in the Central Region[6], and we always knew that you would become a great success someday.

You came to know us and our service well during the past four years, and you know that we stand ready to be of continued service to you in the days ahead.

We extend every good wish to you in this challenging task.

Sincerely yours

Sample Letter 7-34

Dear Mr. York,

I was delighted to learn that you are now establishing your own advertising company. I would like to add my voice to the chorus of congratulations from all sides.

With your brilliant background and long record of fine achievements, I am convinced that the new company will be a great success. I sincerely hope you will find in this new venture the sense of great achievement.

Should there be any way in which we can be of great assistance, please do not hesitate to contact me. I wish your company every success and are looking forward to a closer cooperation with you in the future.

Yours sincerely

7.4 Letter of Sympathy and Condolence

7.4.1 Introduction

Letter of condolence and sympathy are among the most difficult of all letters to write. There can be no set pattern since so much depends on the writer's relationship with the person he or she is writing to and how well he or she knows about him. Nevertheless, it is safe to predict that such letters need to be short and written with restraint, for this is not the time to engage in many words. The important thing is to write promptly and with sincerity.

The purpose of writing letters of condolence is to show your concerns and to cheer up the unhappy victims of misfortune. Therefore these letters should be written tactfully and optimistically.

There are formal and informal letters of condolence. Formal one is more reserved in tone while still being cordial and sympathetic, while informal letters can be more personal and considerate.

The simplest plan for such messages is to (1) start with a statement of sympathy, (2) follow with sentences about mutual experiences or relationships, and (3) close with some words of comfort and affection or if necessary, an offer to help can be presented.

7.4.2 Sample Letters

 Sample Letter 7-35

Dear Mr. Simpson,

We were all very distressed to learn about the fire, which had caused such damages to your plant.

We are wondering whether we can help in any way and hope you will feel free to call on us for any assistance we can render. We would consider it a privilege to help out a friend and customer at such a time as this.

Yours sincerely

 Sample Letter 7-36

Dear Mr. Pierce,

I am extremely sorry to hear that your illness has become more serious, and you have had to go into hospital. Let us hope that it will be for only a short time and that you will soon be out and about again. Everybody here sends his best wishes to you for a quick recovery.

With best regards.

Yours sincerely

 Sample Letter 7-37

Dear Mr. Denton,

I was distressed to learn of your accident when I called you yesterday, but it was good to know that you are now over the worst and are progressing toward recovery.

You have, as always, my kindest regards and best of good wishes.

Sincerely yours

 Sample Letter 7-38

Dear Mr. Jordan,

We understand that, due to the recent flooding of the Yangtze River caused by heavy rains, your factory in Suzhou was severely damaged. It is our sincerest hope that there are no casualties in this terrible incident and that the factory can resume operations as soon as possible.

As a token of friendship and sympathy, we would like to make a contribution of US$100,000 to the rebuilding of your factory.

Please accept the donation as a gesture of our friendship.

Yours sincerely

 Sample Letter 7-39

Dear Sirs,

It was with profound regret that we received the sad news of the sudden and untimely death of your deputy managing director, Mr. Grant. His passing must mean a great loss to your company and his associates and he will long be remembered by all who knew him and who worked with him.

Please accept our heartfelt condolences and convey our deepest sympathy to Mrs. Grant and her family.

Yours faithfully

Sample Letter 7-40

Dear Sirs,

I was deeply distressed to hear of the sudden death of Mr. Thomas Wilson who served at your company for so long. His passing must mean a great loss to your company and his associates.

We have cause to be grateful to him for the kind patronage and advice that he gave us unreservedly. My staff join me in conveying our sincere sympathy to members of his family.[7]

Yours faithfully

 Sample Letter 7-41

Dear Mr. Smith,

We, at William Kent, were shocked and saddened to learn about the tragic, untimely death of your brother.

I know I cannot find any words to comfort you, but I do want to express how deeply we all feel for you.

Please call me if there is anything I personally can do to help.

Yours sincerely

 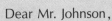

Dear Mr. Johnson,

I was saddened recently to hear of your great loss, and should like to extend my deepest sympathy to you at this time of sorrow. Terry was both loved and admired by all of his colleagues, and his disarming sense of humor will be sadly missed in the office.

I should just like you to know that if you need anything in the coming weeks, I will be more than happy to help out in any way I can.

With much sympathy.

Yours truly

Ralph Kwok

7.5 Letter of Complaints and Claims

7.5.1 Introduction

Complaints or claims may sometimes arise in spite of our well-planned and careful work in the performance of a sales contract. Goods may be shipped to wrong address or arrive in less than perfect condition; details for an order may be confused; badly needed goods may be delayed; quality may be different from the standard. When such situations arise, a claim letter is usually sent. But claim letters can be divided into two groups: routine claims and persuasive claims. Letters about persuasive or non-routine claims assume that the requests will be granted after explanations and persuasive arguments have been presented. If a problem is only a matter of correcting a very understandable situation (possibly because of guarantees, warranties, or other contractual conditions), a routine claim letter is involved. This kind of letter usually assumes that the request will be granted quickly and willingly.

Since routine claim letters are usually associated with relatively minor problems, the requests are not likely to meet resistance. All necessary work to be done is to write a clear, specific, and concise claim letter listing the facts of the situation. Your writing needs to be straightforward, but well planned and documented. Therefore, it is necessary to study the case in question and make certain what the real cause is and who is the party to be held responsible.

How can your complaints and claims receive best adjustment you desired? Here are some guidelines for your reference:

(1) State the request at the beginning;
(2) Explain details to assess the situation;
(3) Name specific actions to correct the problem and politely mention strong terms if you fail to get a satisfactory reply;
(4) End positively—express your appreciation in advance for taking the action requested.

7.5.2 Sample Letters

 Sample Letter 7-43

To Whom It May Concern,

Re: Order FC-996 on Family Computers

Would you please look into the execution of the delivery for our order FK-776 on Family Computers Model HRS-001, which should have reached our warehouse a week ago?

On 25th July our company sent you an order for 300 Family Computer Model HRS-001, stressing the importance of delivery by 5th September at the latest. However, up to now, we have received no acknowledgement of the order, nor have the computers been delivered to us. Apparently some mistake must have been made in the processing of this order.

Failure to collect the goods in time is causing serious inconvenience to our customers. We shall be glad if you look into the matter as an urgency and let us know when the goods can be expected.

We are looking forward to the arrival of the computers.

Yours truly

 Sample Letter 7-44

Dear Mr. Lee,

You will remember that last month we ordered 24 Haide 1 GHz Pentium X Computers.

When we discussed delivery dates, you assured us that you could deliver by 2 December. However, the goods are now two weeks overdue, and I have heard nothing from you to confirm a definite delivery date.

We urgently need these computers to upgrade the administrative functioning of our offices, and your slowness is causing a great deal of inconvenience.

I should appreciate your looking into this matter and arranging for delivery of these computers within the next three days.

I am afraid that if you are unable to deliver within this period, we shall be compelled to cancel our order and purchase from another supplier.

Yours sincerely

Mr Kadir Aboe
Office Manager

KA:lK

 Sample Letter 7-45

Dear Sirs,

When the S. S. "Eancastria" arrived at Tripoli on 10th November, it was noticed that one side of Case No. 5 containing super Earphones was split. We therefore had the case opened and the contents examined by a local insurance surveyor in the presence of the shipping company's agent[8]. The case was invoiced as containing twenty-four "Panda" brand, among which ten were badly damaged.

We enclose the surveyor's report and the shipping agent's statement. Ten replacements of the earphones will be required. Please arrange to supply these and charge to our account.

We hope no difficulty will arise in connection with the claim and thank you in advance for your cooperation.

Yours faithfully

Sample Letter 7-46

Dear Mr. Li,

We received our consignment of hi-density optical disks (Art No. 456) this afternoon.

However, on checking the disks we have discovered that they do not function properly.

They appear to be incapable of storing data for some reason. Therefore, I am afraid they are completely unusable.

We had planned to start a promotion of these disks from Monday. In fact, we already have many advanced orders, which we shall now have to postpone because of your poor quality control. This will cause us a great deal of inconvenience.

I should like you to replace these faulty disks with full-functioning Grade "A" disks within the next week. If you are unable to guarantee delivery for whatever reason, I should be prepared to accept a complete refund of the money, which was paid for the order.

Yours sincerely

Mr. Tsai Hsin-En
Manager

 Sample Letter 7-47

Dear Mr. Johnson,

Re: your S/C No. 2A-667B

We were informed by our agents in Beijing that 200 Tea Sets under the above S/C by S/S "Great Wall" had arrived at Port Amsterdam on July 8. Much to our regret, about 20% of the packages was seriously damaged with contents shattered to pieces and the outer bands broken.

We immediately invited qualified surveyors to the spot to look into the case, and their findings show that this was due to poor packing. A detailed survey report will be dispatched to you subsequent to their further study of individual case.

In accordance with the stipulations of the above Sales Confirmation, we think the tea sets should have been packed in strong seaworthy wooden cases suitable for long distance ocean voyages.

We are obliged to hold you responsible for the damage and claim against you for the compensation for the loss thus incurred.

Meanwhile our buyers are urging us to settle the case immediately. Therefore we would like you to inform us of what you decide to do regarding our losses.

We are awaiting your prompt reply.

Yours sincerely

 Sample Letter 7-48

Dear Sirs,

We are sorry to learn from your letter of August 10th, 2015 that something was wrong with the Cotton Goods we sent to you by S. S. "Peace". We can assure you that the goods in question were in perfect condition when they left here. We have the clean B/L to support what we say. Maybe the damage complained of must have occurred in the transportation or during loading and unloading.

This being the case, we think we are apparently not liable for the damage and would like to advise you to claim on the shipping company who should be responsible.[9]

At any rate, we deeply regret about the unfortunate incident and should it be necessary we shall be pleased to take the matter up on your behalf with the shipping company concerned.[10]

Yours faithfully

Sample Letter 7-49

Dear Mr. Suauki,

The goods we received on July 15 were found not to match our order.

The goods we ordered were Item No. 2345 whereas the goods received were Item No. 2435.

We cannot understand how this kind of mistake could occur at your end. We have decided to ship the goods back to your company by freight at your expense and we ask that you refund the US＄15,000 which we have already paid you. Please remit this amount to our account (A/C No. 1012379) with the Midori Bank, Ltd., Minato Branch, Tokyo. Please note that we hereby also reserve the right to claim any damages arising out of your wrong shipment.

A quick refund will be brightly appreciated.

Yours sincerely

 Sample Letter 7-50

Dear Mr. Skinner,

The one hundred (100) pieces of furniture arrived in Yokohama at the end of October. However, at the inspection, five (5) pieces were found damaged, as fully described in the attached report made by our inspector.

We request that you send five (5) new pieces as replacements as soon as possible.

Yours sincerely

Unit 7 Goodwill and Social Letters

 Sample Letter 7-51

Dear Mr. Nishida,

The cargo of two hundred (200) units of your desktop computers has arrived in New York. Unfortunately, however, our inspection showed that eleven units were missing their connection cords. Attached is the report made by the surveyor who inspected the cargo. As you can see from the report, the eleven cords were already missing at the time the units were packed at your factory.

Please send us the cords free of charge, and no later than March 20th. We await your favorable reply.

Sincerely yours

New Words and Expressions

publicize	v.	宣传，广告
anniversary	n.	周年
specimen	n.	样品，信样
venue	n.	地点，地址
alternatively	ad.	另外地，两者选一地
cordial	a.	热情的，真诚的
courteous	a.	有礼貌的
hospitality	n.	友好，款待
intimacy	n.	亲密，关系密切
monogrammed	a.	有交织字母的
addressee	n.	收信人
plaza	n.	大厦，城市中的广场
notify	v.	通知
buffet	n.	自助餐
exclusive	a.	专有的，独家的，唯一的
audio-visual	a.	音像的
superb	a.	极好的，超等的
sophistication	n.	复杂，尖端

distinct	a.	清楚的，独特的
adjoining	a.	相邻的，毗邻的
acquire	v.	获得，兼并
wholesaler	n.	批发商
acknowledgement	n.	承认，认可
unforeseen	a.	不可预测的，不可预见的
stimulating	a.	激励的，起刺激作用的
deductive	a.	演绎的
reciprocation	n.	回报，报答
showroom	n.	展览室
airfreight	v.	空运
documentation	n.	（所有）单据，单据使用
subsequent	a.	后来的，随后的
breadth	n.	宽度，知识面
commitment	n.	承诺，承担义务；致力，专心致志
associate	n.	同伴，同事
congratulatory	a.	祝贺的，庆贺的
heartfelt	a.	衷心的
conscientious	a.	认真的，自觉的
untiring	a.	不知疲倦的
rejoice	v.	欢乐，高兴
gratifying	a.	令人满意的
chorus	n.	齐声
hesitate	v.	忧虑
condolence	n.	吊唁，慰问
restraint	n.	克制，抑制
optimistically	ad.	乐观地
reserved	a.	有保留的，缄默的
sympathetic	a.	富有同情心的，同情的
affection	n.	情感，喜欢
distressed	a.	悲痛的，忧伤的
render	v.	使成为，提供，给予
privilege	n.	优先给予的权利或机会
casualty	n.	伤亡，伤害
resume	v.	继续
token	n.	标志，象征
untimely	a.	过早的
patronage	n.	资助，帮助

Unit 7 Goodwill and Social Letters

unreservedly	ad.	毫不保留地
disarming	a.	消除怒气的
complaint	n.	抱怨，投诉
persuasive	a.	有说服力的
non-routine	a.	非日常的
document	n.	记录，记载
adjustment	n.	理赔
execution	n.	执行
urgency	n.	紧急的事情，要紧的事
assure	v.	向……保证
overdue	a.	过了付款期的
split	v.	开裂
invoice	v.	（在发票上）载明，列明
high-density	n.	高清晰度
unusable	a.	无法使用的
full-functioning	a.	全面功能的
guarantee	v.	保障，保证
refund	v.	偿还
shatter	v.	粉碎，击碎
seaworthy	a.	适航的
incur	v.	招致（损失），遭受
item	n.	货物
remit	v.	汇寄，寄
hereby	ad.	在此
inspector	n.	货物检验员
replacement	n.	置换品，替代物
in honor of		为庆祝……，向……表示敬意
be affordable to		对……来说能承受得起
electrical appliances		家用电器
as with		与……一样
in advance		事先的
settle one's account		结账
out and about		四下走动
be compelled to		必须，不得不
insurance surveyor		（保险公司）货物检验员
optical disk		光盘

qualified surveyor	有资格的检验员
to look into	调查
sales confirmation	销售确认书
hold sb. responsible for	让某人对……负责
to claim against	向……提出索赔
to settle the case	解决问题
a clean B/L	清洁提单
at any rate	无论如何
be liable for	对……负责
at one's end	在……一方
to ship ... by freight	运输货物
the connection cord	（电）塞线

Notes

1. There are no hard and fast rules in laying out an invitation... 在写邀请函时并没有严格的规定原则……

2. Our new models offer superb quality and sophistication with economy, and their new features give them distinct advantages over similar products from other manufacturers. 我们的新产品具有超一流的品质，而且价格优惠，与同类产品相比，更具明显优势。

3. For the first time this year, an award will be presented to the dealer with the largest percentage of new accounts acquired during the dealer's second year with Stagers Wholesaler. 首先，对于在与斯丹戈批发商进行贸易的第二年中获得最多新订单的交易商，我们将在本年度给予奖励。

4. I thank you for the invitation and hope that my topic will be informative and stimulating to your group. 感谢你的邀请，并希望我的演讲对你有所启发和帮助。

5. It has been of great help to us at a time when we ourselves have been faced with heavy commitments connected with the expansion of our business. 我们自己也面临着业务拓展的艰巨任务，而此刻贵方的及时结款给了我们极大的帮助。

6. Your promotion to national marketing manager certainly came as no surprise to us in view of your brilliant record of achievements while you worked as the regional sales manager in the Central Region... 得知你被提拔为全国营销经理的消息，我们并不感到惊讶，因为你在担任中部地区销售经理时就已经取得了辉煌的销售业绩……

7. We have cause to be grateful to him for the kind patronage and advice that he gave us unreservedly. My staff join me in conveying our sincere sympathy to members of his family.

他给予了我们全心的支持和良好的建议，对此我们表示感激。我和我的员工一道向他的家属表示诚挚的慰问。

8. in the presence of the shipping company's agent   当着货运公司代理人的面

9. This being the case, we think we are apparently not liable for the damage and would like to advise you to claim on the shipping company who should be responsible.   鉴于这种情况，我们认为我们显然不能对这种损失负责，因此我们建议你向货运公司提出索赔，它们应该对此事负责。

10. ... and should it be necessary we shall be pleased to take the matter up on your behalf with the shipping company concerned.   ……如有必要，我们将愿意代表你方就此事向有关的货运公司进行交涉。

Invitation Letter

1. Formal invitation

(1) President/Mr. and/Mrs. ... request, the pleasure/honor of the company of Mr. and/Mrs. ... at Dinner/a Cocktail party/a buffet dinner/banquet/a tea party/a party dance at <u>venue</u> at <u>time</u> on <u>date</u>.

(2) Mr. ... request, the honor of Mr./Miss ...'s presence and reception to be held at ...

2. Accept the formal invitation

(1) Mr. and Mrs. ... thank ... for this kind invitation to <u>event</u> to be held at <u>venue</u> at <u>time</u> on <u>date</u>, <u>month</u>, <u>year</u>, and has/have pleasure in accepting.

(2) Mr. ... accepts with pleasure/honor the kind invitation of Mr./Mrs. to <u>event</u> to be held at <u>venue</u> at <u>time</u> on <u>date</u>, <u>month</u>, <u>year</u>.

3. Informal invitation

(1) We are now planning to celebrate ... and should be honored to have you as our guest, if you could manage it.

(2) We shall be glad if you will join us at ...

(3) We would like to invite you to ...

(4) You are invited to be guest at ...

(5) It is indeed an honor for us to invite you to lecture/give a keynote speech in ...

4. Accept informal invitation

(1) I am pleased to accept your kind invitation to ...

(2) I am delighted to accept your kind invitation to ...

(3) It is with great pleasure/gives me much pleasure to accept your kind invitation to ...

(4) Thank you very much for your kind invitation to ... We would be pleased to come.

5. Decline an invitation

(1) Mr. and Mrs. ... regret that a previous engagement prevents their acceptance of Mr. and Mrs. ... 's kind invitation to dinner.

(2) Thank you for ..., but regret being unable to attend your ..., owing to ...

(3) Much to my regret, I am unable to accept your kind invitation.

(4) Thank you for your kind invitation to ..., but unfortunately I have another engagement on that day.

(5) Please accept my sincere regrets for not being able to join you. I certainly hope you will understand.

(6) Please accept my sincere apologies since, due to a previous arrangement, I will not be able to join you.

(7) Unfortunately, my schedule will not allow me to attend the reception.

(8) I wish I could be at your reception but I am afraid on that day I have some schedule conflicts.

Letter of Thanks

(1) We are writing to thank you for ...

(2) Please accept my sincere appreciation for ...

(3) Thank you for all the kindness you extended to us.

(4) Thank you very much for the hospitality you extended to me during my stay.

(5) Thank you for taking the time to meet with us.

(6) I really appreciate your thoughtful gift and I will always treasure it.

(7) I enjoyed the short stay at your home, which is both delightful and memorable.

(8) Our trip to your country was very much enhanced by your kind arrangements and hospitality.

(9) We must write to you to say how much we appreciate the promptness with which you have settled your accounts with us during the past year.

(10) I look forward to the chance to reciprocate your kindness when you come to us next time.

(11) Our best wishes and warmest regards.

Letter of Congratulations

1. Express your delight in hearing the good news

(1) It is delighted news for me to learn that you have been appointed to Chairman of ...

(2) It came as no surprise to me to learn that you had been awarded the Outstanding Entrepreneur for the year for your excellent work in the field of management.

(3) We were very pleased and excited to hear about your new assignment.

(4) Your appointment came as no surprise to us in view of your unusual abilities.

(5) I was very pleased to learn of your appointment as ...

2. Express your congratulations

(1) Please accept my warmest congratulations on this tenth anniversary of the founding of your business.

(2) Please accept my sincere congratulations on your success.

(3) I would like to extend my warmest congratulations to you on your promotion.

(4) I am sure you will be able to fulfill your new responsibilities with your usual success.

(5) We know that your promotion is a well-deserved reward for your many years of conscientious and untiring efforts for your company.

(6) I would like to extend my warmest congratulations to you on this well deserved recognition of your ability.

(7) It is reassuring to us that someone of your ability will assume this key position.

(8) Congratulations! All of us feel proud of your remarkable achievements!

3. Close with a warm, courteous statement, your best wishes for the future success, or cooperation, etc.

(1) The best luck to you.

(2) My very best wishes to you as you begin your new duties.

(3) Please accept my congratulations.

(4) With kind regards.

(5) Warm regards and best wishes.

(6) I wish you the best of everything for all the years ahead.

(7) Please accept my best wishes to both you and your President.

(8) We extend good wish to you in this challenging task.

(9) We look forward to the continuing growth of your company under your enlightened leadership.

(10) Keep up the good work.

(11) May the success of the years be the foundation for the even more successful future.

Letter of Sympathy and Condolence

1. Letter of sympathy

- **Show your sympathy at the news**

  (1) We were very sorry to learn of...

  (2) I was deeply distressed to hear of...

  (3) I was deeply concerned when I learn of...

  (4) I heard from your secretary the unfortunate news that you are hospitalized.

  (5) We are sorry to learn about the accident in your factory.

  (6) It was terrible to learn that many of your employees were injured in the explosion.

- **Express your wish for early recovery or getting out of difficulties**

  (1) We are all praying for your quick and complete recovery.

  (2) I wish you a complete and speedy recovery.

  (3) We hope you will be able to get over the accident and recover soon.

- **If necessary, offer your help**

  (1) Please feel free to contact me if I can be of some help.

  (2) If there is anything I can do to help you, please let me know.

  (3) Please do not hesitate to ask us if you need any help.

2. Letter of condolence

- **Show your distresses at the sad news**

  (1) It is with great sorrow that we have received the sad news of the loss of...

  (2) We are shocked to hear of the sudden death of...

  (3) I was indeed grieved/deeply distressed to hear of the untimely passing of...

  (4) It came as a surprise to learn of your company president's sad news.

  (5) I was saddened recently to hear of your great loss, and should like to extend my deepest sympathy to you at this time of sorrow.

- **Make favorable comments on the mutual experience and your friendship**

  (1) We know how much he meant to you.

  (2) I had the privilege of knowing him for many years and always admired his integrity and high quality of business conduct.

  (3) His unfortunate passing away will definitely be a big loss to our cooperation.

(4) Mr. Keegan was the person who initiated business with our company and he was always supportive in expanding our mutual business ties.

(5) We know how difficult it will be to replace a man of such exceptional ability and character. He will be missed by all of the people who know him and have dealt with him.

- **Convey your condolences to the family or the company. If necessary, offer your help**

(1) My staff join me in conveying our sincere sympathy to members of his family.

(2) Please convey our sympathy to his family.

(3) Please extend our profound sympathy to everyone in your family.

(4) Please accept our heartfelt condolences and convey our deepest sympathy to Mrs. Grant and her family.

Letter of Complaints and Claims

1. State the request

(1) Would you please correct your shipment by sending the order No. ... by the first available vessel?

(2) I should appreciate your looking into this matter and arranging for delivery of the required goods as soon as possible?

(3) We should like you to replace these faulty goods with full-functioning products within the next week.

(4) I should like you to refund the money we have paid you for these machines.

(5) We should be obliged if you would replace the goods you delivered with the correct ones.

(6) We should be grateful if you would give me/us a complete refund for the defective goods, which were delivered.

2. Explain details to assess the situation

(1) On checking the camera, I discovered that it did not function.

(2) Upon inspection, it was found that the total content had been short-delivered by 1.5 tons.

(3) It was regrettable to see that the chemical content of ... is not up to the percentage contracted.

(4) After having the boxes examined we found that they were not strong enough for the long distance delivery.

(5) When we discussed delivery dates, you assured us that you could deliver by 2 December. However, the goods are now two weeks overdue/late.

(6) There is a mistake in your invoice of 27 July, 2015; you state that we have received 240 Gent's suits.

(7) You have supplied items, which fall far below the standard expected.

(8) The standard of workmanship of your products is inadequate.

(9) Unfortunately, you have sent us the wrong items. We ordered Model 602 but you have sent us the order Model 502.

3. Name specific actions to correct the problem and politely mention strong terms if you fail to get a satisfactory reply

(1) We would like you to send a new shipment at once to replace them. We'll await instructions from you.

(2) We are returning these... today, and request immediate replacement of the damaged goods.

(3) So we request you to bear some part of the airfreight charges. We await your reply as to whether you agree to our proposal.

(4) We hope you to refund US$... that we have paid for.

(5) Therefore, we request you to send us replacements within one week and pay for freight charges thus incurred.

(6) We believe that you should be responsible for the error, and assume all the costs of repairs.

4. Close positively — express your appreciation in advance for taking the action requested

(1) We hope no difficulty will arise in connection with the claim and thank you in advance for your cooperation.

(2) Please give this matter your urgent consideration.

(3) Your early clarification and settlement of the case will be appreciated.

(4) In the future transactions, we assure you of our best service at all times.

(5) We are awaiting your prompt reply.

(6) We shall be pleased to discuss with you where and how the arbitration is to take place.

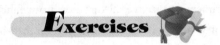

Exercises

I **The following statements are taken from the text of a letter. Rearrange the sentences in a correct order.**

1. However, your invoice states that the consignment contained 230 copies of *China Today* by Shi Xiang.

2. If you check our original order (No. 563487 — copy attached) you will see this was all we ordered.

3. Whereas, in fact, it contained only 200 copies.

4. We have just received the above invoice for a consignment of books which was delivered on May 2015 as part of our exhibition of contemporary Chinese photographers' work.

II Fill in the blanks in the following letter with the words given, and change the form where necessary.

> elapse, value, exhaust, place, event, impress, consequently, compel

Dear Sir or Madam,

I sent you on June 22, 2015, an order for wool to the _____ of $350,000 and _____ upon you that the necessity of delivery within 14 days from the date of the order. In spite of this, 20 days have _____ from that date, and the goods are still unreceived.

We must point out to you that this delay is very seriously inconveniencing us; our present stock of these goods is _____, and we are unable to meet our customers' demands, who, _____, have in many cases _____ their orders elsewhere. We should be glad to hear from you the reason of the non-execution of our order, as in the _____ of your being unable to supply us we shall be _____ to cancel the order and get these goods from another firm.

Yours truly

III Look at the following letter of complaints and decide how it can be revised, and then rewrite it.

Dear Sir or Madam,

I am frustrated and will never believe anyone who sells or represents the AAS Company. I need to tell you that the best way to lose future sales is to misrepresent a product.

When I brought the bike from Drellar Department Store, Main Street, Jonesville, last month this year, I was told that this was the best bike on the market, and its parts would be easy to be obtained.

As you will note, there is a box along with this letter. Inside the box is the broken part, which is the cause of all the trouble.

After having talked to seven repair shops in my city, I was furious at being told, "the company doesn't have replacement parts", and "The big stores sell this bike, and we repairmen get the gripes too. It shouldn't be available on the market."

I wanted to ask you to either replace the enclosed part, or send me a replacement bike. This is not a request but should be done on your part, for you should bear the responsibility for all the trouble that has been caused so far.

Mark Thompson

IV Writing practice.

Situational Writing 1

You have just learned that Mr. John Smith was promoted to the position of Deputy Managing Director. He has been doing business with you for several years. Now at the news, you are requested to write a letter of congratulations on his promotion on behalf of your Dept of Import.

Situational Writing 2

Now you are going to sponsor a forum, and you at your company are to invite a world famous economist Mr. Johnson to give a keynote speech on one of the interested issues prevailing in China. In your invitation letter, you need to design the speech topics for him to choose and tell him that expense incurred during his trip will be cared for by your company.

Situational Writing 3

Suppose you were working in a company, and one of your clients suffered great losses in last month's flooding. You, representing your president, are planning to write a letter of sympathy, in which you express your great concerns and sympathy, and suggest that if necessary, you could offer your financial support.

Situational Writing 4

Suppose your company ordered 50 sets of air conditioners. However, when goods have arrived, you find that there are only 45 sets. Now you are requested to write a letter of claim against the supplier, ABC Company, on the short delivery of the machines.

Unit 8

Interoffice Routine Letters
办公室日常信函

8.1 Letter of Appointment

8.1.1 Introduction

On many occasions, appointment is made through telephone calls or emails and faxes, etc. During the business trips overseas, you may also be convenient in asking for meetings or face-to-face talks. But all these need to be well arranged to the convenience of meeting with your business counterparts. While appointment can be made via above mentioned means, there are some formal occasions which call for written form of appointment. Therefore correspondences are exchanged to decide on the time or occasion for the appointment. In composing such letters, you should always consider the convenience of meeting with the person and you must make it easy for your reader to see at a glance the purpose of the appointment and, above all, the place and time for the suggested meeting. Details are not advisable to be discussed in the letter. Writing principle is prescribed as follows:

(1) Start with the request for appointment and state your reasons;
(2) Give the exact details about place and time or let the other party choose time, if your schedule is not busy;
(3) Ask the other party to contact for confirmation.

8.1.2 Sample Letters

 Sample Letter 8-1

Dear Mr. Johnson,

We should very much like to discuss with you the matter of agency in China, and as our Trade Delegation will be in Sydney early next month, we hope it will be convenient for you if Mr. Deng Guojun of the Delegation calls on you, say, on the 5th, May at 10:00 a.m., or any other time that suits you. Please let us know.

Sincerely yours

 Sample Letter 8-2

Dear Mr. Smith,

I represent the Dellaer maker of machine tools in Munich, and I would like to talk to you about purchasing some of the electronic components you make.

I shall be in Nanjing for a week from September 17 to 23, and would like to see you. Would Wednesday, September 20 at 11:00 a.m. be convenient to you?

I shall be at Jinling Hotel at week and a message or letter will reach me there.

Sincerely yours

 Sample Letter 8-3

Dear Sir or Madam,

I should very much like to see you on a matter which I think you would agree is of special interest to both of us, and as I shall be in Bradford next week I propose to give a call on, say, Thursday morning, the 12th about 11:00 'clock, or at any other time that will suit you.

If the day and time suggested are not convenient and if you would suggest an alternative appointment, I will re-arrange my other engagements as may be necessary.[1]

Yours faithfully

 Sample Letter 8-4

Dear Mr. Jackson,

Mr. John Green, our General Manager, will be in Paris from June 2 to 7 and would like to come and see you, say, at 2:00 p.m. on June 3. about the opening of a sample room there.

Please let us know if the time is convenient for you. If not, what alternative time you would suggest?

Yours sincerely

 Sample Letter 8-5

Dear Mr. Howell,

In connection with the matter of opening a branch in your country, we would like to have the opportunity of a personal meeting with you while we are in your country, and would much appreciate it if you could spare me a few minutes sometime during the stay.[2] Our secretary will call or fax you to arrange a chance of meeting with you.

Yours sincerely

Sample Letter 8-6

Dear Henry,

Please be advised I will be traveling to the United States next month to promote latest products from Hara Software Inc.³ I will be in New York and available for discussions from November 17 till November 19.

I would like very much to pay you a visit. Assuming this is acceptable, please let me know when it will be convenient for you to meet me at your office.

Sincerely yours

 Sample Letter 8-7

Dear Sirs,

Would you be interested in stocking a radical new departure in laptop computers? I would very much like to brief you on this great innovation. Could we make an appointment?

The machine is the same as most laptops but comes with some totally new features. In addition, the retail price will undercut its nearest competitor by at least 20%.

I shall be in the UK from 1st September to 20th October. If you would like to know more, just fax or email me.

Yours faithfully

8.1.3 Reply to Appointment

1. Introduction

Upon receipt of the letter asking for appointment, a prompt reply needs to be given about whether you can meet the request for appointment or you cannot due to some reasons. In reply, you will have to show your appreciations and confirm the date and the place for the meeting if you can meet the appointment. If you cannot accommodate the appointment, you need to explain the reasons to let the person concerned understand the circumstances that prevent your acceptance. If it allows, you can suggest alternative time or place and ask for confirmation.

Writing principle includes:

(1) If you agree, you can give a brief and polite reply with expression of your thanks;

(2) If you cannot meet the appointment suggested, you will be polite in stating your reasons (or if you would like another person to come, you can introduce his or her title or name, etc.);

(3) You propose another time for a possible appointment, if it permits.

2. Sample Letters

 Sample Letter 8-8

Dear Sirs,

I am pleased to learn that your trade delegation will visit this city early next month. I shall be glad to see Mr. Deng Guojun on the 5th at 10:00 a.m.

Yours faithfully

 Sample Letter 8-9

Dear Mr. Johnson,

Thank you for your letter announcing Mr. Pennington's forthcoming trip on business. Our Export Manager, Mr. Li will be very pleased to see him at 11:30 a.m. on 9th June, and would be grateful if Mr. Pennington would confirm the appointment on his arrival in China.

Yours sincerely

Sample Letter 8-10

Dear Mr. Johnson,

Thank you for your letter concerning Mr. Pennington's visit to China. Unfortunately our Export Manager, Mr. Li is in USA at present and will not be back until 19th June. He would, however, be very pleased to see Mr. Pennington if he could be in Beijing after that date.

We look forward to hearing from you.

Yours sincerely

 Sample Letter 8-11

Dear Mr. Rosco,

It was good to hear that you will be here in Beijing from October 10 to 14.

Unfortunately, as I have a previous engagement to be in Japan from October 8 to 15, I will not be able to meet you on October 12, the day you proposed. But I have arranged for Mr Cao Guohua, the Deputy Chief of our Overseas Business Department, to meet with you on the 12th. He will be ready to discuss with you whatever is necessary.

Meanwhile, I do hope we will have another chance to get together soon.

Yours sincerely

 Sample Letter 8-12

Dear Mr. Lyon,

Thank you for your letter announcing your upcoming trip to Nanjing.

I shall be very pleased to see you and discuss your purchase. But I am afraid I cannot manage 11:00 on Wednesday, but I could make 11:00 Thursday, September 21.[4] I hope this will be convenient for you.

I look forward to seeing you.

Yours sincerely

 Sample Letter 8-13

Dear Henry,

Thank you for your letter of October 15 regarding your visit next month.

We would be delighted to meet you to discuss your new products. Could you please come to our office at 11:00 a. m. on November 8th. If your schedule permits, we would like to invite you to lunch after the meeting.

We look forward to seeing you.

Sincerely yours

 Sample Letter 8-14

Dear Bruce,

Thank you for your letter of October 15 regarding your visit next month.

Although we would very much like to meet with you to discuss your new products, I am afraid neither I nor my deputy manager will be available between November 17 and 19, due to our business trip at that time. Therefore, we suggest that you send us a brochure listing your new products. We will study the brochure and contact you for any further information or questions.

We hope to see you next time you are in China.

Sincerely yours

 Sample Letter 8-15

Dear David,

I am very sorry to tell you that it will not be possible for us to meet during your forthcoming trip to China. Unfortunately I will be out of town on June 20, which is the only date when you said you are available in Beijing.

If you are planning to make another visit to China sometime soon and if you can give me some advance notice of your visit, I would be delighted not only to see you again but also to arrange a visit to our factory.[5]

In any case, I look forward to meeting you again in New York on my next trip.

Sincerely yours

8.2　Letter of Introduction

8.2.1　Introduction

　　There are different ways in which you can introduce your friends, acquaintances and business associates. Personal letters of introduction can introduce one friend or acquaintance to another while a more formal letter of introduction could introduce a colleague or business associate to another organization. When you write a personal letter of introduction, it is advisable that you need to mention some points of common interests. In a formal business letter of introduction, a competence and reliability of the person or company being introduced should be stressed. Writing principle is indicated as follows:

　　(1) Introduce the letter bearer, stressing qualification, ability and experience, etc.

(2) Account for your reasons for introduction, and suggest how the addressee could be of help.

(3) Express your thanks in advance.

8.2.2 Sample Letters

 Sample Letter 8-16

Dear Sirs,

It gives us great pleasure to introduce to you by this letter Mr. Fang Tianxiang, a director of this company. Mr. Fang is visiting your city to study the business custom of the Great Britain and we should be most grateful if you would give him any advice or introductions that may be helpful to him.

Thank you in advance.

Yours faithfully

 Sample Letter 8-17

Dear Sirs,

This is to introduce Mr. Tony Blond, one of our senior engineers who is going to help you with your newly-purchased CT system.

Mr. Blond is an expert on CT system and the head of the after-sales service department of our company. His main task is to determine how we can best upgrade the services we offer our major clients. During his one month's stay in your hospital, he will help set up the machine and instruct your personnel on the operation.

Mr. Blond is highly knowledgeable in the workings of his system. We are very proud that he has worked with us for many years, and confident that you will find him easy and pleasant to work with.

Yours faithfully

Sample Letter 8-18

Dear Sung,

We have recently appointed a new Overseas Sales Manager, Mr. D. Thomas, who will be visiting China, and especially Shanghai at the end of next month. We are writing this to you and we should be much obliged if you would extend to him the courtesy and help which you invariably gave to his predecessor, Mr. J. Hilton.

Mr. Thomas is thoroughly conversant with the Chinese market and would like to discuss various schemes which he feels might be to our mutual advantage.

Yours sincerely

 Sample Letter 8-19

Dear Mr. Owens,

In early next month you will receive a call from Mr. Song Qiming, Export Manager of Rainbow Co., who is a very good business associate of ours.

Mr. Song will be visiting the United States in the near future to establish new business connections.

We should greatly appreciate any assistance that you may be able to give him and shall be pleased to reciprocate your kindness if you will give us the opportunity at any time.

Sincerely yours

 Sample Letter 8-20

Dear Mr. Dell,

It gives us great pleasure to introduce to you by means of this letter Mr. Jackson of

ABC Co., Ltd., with whom we have done business for many years. Mr. Jackson will be visiting China in the near future to expand his sales organization and we should consider it a personal favor if you would give him the benefit of your advice and experience.[6]

Yours sincerely

 Sample Letter 8-21

Dear Sirs,

Mr. David Chen, one of our customers in Hong Kong, wants to increase his connections in his country and has asked us to help his representative, Mr. Tommy Liu, by introducing him to the leading import houses in Holland. Unfortunately, we are not sufficiently well known to the Holland import houses to be able to provide Mr. Liu with the letter of introduction he will need, but feel sure that with your connections and facilities you could do so and at the same time help him with information as to the standing of firms.

We should be most grateful if you would cooperate with us in this matter and need hard to say that we should welcome the opportunity to help you in a similar, or in any other way.

Yours faithfully

 Sample Letter 8-22

Dear Paul,

A friend of mine, Mr. David Li, would very much like to meet with you. He is a researcher of business administration at ABC Co., Ltd.

Meanwhile, he is making a study trip to USA in order to contribute to a book which is in publication entitled "Business Administration in USA".

You were kind enough to offer me your assistance when you were here in Shanghai. I would very much appreciate it if you could find time to see Mr. Li, or give him an introduction to someone on your staff. Thank you.

Yours sincerely

8.3 Letter of Recommendation

8.3.1 Introduction

Letters of recommendation are part of positive letters because recommendations may be written to nominate people for awards and for membership in organizations, and they may also be written by employers to appraise the performance of employees, which is known as solicited recommendations. They may be solicited by potential employers or organizations, which are called unsolicited letters of recommendation. The unsolicited letter may be headed by "To Prospective Employers" or "To Whom It May Concern". Sometimes the bearer of the letter is the person recommended.

The writing skill of letters of recommendation is very similar to that of letters of introduction, which stresses the authenticity and sincerity in providing the information about the person recommended. The information will focus on work experience, personality, work capability and communicational skills, etc. of the person in question. It would be best if you could supply a few examples to illustrate your recommendation of above-mentioned aspects of a person recommended.

The following guidelines can be for your reference in writing a letter of recommendation.

(1) Use one or two statements to establish the subject.

(2) Provide only job-related information, namely, a person's qualities, emphasizing the strong points of the person on his capability, personality, potential, or other outstanding features.

(3) Stress the facts. If necessary, provide some of examples to illustrate your recommendations.

(4) Summarize by giving a favorable comment or offer a forward-looking thought at the end of the letter if it is necessary.

8.3.2 Sample Letters

 Sample Letter 8-23

To Whom It May Concern,

I take great pleasure in recommending Mr. Roger Boyer who was a member of my staff in the Transportation Department for three years from April 2014 till 2015.

During his time with us, Mr. Boyer worked very hard, had a strong sense of responsibility, and handled his duties quickly and efficiently. Moreover, his job performance was very satisfactory not only to me but to all my colleagues as well.

Mr. Boyer was always eager to improve himself and, during his tenure with us, he took advanced evening courses to upgrade his computer and English skills. After leaving the company, he attended graduate school at the University of Oregon and he obtained his MBA degree last year.

Mr. Boyer is a capable and reliable person and I have no hesitation in recommending him to any organization.

Yours faithfully

 Sample Letter 8-24

Dear Sirs,

I am happy to recommend Miss Elaine Cross to your company.

Elaine has worked for our company as a designer for the last five years. During that time, she has shown herself to be a conscientious and gifted member of our design department.

Elaine was trained in Australia and USA and her technical skills are unquestionable. She is imaginative and, at the same time, very practical. Her design invariably went straight from the drawing board into the production department.

Elaine has a very pleasant personality and she gets on with people very well. She was a well-liked and valuable member of our company. We are very sorry that she leaves our company.

It is my pleasure to recommend her to you without reservation.

Yours faithfully

 Sample Letter 8-25

Dear Sir/Madam,

At the request of Mr. Dylan Thomas, I am pleased to write a reference for him concerning his career with Pacific Canned Food Co., Ltd.

I came to know Mr. Dylan Thomas in 2000 when he was the Assistant General Manager of Pacific's Sales Department, and since that time, he has been the key person in his company for placing orders with us for canned food.

Mr. Dylan Thomas is a very capable person, whose expertise and experience in marketing canned food is well-recognized and highly valued.

In closing, Mr. Dylan Thomas of Pacific Canned Food Co., Ltd. is well-known in the Japanese canned food industry and his reputation is an excellent one. We would like to recommend Mr. Dylan Thomas to any potential employer, as I am confident that he will justify my confidence in him.

Yours faithfully

Sample Letter 8-26

Dear Mr. Archie,

I am pleased to provide information you requested on Mr. Zhang Hua, who has applied for the position of coordinator with the Atlanta Public school system. Mr. Zhang worked as my full-time secretary from 2013 until 2015 and left to return to college full-time to complete his degree.

Mr. Zhang's overall skills were competent. Although it took him longer than some other secretaries to learn the software program, he eventually mastered each new program. More important, his top-level organizational skills enabled him to handle all tasks assigned to him in an efficient and competent manner.

Mr. Zhang's human relations skills were superb. He had an outgoing personality and cooperative attitude. He got along well with everyone, including high-level executive. If he had stayed with us for another year, I am sure he would have been promoted to be the administrative assistant for the executive vice president.

I enjoyed knowing Mr. Zhang, and I appreciate the competent work he did for me. If I had the opportunity, I would gladly rehire him. Please call me if I can provide additional confidential information to help you in the evaluation process.

Sincerely yours

 Sample Letter 8-27

Dear Sir or Madam,

I am pleased to write this letter of recommendation in support of the application of my student Xu Jia. She was among the top students in our department of English language. Because of her academic excellence, she was awarded the scholarship in her academic year, and she gives us a deep impression that she is a girl of high responsibility, extrovert and enthusiastic, with good organizing skills.

In the third year of her undergraduate study, I taught her the Practical Course of Import and Export, during the time of which I was impressed by her active involvement in class activities and by her performance. Especially on occasions where they were requested to elaborate on a certain set of trade principles and to analyze a controversial trade case, she could be both articulate and accurate in presenting her opinions and analysis. Her arguments are sometimes impressively presented from quite unique perspectives, and her stimulating answers and concise remarks display a fairly good ability of her deep and sharp thinking.

She is a hard working student and shows great interest in studying business and management, and much of her extracurricular time is mostly committed to reading the books of this kind, therefore she has a very good repertory of internalized knowledge of management and business.[7] Her class activities and academic papers, which are characteristically well founded and full of original ideas, can well attest to this, and I think that her potentialities in the field of management and business need to have precious opportunities and intensive training as a must to blossom into actual beings.[8]

In addition, her schedule of the campus is also occupied by lots of social activities. She initiated and organized many activities for the class, such as providing short-run English training courses for hotel waitresses, and coordinating surveys on law consultations, and hosting oral contest, etc., during which she registered herself as a competent and efficient organizer, receiving acclaims from both teachers and the school leadership.

Miss Xu really deserves the chance for further study in the domain of business and management in which she is very much talented and has a consistent interest for ever so long time. I am sure that you will find her an honest and enthusiastic and cooperative student and above all a promising young scholar or a good manager in the future.

I would like to recommend Miss Xu to your graduate program.

Faithfully yours

Shu Guanghui

Sample Letter 8-28

To whom it may concern:

I am writing this letter at the request of Mr. Li Jun who is now applying for the Service Management Postgraduate program in your esteemed university. Mr. Li studied in our university during 2004–2008. He was one of our top students in my management class, and he has been in contact with me over the past 10 years.

During his studies in the university, Mr. Li actively participated in class discussion. I was well impressed by his consistent endeavor to pursue new knowledge and his courage to embrace new challenges in his studies.[9] He always found new topics to study and got much knowledge that is new to his classmates. This made him exceptional among all the students.

All his efforts during the campus life have paved a good way for his career as an insurance consultant after graduation. He is now an expert in risk appraisals and risk management for companies and he has been involved in some of the key projects in the location and won good recognition.[10] His thorough investigation, good insight and valuable recommendations have helped the enterprises reduce great losses and enhance the reputation of the insurance firm.

In addition, he is an amiable, and easy-going person. He is independent, reliable and efficient. I am convinced that the opportunity your school can offer him will be helpful for his ever more brilliant career in the future.

Faithfully yours

8.4 Letter of Notification

8.4.1 Introduction

Under business circumstances, we need to write letters of notification to inform our business partners or our associates of the changes in the company such as personnel changes, changes in premises of the company, opening of new branches, merger and acquisition of the companies, etc.

The style of writing needs to be straightforward and concise in conveying the information. The writing principle is set as follows:

(1) Notify the other party of changes in your premises, the address of your new office or changes in personnel, etc or any necessary background information;

(2) Your expectation for further business transactions.

8.4.2 Sample Letters

 Sample Letter 8-29

Dear Sirs,

This is to inform that we have moved to a much larger and more convenient office building at:

14, Fuxinglu, Xicheng District, Beijing, 100039
Tel: 010-68213319
Fax: 010-68213726

We hope to have the opportunity to welcome you in Beijing and show you around our new building.

Yours faithfully

 Sample Letter 8-30

Dear Sirs,

We have pleasure in informing you of the merger of our company with ABC Trading Co., Ltd., which will come into effect on January 1, 2016.

The new company will do business under the title of Feida Trading Co., Ltd. with the headquarters at the Second Floor, Sun Plaza, Beijing.

Tel: ××××××××
Fax: ××××××××

As the result of this merger, we will be able to supply a wider range of household plastic products to our customers. And with the expansion of distribution channels, the cost can be reduced and the customers can benefit in the form of price reduction.

We look forward to maintaining the good relationship and continuing to provide prompt service to our customers and will always be ready to serve you.

Faithfully yours

 Sample Letter 8-31

Dear Sir or Madam,

We are pleased to announce the establishment of Hene Computer Co., Ltd., a wholly owned subsidiary of Triestar Co., Ltd. Hene will be engaged in the business of importing computers and computer-related items, and Hene's address, telephone number, etc. are indicated as follows:

Address: 1-2-3 Mihogaseki, Minato-ku, Tokyo 105-3786
Phone: 03-3234-7890
Fax: 03-3234-7777
Date Established: 30th June, 2015
President: Kenzo Ichikawa

The company will take over the business currently conducted by our Computer Import Department, and commence operations on 21st July. Therefore, from that date onwards, please direct all your communications to Hene. You may rest assured that you will enjoy the same, or even better, quality and service as in the past.[11]

Yours faithfully

Sample Letter 8-32

Dear Sirs,

This is to formally announce the following changes in our sales personnel.

1. Mr Liu Yi has been appointed Deputy Sales Manager.
2. Mr. Yang Xiaodong has replaced Mr. Ding Wen as our Marketing Manager.

All the other positions remain the same. We trust the new team will strengthen the business of this corporation as well as our service to you.

Your kind understanding of and cooperation with us after these changes will be very much appreciated.

Faithfully yours

 Sample Letter 8-33

Dear Sirs,

The steady growth of our business has made necessary an early move to new and larger premises. We have been fortunate in acquiring a good site on the industrial area at Jiahua in Guangzhou.

The site is served by excellent transport facilities, enabling deliveries to be made promptly. It is also for scopes of better methods of production that will increase output and also improve still further the quality of our manufactures.

We have very much appreciated your custom in the past and hope that the improvements in service which we confidently expect to be able to offer you will result in more business between us when new factory moves into full production.

Yours faithfully

Sample Letter 8-34

Dear Sirs,

To meet the growing demand for a hardware and general store in this area we have decided to expand our business by opening a new department. The new department will carry a wide-range of hardware and other domestic requisites at prices that compare very favorably with any charged by other suppliers.

In order to demonstrate the range of merchandise that will be available, we are arranging a special window display during the week beginning on 15th March. The official opening will take place in the following Saturday, 1st of April.

We hope you will visit the new department during opening week and give us the opportunity to show you that it maintains the reputation enjoyed by our other departments for giving sound value for money.[12]

Yours faithfully

 Sample Letter 8-35

Dear Sirs,

Kindly note that the business carried on by me for the past 20 years at the above address has been taken over by the old established firm of External Company Messrs Peng[13]. The owner of the company will transfer it, as a new department, to their well-known premises at Queen's Building, Central.

Under the terms of the transfer they have taken over all the assets and liabilities of my business. Will you therefore please send directly to them any amount that may be due on your account with me?[14]

My relationship with you over many years has been a very happy one and I hope you will give to Messrs Peng the same generous support as you have always given to me.

Yours faithfully

Sample Letter 8-36

Dear Mr. Ashley,

This is to advise you that after five memorable years in Los Angeles, I am returning to Tokyo at the end of this month to take up my new assignment in our head office. I would like to take this opportunity to thank you for the support and friendship you extended to me during my stay here.

In my new assignment I will be in charge of exporting golf equipment into the US market. Therefore, I will still have the opportunity to work with you, although indirectly through our L. A. office. Hopefully I will also have ample opportunities to see you in the future, either in Tokyo or in the United States.

I leave my responsibilities here in the capable hands of Mr. Yoshio Tanaka who will be arriving from Tokyo next week. Please rest assured that Mr. Tanaka will supply you with the same, or an even better, level of service as you have had from me in the past. I also hope you will give him the same generous support as you have given me during our very agreeable association.

Yours sincerely

prescribe	v.	规定
agency	n.	代理机构，代理公司
delegation	n.	代表团
engagement	n.	约定，安排
stock	v.	安装（程序等）
feature	n.	特点
undercut	v.	减少，削减
forthcoming	a.	即将到来的
previous	a.	以前的，先前的
advance	a.	事先的，提前的

Unit 8 Interoffice Routine Letters

notice	n.	通知
acquaintance	n.	熟人，认识
upgrade	v.	提高，提升
client	n.	客户
appoint	v.	任命，指定
invariably	ad.	必然地，必将
predecessor	n.	前者，前面所提到的人或事
conversant	a.	熟悉，掌握，非常了解
reciprocate	v.	回报，报答
representative	n.	代表
standing	n.	地位，立场
recommendation	n.	推荐
nominate	v.	指定，任命
appraise	v.	评价，评估
performance	n.	业绩，表现
solicit	v.	请求，恳求
authenticity	n.	真实
personality	n.	个性，性格
illustrate	v.	说明，阐明
potential	a.	潜力，潜能
tenure	n.	任期，期间
designer	n.	设计者
gifted	a.	有才能的
justify	v.	认为……是对的，证明……是正确的
coordinator	n.	协调员
competent	a.	有能力的，能胜任的
superb	a.	完美的，极好的
outgoing	a.	（性格）外向的
evaluation	n.	评估
extrovert	a.	性格开朗的，外向的
enthusiastic	a.	热情的
articulate	a.	表达清楚的，表达流利的
accurate	a.	准确的
perspective	n.	视角，角度
stimulating	a.	有启发的
repertory	n.	（信息）储存
internalized	a.	内部消化的，转为自己的

well-founded	a.	有充分根据的
original	a.	有创意的
precious	a.	珍贵的，宝贵的
must	n.	必须
initiate	v.	开创，创立
register	v.	显示
acclaim	n.	喝彩
domain	n.	领域
promising	a.	有前途的
esteemed	a.	受到尊敬的
consistent	a.	一致的，一贯如此的
endeavor	v.	努力
embrace	v.	拥抱，欢迎
appraisal	n.	评价
reputation	n.	名声，声誉
amiable	a.	友好的，快乐的
easy-going	a.	随和的，平易近人的
notification	n.	通知，通告
premise	n.	（常用复数）场地，营业场地
merger	v.	合并，联合
acquisition	n.	兼并，获得
concise	a.	准确的，精确的
prompt	a.	及时的，准时的
wholly-owned	a.	全资的
subsidiary	n.	分支机构，附属单位
assured	a.	确信的
acquire	v.	获得，得到
move	n.	行动，步骤
hardware	n.	硬件，金属器具
requisite	n.	必要，要求
asset	n.	（常用复数）资产
liability	n.	责任，职责
memorable	a.	记忆深刻的
agreeable	a.	令人愉快的，宜人的
electronic components		电子元件
laptop computer		手提电脑

Unit 8 Interoffice Routine Letters

deputy manager	副经理
business associate	商业伙伴
to one's mutual advantage	对双方有利
at the request of	在……的邀请下
elaborate on	详细阐述
attest to	证明
transport facilities	交通设施
compare favorably with	与……相比有优势
in charge of	对……负责

Notes

1. ... if you would suggest an alternative appointment, I will re-arrange my other engagements as may be necessary.　……如果你能建议其他时间的约会，我会根据需要来进行别的日程安排。

2. In connection with the matter of opening a branch in your country, we would ...　有关在贵国设立分公司一事，我们会……　"in connection with" 意为"与……有关"。

3. Please be advised ...　兹通知……

4. But I am afraid I cannot manage 11:00 on Wednesday, but I could make 11:00 Thursday, September 21.　本句中的"manage"是"安排见面"的意思。

5. ... and if you can give me some advance notice of your visit, I would be delighted not only to see you again but also to arrange a visit to our factory.　……如果你能将访问一事事先通知我，我将非常高兴地接见你，而且还会安排你去参观我们的工厂。

6. ... and we should consider it a personal favor if you would give him the benefit of your advice and experience.　……如你能跟他分享你宝贵的建议和经验，我们认为对他将是有益的。

7. ... much of her extracurricular time is mostly committed to reading the books of this kind, therefore she has a very good repertory of internalized knowledge of management and business.　……她的许多课外时间都花在阅读此类书籍上，因此她掌握了大量的管理和商务方面的知识。

8. ... I think that her potentialities in the field of management and business need to have precious opportunities and intensive training as a must to blossom into actual beings.　……我认为她在管理和商务方面的潜能肯定需要宝贵的机会和强化训练才能实现。

9. I was well impressed by this consistent endeavor to pursue new knowledge and his courage to embrace new challenges in his studies.　他对新知识的持之以恒的追求和迎接学习中新挑战的勇气给我留下了深刻的印象。

10. He is now an expert in risk appraisals and risk management for companies and he has been

involved in some of the key projects in the location and won good recognition.　他现在已是公司风险评估和风险管理方面的专家，一直参与当地的一些主要项目，并赢得了好的评价。

11. You may rest assured that you will ...　本文中的"rest assured ..."意为"确信"，"rest"为"半系动词"。

12. We hope you will visit the new department during opening week and give us the opportunity to show you that it maintains the reputation enjoyed by our other departments for giving sound value for money.　我们希望你能在开业的那一周来参观我们的新部门，给予我们向你们展示的机会，展示我们其他部门因提供物有所值的服务所具有的声誉。

13. Kindly note that the business carried on by me for the past 20 years at the above address has been taken over by the old-established firm of External Company Messrs Peng.　句中的"External Company Messrs Peng"为一家公司的名称。其中的"Messrs Peng"是以"彭姓氏"命名的。"Messrs"是"Mr."的复数形式。

14. Will you therefore please send directly to them any amount that may be due on your account with me?　因此，你是否将本来支付给我们的钱款直接支付给他们呢？

Letter of Appointment

1. Make an appointment

(1) I would like to make an appointment with Mr./Ms. ... to discuss future business prospects.

(2) I am writing to find out the possibility of our having a brief meeting some time next week.

(3) Mr. ... and I would like to be in the United States and we would like very much to visit your company.

(4) I am scheduled to visit ... for a couple of days on my way back from Paris.

(5) I represent the company of ABC, and I would like to talk to you about purchasing some electronic components you make.

(6) We should very much like to discuss with you the matter of ... and we hope it would be convenient for you to ... on the fifth at 10:00 a.m. or any other time that suits you.

(7) Would you be interested in discussing ... with me? I would brief you on the matter of ... at 9:30 a.m. on May 5th, 2015.

2. Replies to appointments

(1) We are pleased to learn that you will discuss the matter of ... with us, and we would like

to talk to you at the time you suggested.
(2) Thank you for your letter asking for an appointment, and I will be pleased to see you at ... on ... 2015.
(3) We would be delighted to meet you to discuss your cooperation program. Could you please arrange to have a discussion at ...
(4) I feel it a pleasure to meet with you on the matter of ... , we will manage to talk to you on the schedule you suggested in your last letter.
(5) Our schedule next week is very much engaged and I am afraid it will not be possible to have a meeting. We would appreciate it if you could change the date to ... in the month.
(6) I am sorry that I will be fully engaged with a conference out of this city during that period. So I cannot meet with you on that day.
(7) Unfortunately, I have previous engagements during the period you mentioned.
(8) If you could postpone the meeting until the next day, it would be very helpful.
(9) Please accept my apologies for canceling our appointment at the last minutes.
(10) I am afraid we will have to either cancel or reschedule the appointment as our president was hospitalized after suffering a heart attack.
(11) I hope my cancellation will not cause you any inconvenience.

Letter of Introduction

1. Offer to introduce someone

(1) This is to introduce ... who is ...
(2) We have great pleasure in introducing to you by this letter, Mr./Ms. ...
(3) It gives us great pleasure to introduce to you, the bearer of this letter, Mr./Ms. ...
(4) I am very pleased to introduce ...
(5) Early next month you will receive a visit from Mr./Ms. ... who is ...

2. Thank in advance the other party for his or her help or cooperation

(1) Anything you could do for him will be very much appreciated.
(2) Any assistance you may render to him will be highly appreciated.
(3) Thank you in advance for any assistance in his matter.
(4) I shall consider it a great favor if you could.
(5) I shall be pleased to reciprocate your kindness if you will give us the opportunity at any time.

Letter of Recommendation

1. The opening of the letter

(1) I take great pleasure in recommending Mr./Ms. ... for the position of Sales

Representative.

(2) I have no hesitation in recommendation Mr./Ms. ... to work as a ... in your company.

(3) I would like very much to recommend one of my colleague, Mr./Ms. ..., who is seeking admission to PhD program at your institute.

(4) At the request of Mr./Ms. ..., I would like to recommend him to work as ... at your company.

(5) I submit the following confidential information in support of Mr. ... application for the position of ..., in reply to Mr. Li's request for a letter of recommendation.

(6) This is to recommend Mr. ..., who has been working in our company for 3 years.

2. Information concerning work experiences, capabilities, personalities, etc.

(1) He is always hard-working, helpful, kind and considerate of colleagues.

(2) I do think Mr./Ms. ... is an intelligent and flexible person who is willing to meet any challenges.

(3) His work was perfectly satisfactory and our relations were always most cordial. He is strictly honest, a hard worker and an intelligent man in the best sense of the world.

(4) Mr. ... impressed me as a qualified engineer who is not only an expert on computer softwares, but also has superior interpersonal skills, and enthusiastic.

(5) Mr. ... can fulfill the task to our satisfaction, and is able to meet challenges to prove his success in his work. Mr./Ms. ... is reliable and diligent and, most of all, he/she has 20 years' experience as an accountant.

(6) He served as Sales Manager of ... Inc. and made a great contribution by increasing profits by 10% in 2015.

(7) Mr./Ms. ... was a member of my staff for about 3 years in the Human Resources Department and she showed a real ability and skill in communicating with people.

(8) Mr./Ms. ... has been in our office for three years during which time he/she has faithfully performed his duties, proving himself/herself to be hard-working and thoroughly reliable.

(9) Mr. ... is a pleasure to work with ...

(10) A very friendly disposition, a keen social conscience and an admirable work ethics make Mr. ... a valuable asset in any organization.

3. Closing the letter confidently

(1) I recommend him without reservation and hope that he will soon become one of your promising employees.

(2) I am confident that he will do his best whatever he may be requested to do, and I cordially recommend him to you.

(3) I am sure that he will be fully qualified as one of your research assistants.

(4) We believe he would be a great asset to your organization, a type of assistant a manager will

find indispensable.

(5) She has shown herself industrious, dutiful, conscientious, intelligent and reliable. You will not fail to find her amiable and cooperative.

(6) If any further information is necessary, I will be glad to comply.

Letter of Notification

1. The opening

(1) This is to inform you that we have moved to ... The address of the office is notified as follows:

(2) We are pleased to inform you that ...

(3) We have pleasure in informing you that ...

(4) This is to formally announce that ...

(5) We would like to inform you of the following changes of our company's address.

(6) This is to advise you on the following changes concerning our company.

2. Information on the changes of address or new appointment or merger of the company notified

(1) A new office will be opened at the following address.

(2) We have moved to a much larger and convenient office building at ...

(3) Mr./Ms. ... has been appointed Sales Manager.

(4) We will be pleased to inform you of the merger of our company with ... Ltd., which will come into effect on ...

3. The closing

(1) We hope that the new establishment of our office will facilitate and improve our service to you and we are looking forward to further expansion of our business.

(2) We hope that the new team will promote the development of our business relationship, and improve our service to you.

(3) We are convinced that the merger will enhance our competitive edge and strengthen our relationship. We will always be ready to provide the best service to you.

(4) We are sure that you will enjoy the same, even better, quality service as in the past.

(5) We appreciate your kind understanding of and good cooperation with us after these changes.

(6) We take this opportunity to express our thanks for your cooperation in the past. We hope the new arrangement will lead to even better results.

(7) We look forward to continuing with you the happy business connection that has been so

much to our mutual advantage in the past.

(8) We appreciate the confidence you placed in us in the past and look forward to continued dealings with you.

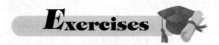

I **The following statements are taken from the text of a letter. Rearrange the sentences in a correct order.**

1. I can recommend Ms. Chan to you without hesitation.
2. Further to your letter of 11 December, I am more than pleased to provide a reference for Ms. Chan, who has worked at this company in the capacity of my Personal Assistant since she joined the company in 2007.
3. Although she does sometimes find it a little difficult to interact with other members of staff, Ms. Chan is extremely hard-working and efficient.
4. I have always found her to be a totally loyal and honest worker who can be relied upon.
5. If you were to appoint Ms. Chan, we should find it very difficult to replace her.
6. However, we appreciate that, in her own interest, it may be time for Ms. Chan to move on.

II **Fill in the blanks of the following letter with the words and expressions given, and change the form where necessary.**

> attend, against, reference, reservation, better, conscientious, opportunity, with,

Dear Mr. Brown,

It is _____ great pleasure that I take this _____ to give Miss Alice Powell a _____.

She was my secretary at the New York office of the Kenyon, Day Company; and I was sincerely sorry to lose her when she left two months ago to _____ her mother's funeral and to live with her father in Chicago.

Miss Powell is an excellent secretary. She is efficient and _____, always pleasant to everyone, tactful and intelligent. I know nothing _____ her character.

I recommend her without _____ as a most helpful and responsible secretary. You couldn't make a _____ choice than Alice Powell.

Sincerely yours

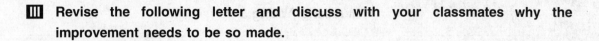

III Revise the following letter and discuss with your classmates why the improvement needs to be so made.

Dear Sir or Madam,

I am writing this letter of recommendation on behalf of Mr. Zhang at his request. He is now looking for a job, which will benefit his career advancement in the future.

I made an acquaintance with him in 2010 and he impressed me as a hard-working, capable and promising young man. Although he worked only for a few years, he can perform his duties successfully. In addition, he could quickly adapt to the new situation and best meet the needs of customers by making a prompt feedback. His work at our company showed that he was an efficient and promising employee.

He is quick to learn, and keeps learning new skills related to his work. I firmly believe that he will play the best role in the new position of your company.

Faithfully yours

VI Writing practice.

Situational Writing 1

Your company is going to import the material from the United States and turn it into finished products, which are in turn exported to the United States. Mr. Li Wenqing, a sale representative of your company who is looking after the business in the Southeast Asia is planning to learn about the whole process of production in the United States. He hopes to pay a field visit to your US supplier's premises next week, and you are requested to write a letter of introduction for him.

Situational Writing 2

Your company is scaling down your business operation in Europe, while consolidating your well-established market position in the Pacific rim area by increasing sales channels and setting up a new regional headquarters in Hong Kong. To accommodate the new changes in the company, a new appointment is made: Mr. Johnson is appointed President of the new regional headquarters. He is going to take his position next month. Please write a letter of notification to inform this personnel change of your company.

Situational Writing 3

Suppose you were a professor of English department of a university, and you are going to write a letter of recommendation for your student who is going to pursue an M. A. degree in the field of business in the UK. Your letter of recommendation needs to focus on the academic performance and the potential qualities of your student.

Situational Writing 4

Please write a letter of appointment in which you are going to talk with your trading partner about the new product sample and the new method of payment.

Unit 9

Memos, E-mails and Notices
备忘录、电子邮件及通告

9.1 Memos

9.1.1 Introduction

The term "memo" (short for memorandum) is used to describe the standard format of internal communication, which an organization uses for its own staff. Memos, including those sent through e-mail, are simple, efficient means of communication within an organization. They are simple in style and are efficient because their format conveys the writer's point quickly and directly to the readers.

Companies use memos to announce policies, disseminate information, delegate responsibilities, instruct employees, and report the result of a research or an investigation. Companies also rely on memos to keep employees informed of company goals, to motivate employees to achieve the goals, and to build employee morale.

The tone of memos tends to be conversational because both the writer and the reader are familiar with each other. Therefore, you may use ordinary words, first-person pronouns, and occasional contractions, like don't, I'm, you're, or we'll. Yet, this does not mean you should be casual with your writing. You should not include any remark that you would not make to the face of your colleagues. But if a memo is written to someone you are less familiar with, particularly to someone in a higher position in the company, it can be as formal as any formal business letters.

Language style of memo can be made more relaxed than in business letters. However, that is no excuse for the sentence to be chatty or impolite. The use of English should be concise and efficient in that memos contain only what you intend to convey. Often you do not have to provide background information when you are certain the reader knows about the subject discussed in the memo, nor do you need to make as much goodwill effort as you do in letters to your business partners outside of the organization. For instance, some sentences like, "I would appreciate it very much if you could have the forms filled in and returned to the Administrative Office by 12 June, 2015." and "Thank you for reminding me of the meeting, and I should like to have an overhead projector for the session." are too polite to be used in memo. Instead, they can be worded as "Please be sure to have the form filled in and returned to the Administrative Office by 12 June, 2015." and "I have been informed of the meeting and would ask for an overhead projector for the session."

You should also avoid wordy expressions and sentences. For example, do not use "because of the fact that...", or "I am writing this memo to inform you that...".

The overall look of memo needs to be neat and can help readers grasp highlights quickly. Effective memo writers can highlight important words, phrases, points, and sections with:

- Numbers or bullets listed vertically;
- Boldface or italics;
- Headings and subheadings.

Memo writers often list their points vertically with numbers or bullets. They capitalize the word at the beginning of each line. They don't use end punctuation unless the statement is a complete sentence. Each item on their list starts with the same parts of speech, say, adjectives, verbs, or nouns.

They may use boldface or italics to draw reader's attention. Bold face is a handy device because it is visually different yet retains the customary shape of letters and numbers. Italics are useful in that they can slow down readers for cautions, warnings, or emphases.

They often use headlines and subheadings to show the hierarchical organization of a message and to help readers grasp the main idea of a section and decide which sections to read.

Let us compare the following two memo formats in Table 9-1.

Table 9-1　Two different memo formats

A Plain Paragraph	A Paragraph with Highlighting Devices
Effective immediately are the following air travel guidelines. Between now and December 31, only account executives may take company-approved trips. These individuals will be allowed to take a maximum of two trips and they are to travel economy or budget class only.	Effective immediately are the following air travel guidelines. • Who may travel: Account executives • How many trips: A maximum of 2 • When: Between now and December 31 • Air class: Economy or budget

9.1.2　Components of Memos

The layout of memos varies from company to company. However, in a broad sense, all memos are made up of two parts: memo headings and body.

Unit 9 Memos, E-mails and Notices

1. Memo Headings

Most companies provide letterhead memo stationery with printed headings on the left near the top of the first page (Figure 9-1). The elements of the headings may appear in a different order (Figure 9-2), decided by custom, by the style manual of the company, or by the file system. Sometimes you may write a memo that is authorized or approved by your supervisor. In this case, you may put your supervisor's name on the "Through" line (Figure 9-3). Please see the following examples of headings.

```
To _____          Date: _____
From _____          To:   _____
Date _____          From: _____
Subject _____         Subject: _____
```

Figure 9-1 Memo heading (1)   Figure 9-2 Memo heading (2)

```
Date: _____
To:   _____
From: _____
Through: _____
```

Figure 9-3 Memo heading (3)

The subject line is the most important element of the headings. It summarizes the main idea of the message. In letters the subject line is optional, but in memos, it is required. It helps readers quickly grasp the main idea and file the message more efficiently. It is usually brief and need not be a complete sentence. You can omit the articles in the subject line and do not need a period at the end.

2. Body

It is the message of the memo, which is separated into paragraphs. Unlike business letters, memos don't need a salutation or complimentary close in the body. But a signature at the bottom of the body may be required by some companies.

To structure the body of a memo, the 4-point plan for composing business letters can be used as a general guide. But close is not necessary for most memos. The following outline is a reminder for composing memo body.

(1) Introduction: Background information, briefly giving the reason for writing.

(2) Details: Facts and figures, separated into paragraphs, each dealing with a particular theme; points are logically presented.

(3) Response: An action statement, requiring action from recipient, or informing action to take.

(4) Close: Not usually needed. It can be a conclusive sentence for ending when necessary.

9.1.3 Samples

 Sample 9-1

To: Edward Smith, Personnel Assistant
From: Don Rily, Corporate Legal Counselor
Subject: Meeting for EEO Report Preparation
Date: July 30, 2015

Let's meet in my office (Suite 165) this Friday at 10:30 a.m. to complete Section 6 of your annual equal employment opportunity report.

You must now provide two items of information that were not required last year:

1. What procedure was followed in advertising available jobs to members of minority races?
2. What procedure was followed to assure that an applicant's place of residency was disregarded in hiring practices?

Please bring this information with you to the meeting in addition to information you normally include in this section of the report.

I look forward to meeting with you on Friday.

 Sample 9-2

To: Department Managers
From: Training Manager
Subject: In-service Computer Classes
Date: 24 May, 2015

We are arranging a training course on computer to improve our staff's ability of computer use. The course is scheduled as follows:

1. From Monday 10 June computer classes will be held in the training center. There will be 2 groups: advanced level (10:30–12:00) and intermediate level (8:30–10:00).

2. Please encourage your staff to attend one of the sessions. All teaching materials will be provided but students will be expected to do homework and preparation outside working hours.
3. Please send me the names of all interested staff by noon on Friday 28 November.
4. The size of each class will be limited to 16 participants.

 Sample 9-3

To: Adam Field. Internal Auditor
From: Philip, Sales Supervisor for Cosmetics
Subject: Response to Request for New-Life Cosmetics Sales Records
Date: 6 March, 2015

I have reviewed your request to see last quarter's Pearl Cosmetics sales records by March 12 with Mary Smith, the assistant to the vice president of sales, Jack Peterson.

Mary and I checked Section 6 of our policy manual and confirmed that Jack must give permission to release many classified records either internally or externally. All cosmetics sales records are classified. Jack is vacationing in Tibet and cannot be reached until he returns to work on March 17. Mary said that these records are complete and can be sent to you on March 17, if Jack approves.

Should you need any unclassified cosmetics records to help you complete your audit by March 30, I can send them to you now. Records such as those of staff hours spent on selling cosmetics are unclassified. Call me at Extension 5168 to tell me what else you need, if anything.

 Sample 9-4

To: D. Wayne Humen
From: Tina Matthews,
Date: April 10, 2015
Subject: Sale personnel resignation in Washington Region

As you suggested, I spent the past week in Washington to see what I could learn about the heavy turnover of sales personnel there.

I was able to get in touch with the six sale personnel who resigned during the past seven weeks. Each spoke highly of our products and the company as a whole. I found that in every instance the overriding reason boils down to money. All claimed big increases in income in the new jobs — in three cases 25% or more. Also, the incentive plans based on increase in sales volume offered by other companies were a powerful inducement. Of the six who left, four went to MC Company, which is our toughest competitor in the Washington area.

I visited seven of our present representatives and the subject of money came up constantly. Indeed, there were veiled threats that they may leave soon if our salary-incentive arrangement is not changed.

It seems to me, Wayne, that we need to take a close look at our compensation policy, and I suggest we name a task force composed of yourself, me, the personel director, and three regional managers. I am sure you know that time is important here, and I hope we can get this task force set up in the next week or two.

Sample 9-5

To: Allan Jackson,
From: Jack Nelson, Manager
Date: 21 April, 2015
Subject: Purchase of Accounting Computing Packages

Your proposal indicated two new packages are suited to our current and projected needs.

Action
1. Please order these packages from the supplier nominated in the proposal and arrange for their installation on our terminals as soon as possible.
2. Could you organize and be involved in training for each of our computer operators?
3. Please see me some time on Wednesday to arrange a reduction of your regular responsibilities to give you time to complete the project.

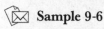 **Sample 9-6**

To: Production Department
From: Marketing Department
Date: May 21st, 2015
Subject: The Proposal of Color Bathtubs Production

According to our recent market research, the sales of white bathtubs are decreasing in the local market because more and more color bathtubs have entered this market from USA, Italy and some other countries, which have been replacing the white ones gradually.

Therefore, in order to maintain our share of the market, we propose that color bathtubs be manufactured by us. If we have our own products, we are, of course, in a stronger position because we can save a lot from import expenses so that we have an advantage in low costs. Moreover, we can get enough pigments in the local market at rather low prices.

We have submitted this proposal to the Management and have got their initial approval. Thus you are responsible for a trial production.

We are anticipating the first products so that we may start an ambitious marketing program at an early date.

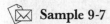 **Sample 9-7**

To: Business Manager
From: Sales Manager
Date: July 15th, 2015
Subject: A Tour to Some Cities in China

I was back yesterday from a ten-day tour in Beijing, Tianjin, Shanghai and Guangzhou. When I was in these cities, I met the officials of the branches of the China Ocean Shipping Corporation and the Head Office in Beijing. Cordial negotiations were made between us and the Chinese parties.

In the negotiations, I introduced the facilities in our dockyard and thanked them for their former patronage. The Chinese parties also introduced the rapid development of their merchant ship fleet, many of which were occasionally repaired in Hong Kong. They complained that we had charged them too high, sometimes even twice than the Japanese charges. I told them that we would reconsider this matter on my return to Hong Kong.

In my opinion, the Chinese parties are interested in our ship repairing facilities and want their big ships to be repaired by us if necessary. In order to accept more ships from China, I propose that our charges be deducted a little so as to have advantage over those by Japanese or Singapore yards.

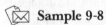

Sample 9-8

To: Miss Mary Smith, Property Sales Department
From: Mr. Richard Berry, Manager
Date: May 8th, 2015

It has come to my attention that there have been complaints about our sending of information.

Several customers complained that information took 2-3 days to reach them. Please make sure in future that details of properties for sales are sent out by first class post on the day we receive the request.

Last week three letters were sent to the wrong addresses. Please double-check the addresses of people you send property details to.

We have a good reputation for efficiency and we mustn't lose it.

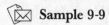

Sample 9-9

To: Personnel Department
From: Services Department
Date: Oct. 21st, 2015
Subject: Deliberate Absence of Some Workers

We applied to you yesterday for the dismissal of Liang Jun, Wang Qiang and Li Yong, who had often been deliberately absent from their posts.

The application was the result of many complaints coming from our customers. They told us that the three workers often came late to their residences for the repairs. It took them half an hour or a total hour to reach the customer's homes, which normally needs only ten or twenty minutes. Moreover, they were also often absent from our department all day long. According to our record, only within this month, Liang had been absent for 3 days, Wang for 4 days and Li for 6 days. They have refused to mend their way despite repeated admonition.

Therefore, we cannot tolerate them to destroy our discipline and we must dismiss them as soon as possible.

9.2 E-mails

9.2.1 Introduction

The wide use of e-mail, standing for electronic mail, shows the importance of this newly developed communication medium. Originally, it was a means of transmitting messages through the computer network within organizations, but now it links people and businesses all over the world.

You often write e-mail messages to your coworkers or supervisors. You may get the response in a few seconds and reply at once as if you were talking with them on the phone. Because of the speed at which messages are transmitted, the back-and-forth interchange taking place between you and your colleagues makes e-mail messages like conversations. As a result, the tone of email tends to be informal and conversational, but if e-mail is sent to a respected person or president of the company, both the format and the tone need to be very formal. Therefore, tone can be varied, depending on different situations. Apart from that, writing of e-mail is similar to correspondence writing, but it cannot be lengthy. So when you send long or complex documents, you should attach them to the message. This feature provides tremendous power to this communication medium.

As for the format, it is different from memo that has an established or all-agreed-upon rules for composing the structure of the message. So you need to check with your organization and follow its conventions and practices. Most email messages contain two major parts: headings and messages. Let us look at the format more closely

9.2.2 Format of E-mails

1. Headings

Generally speaking, headings are similar to those of memo. But people only put the receiver's e-mail address and the sender's address on the To and From lines, while others prefer to include the receiver's and the sender's full names. Under the From line, sometimes, you may see the Cc. It stands for Courtesy or Carbon Copy. You can put in the addresses of those to whom you also want to send the message. As for the subject line, as in memos, you need provide enough information for the reader, so that he or she can immediately identify the contents of the messages.

2. Salutation

Usually people do not start an e-mail message with a salutation, for they think the message is only intended as an internal memo. However, many emails are sent to the outside of the company or business entity, they actually perform the duty of business letter. Therefore, salutation has become a friendly way to greet your readers.

3. Body

The messages in the part of the body can be structured according to your own needs or your company's custom, but the whole looks should be neat and easy-to-read. But be sure not to include any confidential information of your company in the e-mail, because all email messages can possibly be intercepted by someone other than the intended reader.

4. Closing

Conclude your e-mail message with a closing, such as "Best wishes", "All the Best", followed by your name. You can include your title and organization if your reader is not familiar with you.

9.2.3 Samples

 Sample 9-10

Subject: Your account
Date: Wed., 17 June, 2015
To: toyotrdg@wordnet.jp
Attn: Mr. SanroKimura
From: shentoys@pubic.sta.met.cn

We have not received a satisfactory response to the issue raised in our e-mail of 17th May regarding bills. We are therefore obliged to resign your account, effective June 18, 2015.

Your payments are due for all unpaid invoices and for all work in progress as of this date.[1]

Upon receipt of your payment in full we will transfer all artwork, materials, and copy files.

We are doing this with much regret. We all liked working with you and are proud of the results you have been getting.

I will be pleased to see our paths cross again under better circumstances.

Regretfully

Qiao Ni
Senior Vice-President

9.3 Notices

9.3.1 Introduction

Notices are effective means of written communication to reach a large audience. They are often used to announce social events, report on matters of general interest to employees, inform staff of new procedures, advertise posts for internal appointment, remind staff of procedures, and require signatures of staff of agreement or disagreement with some proposed policy of action. There are two main types of notices: notices printed to be circulated among parties concerned and notices intended to be pinned on a notice-board, which are referred to as announcements. And to make all notices on a notice board "immediate", it is important to remove all "dead notices", when they have served their purposes. Like memos, notices are sent to reach a lot of people, however, there is no direct line of communication from the writer of the notice to the people who read it.

9.3.2 Layout of Notices

A notice requires a clear heading at the top, followed by the main body separated into paragraphs. It must have the name and position of the person who wrote it, and the date at the bottom, as shown in Sample 9-11.

 Sample 9-11

New Corporate Staff, Executive Appointments Announced

The company announced today the creation of a new corporate staff: Technical Personal Development.

This new group will promote the technical vitality of the Company's professional engineering, technological, and scientific communities throughout the world and will work to enhance the exchange of technical information among the Company's laboratories and its business units.

Mr. Zhang Qing has been appointed to head the new staff.

Mr. Dan Partridge
Chairman

8 January, 2016

When a notice is meant for notice board display, it has the same layout as the above, but sometimes fully-blocked display of the body is preferred, and the signature of the notice issuer is required before the name in printed form, as shown in Sample 9-12.

Sample 9-12

Notice

Please be informed that Public Health Section will be conducting a Flu-shot March from 8:00 a. m. to 11:00 a. m. in CU 2016 and from 1:00 p. m. to 4:00 p. m. in GLA 101.[2]

Flu-shots are also available during clinic hours daily at the health center. The cost is $2 for faculty, staff, their dependents and students.

Alan Jefferson
Office Manager

3rd March, 2016

In addition, to ensure that the notice is displayed attractively and acted upon where necessary, the following guidelines are helpful.

(1) Use different size print to emphasize headings.
(2) Use asterisks or bullet points to list information.
(3) Leave spaces between headings and different sections consistently.
(4) Use capitals, bold, italics or underlying to distinguish some information when necessary.
(5) Use sub-headings to break up the main information logically.

In closing, sometimes if the event intends to motivate actions, you can specify what should be followed. It is optional but not necessary for notices.

9.3.2　Samples

 Sample 9-13

Red-stone Records
New Store Opening

Red-stone Records are proud to announce the opening of a new branch on Wednesday, 13 February in Anglo Plaza at Jalan Pemuda, Jakarta.

This new branch will feature a complete range of compact disks, ranging from Jazz to Classical, from World Music to Punk Rock.³ Right in the heart of the commercial district of Jakarta.

To mark this very special occasion, customers will be able to take advantage of a special introductory offer. Just complete and cut out this form and bring it to the store with you any time between 13 March and 15 April, and we shall be happy to give you 8% reduction on the price of your purchase.

Name: _____   Tel: _____
Address: _____   Fax: _____

My favorite type of music: Jazz/Classical/Pop/Rock/World/Other
If "Other", please specify: _____
_____

* Offer valid until 15 April, 2015 at Red-stone Records, Anglo Plaza only.

 **Sample 9-14**

SINGAPORE COMMERCIAL BANK CORPORATION
(Regional Training Center)

You are invited to a talk by
Larry Machoski
On "Bank Teller Training"

Date: Thursday, 14 July, 2015
Place: Training Room 4
Time: 2:30 – 3:30 p.m.

The Speaker:

Larry Machoski has worked in the field of Banking since graduating from Harvard in the early 90's. After many successful years in corporate banking training at the Royal Bank of Bangkok, Mr. Machoski moved to First Manhattan Bank's corporate headquarters in NewYork in the mid-2000s. Since 2008, Mr. Machoski has been working with the Regional Training Center of the Singapore Commercial Banking Corporation.

Mr. Machoski has written several successful books on the subject of Bank Telling. These books, and his enduring enthusiasm have established him as one of the world's leading names in the field.⁴

The Talk:

This inspiring talk will consider systems that have been developed for training bank tellers at the Regional Training Center, and how they may be adapted in different contexts. Mr. Machoski's talk will also address the wider issue of "quality" in bank training. The talk should be fascinating.

New Words and Expressions

memo	n.	备忘录
disseminate	v.	散布，传播（思想）
delegate	n.	（权利）下放
morale	n.	士气，精神面貌
contraction	n.	缩略
chatty	a.	非正式的，闲话家常式的
boldface	n.	黑体，粗体
capitalize	v.	将……大写
caution	v.	告诫，警告
hierarchical	a.	等级制度的，等级的
stationery	n.	文具，办公用品
authorize	v.	授权
disregard	v.	不顾，置之不理
cosmetics	n.	化妆品
file	v.	（文件）存档
procedure	n.	手续，程序
manual	a.	手册，指南
externally	ad.	对外地

vacation	v.	度假
audit	v.	审计，查账
turnover	n.	营业额
resign	v.	辞职
overriding	a.	压倒一切的，优先于其他的
incentive	n.	刺激物，激励
inducement	n.	诱导
constantly	ad.	不断地
veil	v.	遮掩，隐藏
terminal	n.	终端
pigment	n.	颜料
initial	a.	开头的，初步的
anticipate	v.	期盼，预期
ambitious	a.	大胆的
dockyard	n.	码头
deduct	v.	扣除
double-check	v.	双重检查
dismissal	n.	解雇
residence	n.	住址，办公场所
mend	v.	修改，改正
tolerate	v.	容忍，忍耐
coworker	n.	同事
intercept	v.	截获
response	n.	回答，回复
circulate	v.	流传，发行
vitality	n.	活力，朝气
motivate	v.	激励
specify	v.	规定
enduring	a.	长久的，长期的
overhead projector		投影仪
end punctuation		句号
classified records		分类记录，保密文件
boil down to		归结为
composed of		包括
stand for		代表
carbon copy		抄送
break up		拆开

Unit 9 Memos, E-mails and Notices

1. Your payments are due for all unpaid invoices and for all work in progress as of this date.　你应该支付尚未付完的货款，以及自本日起所有工作所产生的费用。

   本句中的"as of"有两种意思：一是"到……为止"，二是"从……时起"。本句为第二种意思。

2. Please be informed that Public Section will be conducting a Flu-shot March...　提请注意：保健部门将进行春季预防感冒疫苗的注射……

3. This new branch will feature a complete range of compact disks, ranging from Jazz to Classical, from World Music to Punk Rock.　这个新的分公司的音乐唱片种类齐全，从爵士乐到古典音乐，从世界音乐到蓬克摇滚乐，应有尽有。

   本句中的"feature"是"具有……的特点"的意思。

4. These books, and his enduring enthusiasm have established him as one of the world's leading names in the field.　这些书籍及他对该行业的热情使他成为在该领域中的全球的佼佼者。

Notices

1. The opening

   (1) Please be informed that...

   (2) We regret that the Retail Sales Dept will be closed from... to... for rewiring.

   (3) The company announced today the creation of a new corporate department.

   (4) Hong Kong Book City is proud to announce the opening of a new chain store on..., ... at...

   (5) We are pleased to announce the appointment of Michael Wooden as our CEO.

   (6) All staff are requested to participate in...

   (7) Following a serious accident in the workshop where a member of staff lost his right hand, the company is reminding all the staff to follow the safety requirements.

   (8) It has come to our attention that duplicating machines newly installed in our company often break down, due to...

   (9) Please be advised that...

   (10) This is to formally announce the following regulations made by the Board of Directors.

(11) ABC Company is pleased to announce its establishment. We shall be in operation from . . .

2. Motivate action

(1) The management would appreciate the cooperation of the staff to work for two extra hours in the following two weeks.

(2) It is our company's policy that long-distance calls can be made only on business affairs in the office.

(3) Please be aware of the plan alongside this notice, and note the following parking areas.

(4) The building work is part of our program to improve our facilities so we need your kind cooperation.

(5) Please note that this rule must be adhered to by all members of staff.

(6) We hope that all of our staff members to participate in this program.

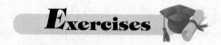

I Revise the following notice and discuss with your classmates why you improve it so.

To: All Staff
From: Board of Directors
Date: May 6th, 2016
Subject: Appointment of a new manager

Dear Staff,

It is our strategic plan to open the new branch in Shanghai, because Shanghai is city with dynamic business activities, which can offer us ample opportunities. Now our scheme has finally become a good reality. We will announce here that we have opened the new branch at Huanhai Road 688.

To look after the business there, we need an efficient manager. After 2 month's consideration, we have decided to appoint Mr. Zhang Jun as the new manager.

Mr. Zhang promises that he will do everything possible to do the management well. We hope that all of you will make efforts to give him a helpful hand.

Sincerely yours

Unit 9 Memos, E-mails and Notices

II Put the following sentences into the right order and make it a complete notice.

1. His place as Managing Director will be taken by me, and Mr. Mann Wang, who has been General Sales Manager for many years, will be filling the vacant place on the Board.
2. Owing to ill health, Mr. Lane Wu, our Managing Director, will be retiring from active business on the 31st December.
3. It is with regret that we have to tell you.

III Fill in the blanks in the following memo with the words given, and change the form where necessary.

> event, possibility, but, run, record, distribute, wear, accuracy

To: Supervisors
From: Gary L. Mayfield, Human Resources Manager
Date: January 2, 2015
Subject: Procedures for replacing damaged badge readers

Our recent transition from a punch clock to badge readers to record employee's time has _____ smoothly. However, we anticipate the _____ of defective badge readers, especially as they become _____ over time.

To ensure the _____ of the payroll, please instruct your employees to follow these procedures in the _____ the reader does not read their badges.

(1) Complete a copy of Form PR-16 (copy attached).
(2) Attach the damaged badge to the completed Form PR-16.
(3) Give the card to Jeanne Saunders in the Payroll Office by 10 a.m.
    She will prepare a new badge and send it to you with Form PR-17 by the end of the day.
(4) _____ the new badge to the employee. Instruct the employee not to use the new badge today _____ to report his/her departing time directly to you.
(5) _____ the employee's departing time on Form PR-17 and return it to Jeanne Saunders in the Payroll Office.

IV Writing practice.

Situational Writing 1

Glob-Finance, an accounting firm, has decided to begin advertising for business for their first time. You are hired as the new advertising director and are now designing an advertising program. You need a 15-minute appointment with each of the firm's 15 account supervisors to discuss their ideas about how best to advertise the firm.

Write a form memorandum to be sent to each of supervisors.

Situational Writing 2

You are one of the account supervisors mentioned in Situational Writing 1. Write a memorandum to the new advertising director telling him that you will be glad to meet with him to discuss the new advertising program. Suggest that you meet next Wednesday morning or Thursday afternoon in your office. Address Chevel Lopez, Advertising Director, Suite 495, Hi-tech Building.

Situational Writing 3

You are office supervisor of a large company. Your company has installed a large number of photocopiers in its offices. This has facilitated the duplication of documents. However, you have found that many people don't know how to operate the photocopiers properly, and breakdowns and waste of photocopying paper are on the increase. Write a memo to all office clerks giving a brief instruction on use of photocopiers in your company's office.

Situational Writing 4

You are requested to write a notice about a sight-seeing trip organized by your company. In your notice, you will inform your co-workers of the trip arrangement including: itinerary, accommodations, and traffic fares, and any other particulars that you think are relevant to your trip.

Situational Writing 5

There will be an International Trade Conference to be held in Nanjing from June 16 −19, sponsored by the International Chamber of Commerce. By the time, many businesspeople, scholars, investors, or economists from both home and abroad will attend the conference. The gathering will provide good opportunities to get latest business information and establish contacts with the business circles both at home and abroad. Mr. Li Xiang, Sales Manager of the Fortune Trade Co., Ltd., wants to attend the conference. He writes a request memo to President, Mr. William Zhang, to get the permission.

Unit 10

Sales Letters and Advertisement
销售信函与广告

10.1 Introduction

10.1.1 Writing for Persuasion

Persuasion is the art of influencing others to accept your point of view. It is not an attempt to trap someone into taking action favorable to the writer. Instead, it is an honest, organized presentation of information upon which a person may choose to act.[1] In all occupations and professions, rich rewards await those who can use well-informed and well-prepared presentations to persuade others to accept their ideas or buy their products, services, or ideas.

For persuasion to be effective, you must understand your product, service, or idea; know your audience; anticipate the arguments that may come from the audience; and have a rational and logical response to those arguments. Remember, persuasion needs not to be a hard sell; it can simply be a way of getting a client or your supervisor to say "yes". As for knowing the features of the products or services, you need to focus on their superior features (e.g., design and quality or receiver-benefit) and what the product, service, or idea do for the audiences and sometimes what the cost is to the readers.

It is equally important to understand the needs of the readers. Is a persuasive message to be written and addressed to an individual or to a group? If it is addressed to a group, what characteristics do the members have in common? What are their common goals, their educational status? To what extent have their needs and wants been satisfied? Some people may respond favorably to appeals to physiological security, and safety needs (to save time and money, to be comfortable, to be healthy, or to avoid danger). People with such needs would be impressed with a discussion of such benefits as convenience, durability, efficiency, or serviceability. Others may respond favorably to appeals to their social, ego, and self-actualized needs (to be loved, entertained, remembered, popular, praised, appreciated, or respected). We need to identify the needs or needs category of readers, and try to single out the most obvious needs to satisfy.

10.1.2 Applying Effective Writing Principles

The principles of unity, coherence, and emphasis are just as important in persuasive messages as in other messages. In addition, some other principles seem to be especially helpful in persuasive messages.

1. Use Specific Language

General words seem to imply subjectivity unless they are well supported with specifics. Therefore, try to use concrete nouns and active verbs, which can help receivers see the product, service, or ideas more vividly.

2. Let Receivers Have the Spotlight

If receivers are made the subject of some of the sentences, if they can visualize themselves with the product in their hands, if they can get the feel of using it for enjoyment or to solve problems, the chances of creating a desire are increased.

3. Stress a Central Selling Point or Appeal

Few products, services, or ideas have everything. A thorough analysis will ordinarily reveal some feature that is different from the features of competing products or some benefit not provided by other viable alternatives.[2] This point of difference can be developed into a theme that is woven throughout the entire letter. Or, instead of using a point of difference as a central selling point, writer may choose to stress one of the major satisfactions derived from using the item or doing as asked. A central selling point (theme) should be introduced early in the message and should be reinforced throughout the remainder of the message.

4. Be Certain Your Persuading Message Presents the Facts Honestly, Truthfully, and Objectively

Overzealous sales representatives or imaginative writers can use language skillfully to create less-than-accurate perceptions in the minds of receivers. However, legal guidelines related to advertising provide clear guidance for misrepresentation of products or services. If you exaggerate or mislead in your sales letters or advertisements, you will run risk incurring penalties and losing your loyal customers.

5. Use an Inductive Outline

About ninety years ago, Sherwin Cody summarized the persuasive process into four basic steps called AIDA. The steps have been varied somewhat and have had different labels, but the fundamentals remain relatively unchanged. The AIDA steps for selling are:

A — get the reader's *attention*;

I — introduce the product, service, or idea and arouse *interest* in it;

D — create *desire* by presenting convincing evidence of the value of the product, service, or idea;

A — encourage *action*.

A sales letter written by following these steps is inductive. The main idea, which is the request for action, appears in the last paragraph after presenting the details — convincing reasons for the receiver to comply with the request. Each step is essential, but the steps do not necessarily require equal amounts of space. Good persuasive writing does not require separate sentences and paragraphs for each phase of a letter: ① getting attention; ② introducing the product, service, or idea; ③ giving evidence; and ④ stimulating action. Points ① and ② could appear in the same sentence, and point ③ could require many paragraphs. Blend the steps in the four-step outline to prepare effective and persuasive sales letters and booklets or other advertisements.

10.2 Sales Letters

10.2.1 Writing Skills

1. Get Attention

In writing sales letters, we need to make impression on the goods you wish to promote, we, therefore, need to catch the reader's interest in the opening paragraph. For that, various techniques can be used successfully in convincing receivers to put aside whatever they are doing or thinking about and consider your sales letter. Here are some commonly used attention-getting devices.

- **A personal experience**: When a doctor gives you instructions, how often have you thought, "I wish you had time to explain" or "I wish I knew more about medical matters".
- **A solution to a problem**: Just imagine creating a customized multimedia presentation that ...
- **A startling announcement**: More teens die as a result of suicide each month than die in auto accidents in the same time period.
- **A what-if opening**: What if I told you there is a saving plan that will enable you to retire three years earlier?
- **A question**: Why should you invest in a country that has lost money for six straight years?
- **A story**: Here's a typical day of a manager who uses Wilson Enterprises Voice Mail.
- **A proverb or quote from a famous person**: P. T. Barnum supposedly said, "There's a sucker born every minute." At Northland Candy Factory, we make the saying come true!
- **A split sentence**: Picture ... ;
  Your audience's enthusiastic response to eye-catching graphics and colorful visuals to support your major points.

The beginning sentence must suggest a relationship between the receiver and the product, service, or idea. It must pave the way for the remainder of the sales letter. The sentences that follow the first sentence should grow naturally from it. If receivers do not see the relationship between the first sentences and the sales appeal, they may react negatively to the whole message— they may think they have been tricked into reading.

2. Focus on a Central Selling Feature

Almost every product, service, or idea will in some respects be superior to its competition. If it is not, such factors as favorable price, fast delivery, or superior service may be used as the primary appeal. This primary appeal (central selling point) must be emphasized, and one of the most effective ways to emphasize a point is by position in the letter. An outstanding feature mentioned in the middle of a letter may go unnoticed, but it will stand out if mentioned in the first sentence.

Good sales writing often reveals in the first sentence how a product, service, or idea can solve a receiver's problem. However, when mentioning the feature, do not use the same peculiar combination of words other people are known to use. That is a bad sales technique; it is also poor composition. People like to read something new and fresh; it gets their attention and interest. Writers should enjoy creating something new.

A persuasive message is certainly off to a good start if the first sentences cause the receiver to think, "Here is a solution to one of my problems", "Here's something I need", or "Here's something I want". You may lead the receiver to such a thought by introducing the product, service, or idea in the very first sentence. If you do, you have succeeded in both getting attention and arousing interest in one sentence.

3. Sustain Audience's Interest

1) Let facts speak for themselves

After having made an interesting introduction to your products, service, or idea, you can present enough supporting evidence to satisfy your receivers' needs. When presenting evidence, choose evidence that supports the outstanding features. For instance, if you say a certain machine or method is efficient, it is not enough. You must say how you know it is efficient and present some data to illustrate how efficient. Saying a piece of furniture is durable is not enough, because durability exists in varying degrees. You must present information that shows what makes it durable and also define how durable. The convincing-evidence portion of the sales letter needs to include all the information about the product, service, or idea. You can establish durability, for example, by presenting information about the manufacturing process, the quality of the raw materials, or the skill of the workers:

> KCC Publishing Garnet Classics will last your child a lifetime—Pages bound in durable gold-embossed hardback, treated with special protectants to retard paper aging, and machine-sewn (not glued) for long-lasting quality.
>
> The 100-percent cotton fiber paper can withstand years of turning the pages. The joy of reading can last for years as your children explore the world of classic literature with KCC's Garnet Classics.

It is another way to present research evidence to support your statements to increase your chance of convincing receivers to buy; in addition, experimental facts also present more convincing messages to consumers than general remarks about the distinctive features of products, although they take more space and time.

But your evidences presented should sound authentic, although they are authentic by nature. Facts and Figures help. However, you cannot go overboard and inundate your receivers with an abundance of facts or technical data that will bore, frustrate, or alienate them.[3] Never make your receivers feel ignorant by trying to impress them with facts and figures they may not understand. Therefore, use of language should help letters sound authentic. As we know, specific, concrete language can play such a role, for they can create an impressive image of the products for sales in the minds of consumers, while unsupported superlatives, exaggerations, flowery statements, unsupported claims, incomplete comparisons, and remarks suggesting certainty all make letters sound like high-pressure sales talk. Just one such sentence can destroy confidence in the whole letter. Look at the following statements to see whether they can give convincing evidence:

> This antibiotic is the best on the market today. It represents the very latest in biochemical research.

The above stated is nothing but a few abstract words linked up, giving no vivid picture of the product. As a matter of fact, the way to tell antibiotic is best to gather information about all antibiotics marketed and then choose the one with superior characteristics.

Let us examine the following statements to see if they are persuasive enough.

> Our recent research and tests have showed that rooms with our newly developed Energy Savers stay warmer and require 20 percent less fuel than those rooms of the same size without the usage of the savers. The new savers are popular because they are able to store and reflect heat in a much more efficient way.

This passage emphasizes the fact that less fuel is consumed and easy way in installing by giving specific facts. The author mentions the research and tests to show the scientific authenticity and authority.

2) **State prices logically and tactfully**

Price is a sensitive issue in most sales letters, and we need to be careful with it in our statement. Logically, price should be introduced late in the letter—after most of the advantages have been discussed. Few people want to part with their money until they have been shown how they can benefit by doing so. Thus, we need say something to assure the receiver that the price is not unreasonable. Here are some ways to help people to react positively to price.

- Introduce price only presenting the product, service, or idea and its virtues.
- Keep price talk out of the first and last paragraphs — unless, of course, price is the distinctive feature.

- Use figures to illustrate how enough money can be saved to pay for the expenditure (For instance, say that a US$ 60 turbo-vent that saved US$ 10 a month on summer electric bills would save approximately US$ 60 in two, 3-month summers and that the vent would last for many summers.).
- State price in terms of small units (Twelve dollars a month seems like less than US$ 144 a year.).
- Invite comparison of like products, services, or ideas with similar features.
- Use facts and figures to illustrate that price is reasonable.

4. Motivate the Receiver to Action

After a sufficient amount of facts and evidences is provided convincingly to arouse reader's interest in or desire for buying the goods you are advertising, it is your turn to motivate them to move, and it is helpful to increase your chances of getting action if you:

- allude to the reward for taking action;
- present the action as specific and being easy to take;
- provide some stimulus to quick action.

1) Allude to the reward for taking action

For both psychological and logical reactions, receivers are encouraged to act if they are reminded of the reward for acting. A well-written sales letter mentions outstanding selling features in the early paragraphs but emphasizes the particular rewards that consumers can get, for instance, discount or best quality after-sales. Let us look at the following examples.

> (1) If for any reasons you find the model machine unsuitable to your needs, we will replace your order or refund you.
> (2) Use our Microwave Oven for two weeks — absolutely free.

2) Present the action as specific and being easy to take

You need to define the desired action in specific terms by asking receivers to fill out an order blank and return it with a check, or place a telephone call, or return an enclosed card, etc. However, if your order forms or return cards and envelope, etc are difficult and time-consuming to fill out, receivers will hesitate to attempt doing that. Therefore, it is advisable to streamline items in the forms or on cards so that receivers can have the pleasure in taking the desired action. For instance:

> (1) Just give us a call. The beauty with the dress will be yours in only one week.
> (2) Please fill out the enclosed order form and return it with a check. We will effect the shipment immediately after we see your instruction.

3) Provide some stimulus to quick action

The longer the receiver waits to take action on your proposal, the persuasive evidence will be harder to remember, and the receiver will be less likely to act. Therefore, you prefer for the receiver to act quickly. Reference to the central selling point helps to stimulate action. Here are some commonly used appeals for getting quick action:

(1) Buy while present prices are still in effect.

(2) Don't delay! Those who order by Oct. 6 will receive a microwave oven free.

(3) Please come and buy right now since a special discount of 16% will only be offered for a month.

(4) Buy now while a rebate is being offered.

(5) Order it today. You will see 30% less cost for your next bill by using your newly purchased heating saver.

10.2.2 Sample Letters

 Sample Letter 10-1

Dear Mr. Smith,

Did you know it costs US$6 for each letter your staff types and your typical employee spends 20% of his or her time at work writing?

Of course you know the ability to write well gets the results you want. Contracted training saves your bank money.

To upgrade the writing skills of your employees, you may now contract WRITING SKILLS & EFFICIENCY, a training seminar tailored to your employees.[4] Furthermore, we will organize the seminar at your bank during the time when it is most convenient for your busy staff.

WRITING SKILLS & EFFICIENCY reviews troublesome mechanics, grammar, and usage as well as offers indispensable suggestion on correspondence, report writing, and much more. An experienced instructor will tailor the materials to your specific needs. Over 36 banks in New York will attest to the practicality of this training program.

May I make an appointment with Mr. Smith to discuss course contents, prices, and times? I will call your office within the next ten days.

Truly yours

Edgar P. Fowler
Writing Consultant

Sample Letter 10-2

Dear Car-owners,

CARE FOR YOUR CAR

Congratulations on your new car! I am sure that you are delighted with it and now look forward to countless days of motoring during the coming summer. I certainly wish you a great joy.

But delightful though motoring can be in good weather, it is quite another story in rain or fog. Then you will have the misery and also the fear for having to drive in the worst of conditions, and at the same time have the trouble of keeping your windscreen clear so you can see what the traffic condition in front of you is like. We have all experienced this kind of thing and, believe me, I hate it.

Now, however, we at Sunny Textiles Corporation have been able to produce what every motorist has been praying for — the **MAGIC CLOTH**. Far more than any similar cloth, it keeps windscreens and rear windows clear in that bad weather we all dread, but which will certainly be with us again as soon as the summer is over. When you wipe only with the **MAGIC CLOTH**, your car windows will remain beautifully clear for at least six days. And how is this? Well, the **MAGIC CLOTH** has been specially treated so that it will prevent fog, mist and frost from forming. As you must know yourself, your new car deserves all the care you can give it — it deserves the best you can get it ... and the **MAGIC CLOTH** will prevent you from having a lot of nasty accidents.

Will a **MAGIC CLOTH** cost a lot of money? Not at all, for we offer this great aid to all motorists for only £4 for five cloths — and those five will be quite enough to keep all your car windows clear for at least a year. Moreover as a special gift to you and your car, we will send you a 150 gm can of "Glux", the new combination car cleaner and polish, with your order for five **MAGIC CLOTH**.

What should you do now? It's all so simple — just complete the order form I enclose and return it to us with your remittance for £4 in the stamped and addressed envelope also enclosed, and we will immediately send your five **MAGIC CLOTH** and your free can of "Glux", I am sure you will agree you now have the answer to your problem, but if at the end of ten days you are not completely satisfied, just return the cloths for a full refund of the price — and you can still keep the can of "Glux".

Hope you will get satisfied with our product.

Yours sincerely

Mary Jones
Sales Manager

 Sample Letter 10-3

Dear Customer,

Have you ever felt anything both soft and strong?

Believe it or not, this enclosed small sample of leather used in our new Rainbow leather bags will offer you such a feeling.

Give a touch to the sample and you will find that the leather our manufacturer is going to use is just as soft as a piece of cloud. But top quality leather is only one feature of the new Rainbow line, and style is another. Consequently it has won this year's First National Award for its gentleness and elegance. Wherever you go with it, you may be sure that your Rainbow leather bag will draw attention from your companions.

In addition, the Rainbow leather bag has plenty of room for different items, and it even has a secret compartment for heaven-knows what.[5] For your information, the leather bags are designed in a variety of colors available in camel, white, navy blue, brown, and black.

As a result of the recognition, it is not surprising that this fashion line of our leather bags is being sold by all the top department stores in our country and has also been accepted by many dealers from European markets.

Complete the order form and return it right now. We trust that your trial order may convince you that this 90-dollar leather bag is of excellent value. You will receive a bottle of foam cream (leather clean) as a gift if you let us have your preference by sending the completed order form before August 10.

Yours sincerely

Sample Letter 10-4

Dear Sirs,

You can have a green, weed-free lawn this summer with a revolutionary new fertilizer. And we can do all the work for you.

Once every two weeks, our well-trained experts will visit your home to apply Green-Dew, a liquid fertilizer developed by Grand Tree Fertilizer Co., Ltd. It kills weeds and strengthens the root fibers of the grass. It works in both shady and sunny areas and is particularly effective in our area.[6] This product is safe to use around pets or birds.

All you have to do to have a beautiful lawn for the entire season is to water it and keep the grass cut. Green-Dew will do the rest excellently.

Don't wait. If you buy it now, you can enjoy 20 percent discount, for it is our sale week. Your green lawn will be a soothing cool paradise all summer.

Faithfully yours

 Sample Letter 10-5

Dear Sir or Madam,

More people are now saving their time and efforts by preparing meals the modern way — the microwave cooking way.

No longer do you need to wait hours for food to be prepared. Microwave cooking is quick, convenient and inexpensive. What you need to do is just to press the button, and then this new cooker will permit you to serve mouth-watering meals in no time at all.

Read the enclosed brochure and learn why more and more people are rushing to buy microwave ovens. During the month of September, we are ready to offer you Glaze Microwave ovens at a 15% saving on the regular price.

Please fill out the enclosed order form and we are sure to deliver the goods you need promptly.

We are sure that our ovens will give your life convenience and good taste.

Truly yours

 Sample Letter 10-6

Dear Customer,

**IRON AWAY YOUR BLUES WITH A STEAMEASY
STEAM IRON AT THE UNBELIEVALBLY LOW PRICE OF
$60.99!**

Wouldn't you love to whisk your way through those piles of ironing on washday?[7] Free yourself to do more interesting things?

Well now you can with the **SteamEasy** steam iron. Scientifically designated to make ironing easier, the **SteamEasy** is not only incredibly light, but also extremely versatile. What is more, its built-in overnight charger means that the **SteamEasy** is always ready to use, day or night.

Laboratory reports show that the **SteamEasy** is up to twice as reliable as some of the "big name" brands. And to show how confident we are, the **SteamEasy** comes with a two-year guarantee.

At just $60.99, the **SteamEasy** is irresistible. Post the enclosed pre-paid card today and you will get your **SteamEasy** within seven days. **SEND NO MONEY NOW**. Then you can start planning how you are going to use all the free time that the **SteamEasy** will bring you.

Juan Wang
Vice-President
Sales Department

Sample Letter 10-7

Dear Customer,

Isn't it time you put your teeth in the hands of a professional?

How often have your teeth let you down? At that all important interview? Or on that date? Did you wish that you could have got your teeth cleaner, whiter, fresher?

Well now you can with the **Pearl White-1** electric toothbrush.

Scientifically designed to reach the parts of your mouth conventionally brushing can never reach, the **Pearl White-1** electric toothbrush will guarantee that your breath is always fresh and your teeth are sparkling clean. Laboratory reports show that regular use of the **Pearl White-1** electric toothbrush can result in significantly less dental repairs, too.

One happy customer, Mr. Liu of Kennedy Road told us that his dentist had advised his having all his teeth removed until Mr. Liu tried the **Pearl White-1**. The improvement, according to his dentist, was "amazing".

The **Pearl White-1** electric toothbrush is beautifully compact (ideal for the busy executive or tourist) and comes in a range of ultra-clean colors: Marine Blue, Lightning White and Flame Red. It comes with a set of assorted heads suitable for children, and those with tender gums or dentures. The **Pearl White-1** also has a built-in battery charger for overnight charging.

At just HK$268, the **Pearl White-1** is irresistible. Post the enclosed pre-paid card today and you will get your **Pearl White-1** within ten days.

SEND NO MONEY NOW. Then you can look forward to healthier, brighter and more attractive teeth than you've ever had before.

Mr. John Lo
Customer Service Manager

Sample Letter 10-8

Dear Sirs,

We learn from your ambassador that you are interested in wool carpets and think we may help you, so we write this letter to let you have a general idea about our products.

Our company has exported large quantities of wool carpets to many countries of the Common Market, where our carpets have become very popular. We are sure that your order of the goods will prove profitable to you.

We would like to tell you that our yearly production is about 60,000 pieces — the largest carpet manufacturer in China and the quality of our carpets is surely the best, but the price is always 15% lower than that of others.

Recently, we have received many enquiries from Europe, South Africa and America. We are convinced that our carpets will be exported to more countries. So we wish we will have your order at an earlier date. Enclosed please find our illustrated catalogue and price list for your reference.

We are looking forward to your orders.

Yours faithfully

Carmen L. Rankin

10.3 Advertisement

10.3.1 Introduction

In terms of written documents, advertisements may take the form of line advertisements, as in "Classified Advertisements" sections of newspapers, in which information runs on from line to line, then using the same typeface throughout, with no special layout, and display advertisements, which use a variety of typefaces and sizes, and may be illustrated with artwork or color. What we mainly deal with in this chapter is display advertisements, with more emphasis on composing the advert copy (the message) than on artwork or color.

Designing an advertisement is actually an exercise in summarizing. It is important to pick out the main points, features, advantages, or whatever is relevant to the theme of the advertisement. It is essential to try to ensure that your advert will be "seen" on the page of the newspaper or magazine. If it is displayed unattractively, it will not achieve this objective. Here are some guidelines for designing advertisements.

(1) Use a company logo, prominently displayed.

(2) Whatever is being advertised (whether it is a job, product or special event) display a headline prominently in capitals, spaced capitals or bold type.

(3) Use your initiative to break up the information; perhaps various points should be listed (use an asterisk or bullet point to display each point on a new line).

(4) Use spacing to advantage, giving special items prominence.

(5) Try to achieve a progressive display, categorizing information, leading finally to action from the reader.

(6) Make the advertisement eye-catching and ensure that it stands out from other advertisements, which will be placed alongside it.

Read the following advertisement and get better understanding of the above guidelines.

10.3.2 Samples

 Sample 10-9

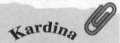

Sales Representatives

Already one of the fast-growing garden products companies in USA, Kardina will soon be selling its high-quality garden furniture in the UK.

We are looking for experienced sales representatives to help us set up a distributorship in the UK. If you happen to be aged 20–30 and

√ **possess good sales and communication skills;**
√ **be able to manage people effectively;**
√ **have an excellent track record.**

Why not join Kardina and enjoy the attractive starting salary of US$ 60,000, plus attractive incentive and scheme and fringe benefit in keeping the image of a young, dynamic company.

Interested?

For an informal discussion, contact our consultant Mr. William Kent at 03 xxxxxxx. Alternatively, write to: Kardina furniture plc, 54 York Road, Chicago, Illinois, USA.

Sample 10-10

A Human Resources Manager Can't Afford to Miss

Michael Chang, one of the world's best lecturers on HR management, is holding a 6-day advanced management course.

When? Monday 3 June to Friday 7 June
9:30 – 16:30
Venue? The Westing Hall
A thick note-book is required!

The lecture makes you a different manager.

Contact

Mark Wright
Office Manager

Newgate Road
London
NW2 5CC

Tel: 2 xxxxxx
Fax: 2 xxxxxx

Issued on 26 May, 2015

Sample 10-11

The transparent facial wash
Neutrogena original formula
Once a day
Purify your skin

Think how healthy your face would feel if you could bring back your skin's natural purity. Mild Neutrogena gently frees the day's accumulation of pollutants, cosmetics, and other impurities, and then rinses off completely. No residue is left behind to dry or irritate your skin. Your face is just as it should be: pure... and radiantly healthy.

 Sample 10-12

New GEICO customers report average annual savings over US$500 on car insurance.

No wonder 3 million drivers
Switched to us last year

Get a FREE rate quote today.

1-800-624-9505

GEICOM
Geicom. com

Unit 10 Sales Letters and Advertisement

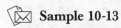 **Sample 10-13**

**Life insurance isn't for the people who die.
It's for the people who live.**

When Michael Rausch was just one year old, his mom, Julie, was diagnosed with a malignant brain tumor. The news devastated his father, Bill, and severely affected the concrete business he and Julie ran together. Sadly, the company failed shortly before Julie's death. But the story doesn't end there. Life insurance meant Bill was able to restart the business and provide a secure and loving home for Michael.

Are you prepared should the very worst happen? Without adequate life insurance, your financial plans may be just a savings and investment program that dies when you do. Consult a qualified insurance professional to help you create a plan that will continue to provide for the ones you love.

LIFE
A Non-profit Organization
WWW. life-line.org

The Life and Health Insurance Foundation for Education is a nonprofit organization dedicated to helping consumers make smart insurance decisions to safeguard their families' financial futures. For more information about life insurance or tips on finding a qualified insurance professional, visit www.life-line.org or call 1888-E-777.

New Words and Expressions

rational	a.	合理的
physiological	a.	生理上的
entertain	v.	满足（需求）
visualize	v.	想象出
reveal	v.	揭示，表明
viable	a.	可行的
derive	v.	获得，得到

reinforce	v.	强化,加强
overzealous	a.	过于热情的
perception	n.	认识,观点
exaggerate	v.	夸大,夸张
blend	v.	融合,结合
customize	v.	按要求改变,使……适合
gold-embossed	a.	烫金的
retard	v.	阻止,妨碍
withstand	v.	承受,抵挡
explore	v.	探索,寻找
inundate	v.	淹没
alienate	v.	使……疏远,陌生
superlative	a.	极好的,最好的
flowery	a.	(文体)华丽的
antibiotic	n.	抗生素
sensitive	a.	敏感的
distinctive	a.	鲜明的,独特的
like	a.	相同的
rebate	n.	回扣
contract	v.	与……签订合同
troublesome	a.	麻烦的
indispensable	a.	必不可少的
correspondence	n.	信函
windscreen	n.	挡风玻璃
frost	n.	霜
nasty	a.	坏的,糟糕的
remittance	n.	汇款
compartment	n.	分隔空间
heaven-know	a.	秘密的
weed-free	a.	无草的,除草的
fertilizer	n.	肥料
shady	a.	树阴的,阴面的
soothing	a.	凉快的
versatile	a.	多方面的
built-in	a.	内置的
irresistible	a.	不可抵挡的,不可拒绝的
sparkling	a.	闪耀的

Unit 10 Sales Letters and Advertisement

ultra-clean	a.	超洁的
assorted	a.	分类的，各式各样的
gum	n.	（常用复数）牙龈
dentures	n.	一副牙齿，假牙
typeface	n.	铅字面
prominently	ad.	显眼地
eye-catching	a.	令人注意的
distributorship	n.	分销
dynamic	a.	有活力的
transparent	a.	透明的
formula	n.	配方
accumulation	n.	沉积，积累
rinse	v.	清洗
residue	n.	残留物
radiantly	ad.	耀眼地
malignant	a.	恶性的
tumor	n.	肿瘤
devastate	v.	破坏，毁坏
consult	v.	查阅，咨询
tip	n.	（常用复数）建议，告诫
be impressed with		对……留下深刻印象
go overboard		超越
allude to		提到
in effect		事实上，实际
microwave oven		微波炉
tailored to		符合，适合
root fiber		根纤维
mouth-watering		令人流口水的，令人垂涎的
to whisk one's way through		快速完成
let someone down		让人沮丧
stand out		突出，突现
track record		跟踪记录
fringe benefit		福利
be dedicated to		致力于

Notes

1. Instead, it is an honest, organized presentation of information upon which a person may choose to act.　相反，这是一种诚实的、有条不紊的信息展示，人们有可能会依照这些信息的要求去做。

2. A thorough analysis will ordinarily reveal some feature that is different from the features of competing products or some benefit not provided by other viable alternatives.　仔细研究你就会发现该产品的一些特点，它们与众不同，同时还具备其他类似产品所不具备的优势。

3. However, you cannot go overboard and inundate your receivers with an abundance of facts or technical data that will bore, frustrate, or alienate them.　然而，你应该把握好度，不要让你的读者接受一大堆技术数据，这样只能使他们感到枯燥乏味、沮丧和陌生。

4. To update the writing skills of your employees, you may now contract WRITING SKILLS & EFFICIENCY, a training seminar tailored to your employees.　为了提高贵公司员工的写作技巧，你们可以和写作技巧与效率培训班签订合同，它能满足你们的要求。

5. ... and it even has a secret compartment for heaven-knows what.　……该款皮包甚至还有一个密层，可以放一些私人物品。

6. It kills weeds and strengthens the root fibers of the grass. It works in both shady and sunny areas and is particularly effective in our area.　该产品可以除草，增强草的根部纤维。无论是在树阴下还是在阳光照射到的地方，该产品都能有效，尤其在我们本地。

7. Wouldn't you love to whisk your way through those piles of ironing on washday?　难道你不希望在清洗日能快速地完成大堆衣服的熨烫吗？

Sentence Menu

1. Get attention

- Adopt "raise a question" sentences

（1）What can you do about conservation?

（2）What if the boss came to your desk and said, "We're going to increase production by 13 percent this week"?

（3）Why not enjoy the colorful spring by joining our tourist group after a busy winter?

（4）Have you ever thought of investing in the Stock Exchange, but then dismissed the idea because of the size of your investment? Well, why don't you think about an investment portfolio?

Unit 10 Sales Letters and Advertisement

(5) Would you be interested in a car which runs on neither conventional gas nor electric power?

(6) Would you like to reduce your rising domestic fuel costs?

(7) Wouldn't it be magic to ...

(8) Have you ever felt anything quite as soft and quite as strong?

- **Adopt "just imagine" sentences**

(1) Just imagine how comfortable it will be when you stretch out your tired limbs on our newly developed White-cloud waterbed?

(2) Just imagine you wake up to find that your face has become radiant with charms after you try our product only for a couple of days.

2. Sustain audience's interest

(1) It is easy, comfortable for ..., which ...

(2) The rugs are hard-wearing, and do not soil easily. You will find that the consignment supports our claim to sell the best rugs of this kind at a reasonable price at any time to any persons.

(3) The product weighs ... ; its dimensions are ... , with colors ranging from ... to ...

(4) Compared with other products, this product has the advantage of ...

(5) Unlike other products, our product is superior in terms of performance, physical features and etc.

(6) They are 20% lower in cost compared with our precious ones and other competitors.

(7) A discount of 2 percent on the total value will be granted if you could make payment within 15 days of delivery.

(8) We are confident that the product will offer you most convenience and efficiency in your work.

(9) I am certain that you will be interested in our new toothpaste.

3. Motivate the audience to action

(1) Remember this offer is only open for two weeks.

(2) You can try our product for one week free of charge.

(3) If you are not completely satisfied, return ... to us with no obligation.

(4) We will take care of fixing, repairing or even replacing it if there is anything wrong.

(5) Try this product for 15 days. Then go back to your old ... We guarantee you won't want to go back.

(6) Order it now, you will see a 20% discount granted to you.

(7) Fill in the enclosed order form and airmail it to us by ... We will ship you the product by the end of ...

(8) Fill out the enclosed order form and return it with a check, we will effect the shipment

immediately upon the receipt of your order.

(9) If you order ... by Oct. ... , you can receive 3% more of goods free of charge.

(10) Please order without delay since our products may well be out of stock.

(11) Fill in the attached form and fix it off to us.

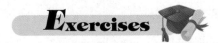

1 Please revise the following sales letter and discuss with your classmates why you need to improve so.

Dear Customer,

Will you please take a few seconds to go through this letter? It describes an excellent proposition we are sure you will not want to miss.

We want you to be aware of the handbook of Window 2000, which is a wonderful book we have recently published and is worthy of your money.

This handbook is a masterpiece composed by so many experts who have used the Window 2000 for a few years. It can be claimed that it is the superior one. It has got many good answers to typical problems caused in using systems. Once you have one, we are sure that all your problems will be over. What is more, both explanations in English and Chinese will offer you a perfect version, whether you speak Chinese or English.

The subscription price is only RMB 25, just about 3 dollars, which definitely costs nothing to you.

Enclosed is a subscription form. Please return it with the number of the copies you need by the end of May.

Yours faithfully

Unit 10 Sales Letters and Advertisement

II Fill in the blanks of the following message with the words given, and change the form where necessary.

> renewable, clean, on, difference, reduce, amazing, alternative

Corn can do _____ things. Corn can be refined into E85 ethanol — an _____ fuel made up of 85% ethanol and 15% gasoline that not only burns _____ than fossil fuels, it's also a homegrown _____ energy source that can help _____ our dependence on oil. GM already has 1.5 million FlexFuel Vehicles on the road that can run _____ gasoline or E85 ethanol. And it's just the beginning. Join the ride. Learn more about E85 Ethanol, which GM vehicles can run on it, whether you can get it and how you can make a _____. One car company can show you how.

III Writing practice.

1. Write a sales letter according to the following situation.

> A company has not paid the overdue balance of your goods, and during the past two months, you wrote 3 letters to ask the company to settle the balance, but that company just responded by explaining away their difficult situation. Now this time you are going to write a letter to persuade that company to settle the outstanding account immediately with a appeal to reputation.

2. Write a sales letter based on the following ideas.

> (1) A survey shows that air-conditioner Haier can raise the work efficiency of office staff by 10% during summer time.
> (2) The improvement in work efficiency means an increase in profits, which in turn can help quicken the recovery of costs.
> (3) The product has its outstanding features... And price is 5% lower than the like products.
> (4) If your order is large, installment is acceptable but payment period is within 2 months.
> (5) Our after-sales are good.

3. Write a sales letter according to the following situation.

> You are now working on a sales letter to publicize your employment service that your center offers to those job hunters. Your letter can focus on the selling points of your center including history, good connections with major corporations and public service, your high work efficiency...
> Please write a sales letter for your employment service center.

4. Write an advertisement according to the following situation.

> You are requested to write a promotional material to introduce an economic development zone. Can you go to library to find out relevant literature and write an introduction to an economic development zone? Your writing can go along by following the writing principles involved in advertisement and sales letter.

Unit 11

Business Reports (I)
商务报告（一）

11.1 The Introduction to Reports

Business report is an orderly, objective message used to convey information from one organizational area to another or from one institution to another to assist in decision-making or problem solving. Although they can take the form of verbal presentation, business reports are usually produced in writing. Usually business people write reports for at least two purposes: to provide information and to analyze the collected data and to supply conclusions and recommendations if requested.

The length of a report depends much on its purpose and the nature of information it will contain, ranging from informal one-page trip reports to formal 200-page financial forecasts. Business reports can be classified in a number of ways.

In general, they can be classified by formality into: formal and informal and by function into: informational reports and analytical reports.

Formal report is carefully structured; it stresses objectivity and organization, contains much detail, and is written in a style that tends to eliminate such elements as personal pronouns. An informal report is usually a short message written in natural or personal language. It is produced as accounts of daily business matters, or anything requiring quick decisions. These reports often take the form of a memorandum, with simplified layout.

Informational report carries objective information from one area of an organization to another to present data without analyses or recommendations.

Analytical report provides data, analyses, and conclusions on the issue that the writer has been asked to investigate. Such report usually provides recommendations for the readers to consider, but only on request. Feasibility reports, justification or recommendation reports, and yardstick reports belong to this category.

11.1.1 Layout

Almost all business reports have the same structural parts — head, introduction, middle, end and bottom. And these five parts incorporate more specific components, which are determined by the subject, the purpose, the information to be used, etc.

11.1.2 Format and Length of a Report

As you are writing a report, you need to know what format you should follow and how long the report should be. Very often you have the freedom to choose the format, based on the reader's need. There are four commonly used formats that we can refer to in composing your business reports.

1. Preprinted Form

Many companies prepared the forms for certain type of reports. These reports usually deal with routine information. You just supply information asked for by filling out the items on the report.

2. Letter

Reports in letter format are usually adopted as an external means of communication, and usually have letter components and report sections.

3. Memo

Reports in this form are usually informal reports, which can be for both internal use and external use. The headings of memo can help audience to immediately identify the major contents of the report.

4. Manuscript

Reports in manuscript format are formal reports, ranging from a few pages to several hundred pages. Long reports need special parts before and after the text.

The length and the kind of format that your report will have are usually determined by the subject and purpose of the report and knowledge of the subject and possible conclusions. But a writer needs to bear it in mind that clear-cut messages ought to be conveyed in composing business reports.

11.1.3 Language and Writing Style

In report writing, the style should be objective, impersonal, specific and factual, and consistent and coherent. The tone of business reports depends on the audience, which reflects the relationship between the writer and the reader of the report. Visual aids contribute a lot to the effectiveness of a report.

Unit 11 Business Reports (I)

1. Objective and Impersonal

The author of the report should be free of any bias or prejudice caused by personal feelings, and the report is required to be based on facts rather than assumptions.

Writing in the first or second pronoun (I/we/you) is not recommended and the style of writing using third person forms is mostly employed. Let us look at the following examples.

> (1a) I have noticed that recently some staff members park their cars in the non-parking zones outside our office building. (✘)
> (1b) It has been noticed that recently some staff park their cars in the non-parking zones outside our office building. (✓)
> (2a) We should like the executive's seats to be high-backed. (✘)
> (2b) It was felt that the executives' seats should be high-backed. (✓)

2. Specific and Factual

The results provided in the report are expected to be particular and supported with details and facts to avoid vagueness. The report consists of the truth only or just includes those things that are real or actual. Let's compare the following writing (see Table 11-1).

Table 11-1 Poor writing and better writing

Poor Writing	Better Writing
Great damage	60% damage
In the near future	By Monday morning
Light in weight	Feather-light
The majority	90%
Some autos have risen sharply in price in recent months.	Such autos as Buick and BMW have risen 50 percent since this week.

3. Consistent and Coherent

It needs to ensure clarity and give a good impression by making sure all sentences consistently follow the same grammatical patterns (grammatical parallelism). Spacing in various parts of the reports should also be consistent, with identically displayed sub-headings and enumeration. If such devices are used, each sentence seems to be joined smoothly to the next, and can help keep you from making abrupt changes in thought.

4. Graphics

It is very common to employ graphics including figures, charts and other statistical data in producing a report. They use visual techniques to focus the reader's attention on the main points and to clarify discussion and findings.

The choice of any specific tool depends on the specific type of the message. We just choose the form that best suits our message and that communicates our message most clearly to the audience. Generally, we have the following choices.

1) Types of graphics

(1) A table, which is a systematic arrangement of data in columns and rows and is efficient in presenting detailed, specific information (see Table 11-2).

Table 11-2   Tax brackets — 2015 taxable income

Joint Return	Single Taxpayer	Rate
$0 – $14,600	$0 – $7,300	10.0%
$14,601 – $59,400	$7,301 – $29,700	15.0
$59,401 – $119,950	$29,701 – $71,950	25.0
$119,951 – $182,800	$71,951 – $150,150	28.0
$182,801 – $326,450	$150,151 – $326,450	33.0
$326,451 and up	$326,451 and up	35.0

(2) A line chart, which illustrates trends over time or plots the relationship of two variables and involves a vertical axis and a horizontal axis (see Figure 11-1).[1]

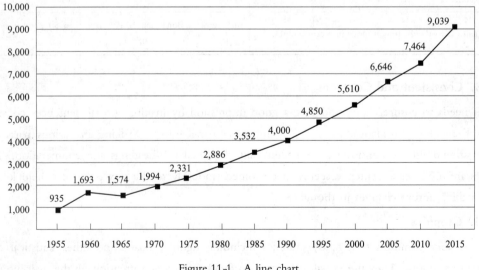

Figure 11-1   A line chart

(3) A bar chart, a chart in which amounts are visually portrayed by the height or length of rectangular bars (see Figure 11-2).

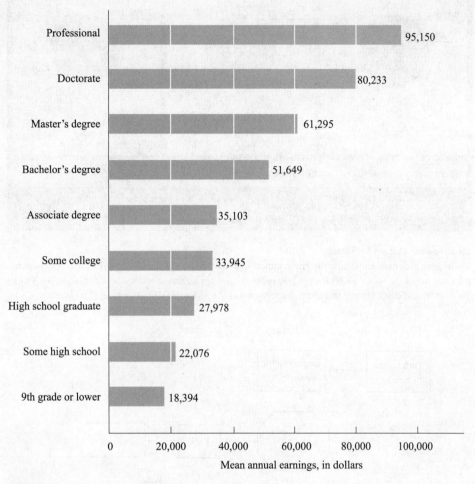

Human Capital
People gain value in the job market by increasing their skills and abilities, or human capital. As a result they can often get higher-paying jobs. This chart shows that people in the United States with more schooling and advanced degrees earn higher incomes, on average, than those with less schooling. Professional degrees include degrees in medicine, law, dentistry, and theology.

Figure 11-2　A bar chart

(4) A pie chart, a chart in which numbers are represented as slices of a complete pie (see Figure 11-3).

(5) A flow chart, which illustrates a sequence of events from start to finish (see Figure 11-4).

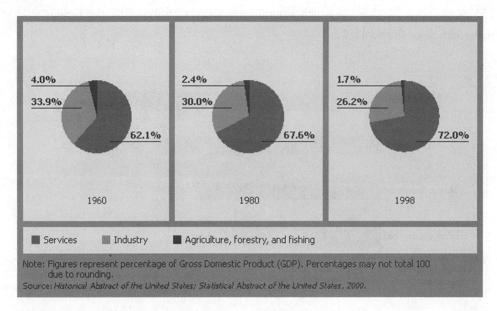

US Economic Output by Sector
These three pie charts show how the gross domestic product (GDP) of the United States was split among the three major economic sectors: services, industry, and agriculture, forestry, and fishing in the years 1960, 1980 and 1998. During this time, the service sector's share of GDP increased significantly.

Figure 11-3　A pie chart

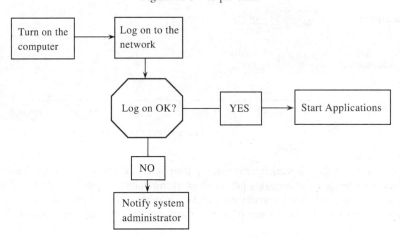

Figure 11-4　A flow chart

A flowchart is a pictorial representation showing all of the steps of a process and is used for:
- defining and analyzing processes;
- building a step-by-step picture of the process for analysis, discussion, or communication purposes;
- defining, standardizing, or finding areas for improvement in a process.

The checklist shown below is recommended for the production of a flowchart.
- All major elements of the project are indicated.

- The elements are clearly labeled.
- Sequence of elements is clear and there are no gaps or dead ends.
- Sequence of elements is logical from user's point of view.
- Flowchart symbols are used correctly.

2) **Narrate the trend in the graphics**

(1) Upward trend:

- go (move) upward
- to grow to ..., up ____% over that of last year
- to rise to ..., up ____%
- to climb to ..., up ____%
- to grow by ____% to reach
- to rise by ____% to attain
- to climb by ____% get to/arrive at ..., to reach a peak of 9.7 million in 2000

(2) Downward trend:

- to move downward
- to decline, decrease, fall, go down, drop, dwindle, slump/slip/slide
- to decline to ..., down ____% over that of last year, compared with that of last year

(3) Level-off trend:

- to level off and to reach a plateau
- to remain constant
- to stand at

(4) Extent to which the trend develops:

- steeply, dramatically, greatly, considerably, significantly, a great deal
- rather, somewhat, a bit, a little, slightly, to some extent

(5) percentage:

- take up ____%
- occupy ____%
- account for ____%

3) **Compare and analyze the data**

(1) Compare:

- Between 2008 and 2014, sales decreased, but in 2015, it rose to US$ 400,000.
- As comparison of sales between 2009 and 2015 shows, the sales rise sharply to _____.
- In April, they rise to _____ up _____% over last rear.
- Sales between years of _____ and _____ are projected to rise (decrease) markedly.
- Prices leveled off slightly in 2014 and 2015, but rose sharply again at _____.

- The sales value remains constant at _____.
- The graph shows the growing rate of _____. between _____ and _____, the sales increased steadily from _____ to _____. But in _____, it started to fall from _____ to _____, and then recovered in the following year to _____. In the year of _____, it stood at _____ and then from the year to _____, the sales leveled at _____. Since then it started to _____.

(2) Analyze:

- As for the increase, I think there are a few factors behind it.
- The fact that there is a big increase in _____ is attributed to the following reasons.
- There are such reasons to account for the decrease of the sales.
- The _____ come from _____.
- I think that a number of factors could account for/lead to the change in _____.
- There are several reasons for this phenomenon/trend/change. In the first place, _____.
- Why are/do/did _____? For one thing, _____; for another _____. Perhaps the primary reason is _____.
- There exists a great variety of reasons to account for this social phenomenon/this problem, but in general, it comes down to three major ones.

(3) Sample:

> The major trend in computer production are clear from the graph above. Production rose steadily in all three countries between 1971 and 1972, but by 1973, production had already started to <u>increase/rise</u> in the UK. In contrast, output in the US <u>descended/fell/dropped</u> to reach a peak of 9.7 million in 1973. The financial crisis in 1974 led to a large <u>drop/fall</u> in output in all three countries, but especially in the US where it <u>fell/dropped</u> from 9.7 to 6.7 million in 1975. The downward trend was <u>brought</u> to a halt in the US and Japan but production continued to <u>descend/drop</u> in the UK after 1975. In the US, production leveled off at 9.2 million while in Japan, it <u>rose/grew</u> steadily so that in 1980 it actually overtook American output.[2] In fact, after 1978 US production <u>fell/dropped</u> in the following three years <u>by</u> 2.9 million.

11.2 Components of a Business Report

The various business reports, despite their types, can be divided into three parts, including heading, instruction, body, conclusion and recommendations.

1. Heading/Title

First of all, all reports must have a heading/title, which briefly gives the subject matter of the report

2. Introduction/Purpose

It means that why the report is being written, who is going to read the report, and what information is required. For instance, the statement can be made by using the phrases like, "The purpose of this report is to investigate/evaluate/study . . ." or "This section of the report gives some background information to the circumstances behind the report."

3. Procedure/Proceedings

It is a brief description of the methods used to collect the information, for instance, questionnaires might have been issued, interviews held, visits made.

The parts of purpose and procedure can be linked into one section known as "Introduction" in some business reports. The following is an example.

> **Introduction**
> The Director of Environment Health and Cleansing Services has asked me to prepare a report on rubbish collection in the borough for the Environmental Health Committee. I have questioned staff, analyzed statistics, collected newspaper articles and spoken to representatives of various local committees.

4. Findings

It is the main body of the report based on the methods described in "procedure", and the information needs to be presented in sections and arranged logically. Sub-headings and enumeration are usually used for clarity.

5. Conclusion

It is the logical implications of the findings. No new facts should appear in this section. Please do not mix up the findings and conclusions. Please note that conclusion is the interpretation of your findings.

Here are two sentences for us to distinguish:

(1) The cost of employing an external consultant is HK$ 1,200 per hour. (findings)
(2) The cost of employing an external consultant is unacceptably high. (conclusion)

6. Recommendations

They are suggestions for actions, which are made on the basis of the Findings and Conclusions. For reports giving a number of recommendations, there is no need to state the reasons, as one cannot tell which pertains to which of the recommendations. [5]

7. Executive Summary

As a long section of a long report, the executive summary aims to present the main body of the report in summarized form so that the main facts can be digested quickly if the reader is in too much of a hurry to read the whole report. The executive summary is usually limited to two paragraphs: one for stating the purpose of the report; the other for stating the basic findings, conclusions and recommendations.

New Words and Expressions

formality	n.	格式
eliminate	v.	删除，消除
yardstick	n.	准绳，衡量标准
justification	n.	认为有理，辩护
manuscript	n.	原稿，手稿
impersonal	a.	客观的，非个人的
consistent	a.	一致的，调和的
coherent	a.	一致的，连贯的
bias	n.	偏见，偏爱
prejudice	n.	偏见，成见
assumption	n.	假定，设想
parallelism	n.	平行，对应
graphics	n.	图形，制图
variable	n.	变量
portray	v.	描绘
rectangular	a.	矩形的，长方形的
financial forecast		财务预测
informational report		信息报告
analytical report		分析报告
feasibility report		可行性报告
preprinted		预先打印
line chart		坐标图
bar chart		柱形或条形图
flow chart		流程图

Notes

1. A line chart, which illustrates trends over time or plots the relationship of two variables and

involves a vertical axis and a horizontal axis. 坐标图有纵轴和水平轴，用来描述随时间变化的趋势或两个变量之间的关系。

2. In the US, production leveled off at 9.2 million while in Japan, it rose/grew steadily so that in 1980 it actually overtook American output. 美国的产量稳定在 920 万左右，而日本则是稳定增长，1980 年实际上已经超过了美国。

3. For reports giving a number of recommendations, there is no need to state the reasons, as one cannot tell which pertains to which of the recommendations. 对于给出许多建议的报告，因无法说明哪条原因和哪条建议相对应，故没有必要列出理由。

Sentence Menu

1. Introduction

(1) Following the request of ... to compile a report on ..., I have consulted the statistics and spoken to many members of staff in the company.

(2) Mr. ... asked me to write this report on May 25, 2015 to ...

(3) Here is the report you requested on June 5, 2015 on ...

(4) The purpose of this report is to ...

(5) The report is based on ...

(6) In response to your request, my staff and I investigated the potential for ...

(7) This report proposes a means of ...

2. Findings

(1) A selection of members of staff was questioned from various departments.

(2) We have found three causes relating to ...

(3) The following points summarize our key findings.

(4) There are a number of reasons for ...

(5) There are several factors which affect ...

(6) Contrary to expectations, ...

3. Conclusion

(1) The studies we reviewed showed that ...

(2) It was agreed that ...

(3) No conclusions were reached regarding ...

(4) On the basis of these details, I firmly believe that ...

4. Recommendations

(1) After analyzing... and studying..., we have three recommendations.

(2) Based on what I found when inspecting the two sites, I think we must...

(3) The firm needs to take some measures to control the expenses.

(4) It is essential to...

(5) We strongly recommend that...

(6) The solutions to the problem are clear.

(7) We think something has to be done immediately, otherwise there would be a disaster.

5. Ending

Thank you for giving us the opportunity to work on this assignment. If you have any questions about the report, please call me.

I Rearrange these sentences to form a paragraph about part of the Economic Report of the US President.

1. We will increase the use of health information technology that will make health care more efficient, cut down on mistakes, and control costs.
2. We have created health savings accounts, which give workers and families more control over their health care decisions.
3. We are working to make health care more affordable and accessible for American families.
4. The medicare modernization bill I signed gives seniors more choices and helps them get the benefits of modern medicine and prescription drug coverage.
5. To help control health costs and make health care more accessible, we must let small businesses pool risks across states so they can get the same discounts for health insurance that big companies get.
6. We will open or expand more community health centers for those in need.

II Compare the following versions and tell which one is better and then give your reasons.

Version A

On the committee, we have spent a lot of time and effort on the question for hours. I mean, different people have different opinions, obviously, and it doesn't matter whether you ask people here or outside, they all have their own opinions about whether it is a good idea or not. And since you get so many different opinions, it is not easy for a committee to come to a final decision, but we have done what we think is right, and we hope that if anybody is not completely happy, they will not take our ideas personally. Since 2014 everybody in this firm has worked 40 hours per week, and we have no intention of changing the total. In any case, a change in the total number of hours would only be possible after proper negotiations between management and union representatives, and this is not the place to anticipate any such negotiations in the near or distant future.

Version B

This report concerns the feasibility of allowing members of staff to start and stop work at the times that suit them best; the obvious provision is, of course, that everyone should still work a total of 40 hours per week, as we do now. The flexible working hours scheme was proposed to the directors by certain members of staff, particularly those who have young children at school.

III The following is a chart taken from 2005 World Trade Report. Please use proper words to describe it.

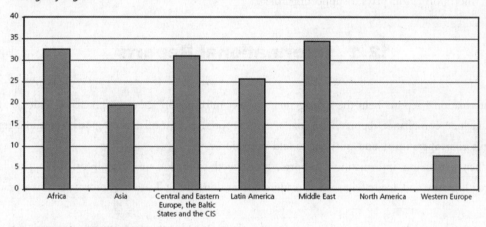

Chart 6
Share of mandatory standards in total number of standards developed by national standard bodies, average by region

Source: ISO Members Directory 2003.

IV Writing practice.

A Factory Inspection

As an employee of the XYZ foreign trade company, you have been assigned to inspect some of its factories/suppliers.

Your task: Visit a factory, and report back to your Director (Ben Franklin) on the factory that you have inspected. Your report should include at least the following information: the date and time of your inspection, a general description of the factory and its equipment, the progress of the production of your company's last order, conclusions about the general condition of the factory, and a statement of any problem that may exist. Show in the report that you have inspected the factory carefully.

Unit 12

Business Reports (Ⅱ)
商务报告（二）

Reports can be classified into informational reports and analytical reports by function. The former focuses on facts and is generally organized around subtopics, while the latter includes analysis, interpretation, conclusions and recommendations, and is usually organized around logical arguments and conclusions.[1] Informational reports are intended to inform the audience, but analytical reports are designed to persuade readers to accept certain conclusions or recommendations. In analytical reports, the information plays a supporting role.

12.1 Informational Reports

Informational reports help the management collect information about corporate operations. They usually include compliance reports, personal activity reports, and justification reports, and those reports on monitoring operations, and on policies and procedures.

When producing informational reports, you need to make sure the information should be presented logically and accurately so that readers will understand and use the information in a practical way.

Here we introduce three major types of informational reports: situational, periodic, and investigative reports.

12.1.1 Situational Reports

Situational reports convey nonrecurring situations, including trip reports, progress reports, etc. They are often prepared in memo formats like other informational reports.

The tone of these reports is informal and the length varies, depending on the actual situation and reader's expectation. You may start a situational report with a brief introduction of the situation to familiarize readers with the topic and end it with a closing.

1. Trip Report

The trip report calls for description of what occurred during a conference, convention, trip or other activity. Such reports are often prepared in a memo format and the tone of these reports is informal and the length varies. It usually includes the following items.

- Brief introduction which usually supplies information about the topic.
- Purpose of the trip.
- Description of activities. The description shall be to the point and in time or place sequence.
- Evaluation of the trip. You can evaluate your trip by describing what you have done and what remains unfinished, and your future plan or your suggested solutions or recommendations.

Sample 12-1

To: Head of the trade department
From: Dan Andrew, assistant of the trade department
Date: November 29, 2015
Subject: Trip to Santiago

Introduction and Purpose

I visited our Santiago offices on Nov. 27th and 28th, and the purpose of the trip was to learn of the problems associated with the establishment of a distribution network security program.[2]

As instructed, I visited the above sites on 27th and 28th November. My purpose of the visit is to look at the business conditions of the offices and try to seek the possible measures to improve our business.

Agenda and Evaluation

I visited four customers during my stay there.

The Denver Trading Inc.

On the morning of November 27th, 2015, I went to the Denver Trading Inc. This company has been trading with us for more than five years and is a regular importer of our electronic products. Mr. Roger Chen, the President, is anxious to import more goods from us and said that he would like his company to be our exclusive agent in Santiago. I promised to mention this to you and inform him if we agreed.

P&Q Watson Ltd.

On the afternoon of November 27th, I went to P&Q Watson Ltd and visited their factory just outside Santiago and was very impressed by the quality of the household utensils they produce. I suggest that we ask them for their export terms.

Johnson Steven & Harry Company

On the morning of 28th, I visited Johnson Steven & Harry Company. This company has been ordering goods from us for the last ten years, but it is clear that the value of their orders has decreased dramatically in the last year or two. I asked why this was so, but was not given a clear answer. When I was in conversation with a number of other traders I met, I learnt that the company has come across some financial difficulties recently and is expected to close down in the fairly near future.³

The Sandstorm Import Company

On the afternoon of 28th, I investigated the Sandstorm Import Company. This is a newly opened company that you asked me to visit. It has received a good deal of support from the Metro Bank in Santiago and is therefore in a strong financial position.⁴ It is clear that they are very keen to do business with us and that they will be important customers in the future, I therefore suggest we offer them our best terms.

 Sample 12-2

To: John Smith
From: Mary Waters
Date: March 29, 2015
Subject: Trip to two operation sites in China from March 25 to 28

Introduction

On March 25, I visited two of our factories in Anhui and Hubei provinces and discussed with the management about the need for drafting a crisis plan. Based on what I found when inspecting the two sites, I think we must force two factories to draft a crisis plan and make sure that plan will take effect as soon as possible to prevent any incident from happening.

Visit to Our Factories in Anhui and Hubei

Wang Ling, the branch office's manager in Beijing, and I met with Zhao Ming and

Zhang Jun, directors of the two factories respectively. This was the third attempt by the Beijing office to urge them to draw up a crisis plan. We explained again the importance of such a plan in reducing the possibilities of accidents in the factories. We were disappointed when we learned they were still working on the plan and had not established an effective system for dealing with emergencies.[5] When inspecting the factories, we did find some hidden hazards in some workshops.

Hidden Hazards

We saw places where incidents might occur. The directors agreed that they had to do something about them. The hidden dangers were:

- In one workshop, chemicals were left near cotton piles and plastic.
- A number of fire extinguishers were out of date.
- Some water hoses couldn't be connected to the faucets.
- The water pressure was low.
- One of the four doors of one workshop was blocked with raw materials. The workers wouldn't be able to evacuate quickly if the place were on fire.
- No strict regulation has not so far been formulated to forbid workers to smoke in the workshop.
- Top management didn't inspect the factories for any hidden danger.

Recommendations

We think some measures or effective ways need to be taken immediately, otherwise there would be a disaster. The two factories wouldn't be able to handle an incident. We suggest the following measures:

- Draft a crisis plan and make it publicized throughout the factories.
- Entrust one manager with the responsibility for implementing the plan.[6]
- Set up a team that inspects the factories regularly. The team has the authority to address any problems that might lead to an incident.
- Keep dangerous materials in the special storage away from the workshops.
- Build a water tank to restore water in case the water pressure is low when the factory is on fire.
- Establish effective communication channels with the company headquarters, local government, and local media.

We talked to the director before we left. They admitted their negligence, accepted our recommendations, and promised to take action immediately.

2. Progress Reports

It describes the progress of a plan being carried out or a project which is underway or whether it is within the budget or not so that managers can have the updated information about the business activities or project worked on. General speaking, the progress report includes the following items.

(1) Summary. It includes the process of a project, describing the status, whether it is on schedule and within the budget, or how is the work performed, when the project will be finished or whether the remaining costs will be within the fiscal limits or not. Are there any possible problems that will arise?

(2) Work already accomplished.

(3) Work that is to be completed.

(4) Your future plan or your forecast.

Sample 12-3

To: Jimmy Li, Manager of Information Department
From: John Brown
Date: November 30, 2015
Subject: Progress on the installation of the GXP information system

As of this date (Nov. 30), the installation of the GXP Information System is ahead of schedule and within the budget.[7] The January 1 operational date should be met as planned.

Work Completed

The "JP Link" cables from the trial installation were left in place after the trial, even though the rest of the equipment was temporarily removed. Accordingly, there was no need to remove ceiling panels to install the cables. In addition, the individual video display terminals and the master printing station have been installed and are awaiting hookup and testing.[8]

Work to Be Done

All system components have to be connected, and a thorough system check performed. This work should be completed by mid December.

Forecast

Acceptance of the system should be possible in December. Our assuming control of the system depends on two items:

- Completion of final testing and
- Our payment of the amount specified in the contract.

12.1.2 Periodic Reports

A periodic report is designed to describe what has happened in a department during a particular period. Some periodic reports are written in memo format, and sometimes a standard format is provided by some companies for employees to fill out the needed information.

In writing a periodic report, we need to give complete facts and figures, which will help the management to make the best decisions. We may pay attention to the following points when composing a periodic report.

(1) Summarize regular activities and events during the reporting period.
(2) Describe unusual events to which the management should pay attention.
(3) Highlight problems and needs.

Most periodic reports are organized in the following sequence: overview of routine responsibility, discussion of special projects, plans for the coming period and analysis of problems.

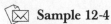 **Sample 12-4**

To: Alan Blaire, President
From: John Li, Manager of Marketing Department
Date: September 1, 2015
Subject: August work on new business development

Introduction

Last month, I visited three locations for our books outlets in Beijing. Alfred recommended these sites in his business development report, and you may find that report on our intranet if you would like to review it.

Comparison of the Three Sites

The following is a quick look at the basic aspects of each location. Lease rates are comparable at these sites, ranging from 22 Yuan to 30 Yuan a square meter per month.

	Space	Rents (a square meter per month)	Availability	Competition	Readers' Density	Marketability
Wudaokou	200 square meters, the first and second floors	30 Yuan	January	Xinhua has opened a branch 7 blocks north; no other big store within a 3 km radius	High; 5 universities and 3 primary and middle schools nearby	Non-marketable

(continued)

	Space	Rents (a square meter per month)	Availability	Competition	Readers' Density	Marketability
Shangdi	347 square meters, the first floor	26 Yuan	Now	No bookstore with a 2 km radius	High; 4 primary and middle schools nearby	marketable
Huilongguan	500 square meters	22 Yuan	Now	No bookstore with a 6 km radius	High; 4 colleges and 12 primary and middle schools in this area	marketable

Scouting Plans for October

Our schedule has been tight for the last 3 months. Following are the plans for our efforts in September:

Perry: I will contract CVBC Consultancy to conduct foot traffic counts at all three locations, and I may get those results in 7 days.[9] I have asked Jack's team to do a permit search to study future decorating plans in each site. I will be talking with Adam Huang next week about decoration restrictions. Adam Huang helped us decorate the Gulou bookstore last year.

Arthur: Charlie Qi wants us to review several other sites he has had his eye on. I will visit them myself in the next two weeks.

Robin: We have run into some problems with the lease negotiations at the Dongcheng site. I will investigate and try to clear it up by September 10.

12.1.3 Investigative Reports

Investigative reports are written in response to a request for information. The purpose of such report is to provide data for a specific situation. They have the heading of a memo, and include the components of introduction, findings, summary and conclusion and recommendation. The whole layout of investigative reports is indicated as follows:

1. Heading/Title

First of all, all investigative reports must have a heading/title, which briefly gives the subject matter of the report.

2. Introduction

This section of the report tells the readers about the purpose, previews its contents or gives some background information to the circumstances behind the report. Apart from what is mentioned above, a brief description is necessarily made of the methods or procedures adopted to collect the information, for instance, questionnaires, personal interviews, or statistics consulted.[10] Let us look at the following example:

> The Director of Environment Health and Cleansing Services has asked me to prepare a report on rubbish collection in the borough for the Environmental Health Committee. I have questioned staff, analyzed statistics, collected newspaper articles and spoken to representatives of various local committees.

3. Findings

It is the main body of the report, and the information needs to be presented in sections and arranged logically. Sub-headings and enumeration are usually used for clarity.

4. Conclusions and Recommendations

In this section of the report, you should discuss what your findings mean. This will answer the question that has caused you to write the report. In addition, you need to present your suggestions for actions to be taken on the basis of the findings and conclusions.

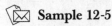

Sample 12-5

To: The Managing Director
From: Yvette Forbes, Safety Officer
Date: 10 July, 2015
Subject: Safety at work

Introduction

Following the request of the Managing Director to compile a report on the company's safety record, I have consulted the statistics and spoken to many members of staff in the company.

Findings

Accidents statistics 2013–2014:
With 18 men and 29 women per 100 employees involved in accidents in the last year, the figures make pretty depressing reading. The accidents are spread across all departments but there are concentrations for men in the dispatch department and for women in production. Compared to other local firms our figures are almost 3 times higher.

Staff Opinions

A selection of members of staff was questioned from various departments. In the dispatch department in the last 3 months there have been 10 accidents involving drivers with inadequate training. In production there were 30 accidents in the last year. Here the monotony of piecework is a particular problem for married women who seem to be the most accident-prone. Tiredness among workers caused by lack of sleep, overeating, over heating of the factory and stress are all given as reasons, but in general it must be said that workers are not safety conscious.

Recommendations

1. To check that the company is complying with all the relevant Health and Safety requirements.
2. To encourage greater staff awareness with regard to accidents.
3. To hold safety courses for staff.
4. To carry out research on causes of accidents.
5. To ensure all workers are adequately trained.
6. To turn down the heating in the factory.
7. To investigate ways of relieving the monotony of piecework.

Sample 12-6

Proposed Flexitime Scheme at Roche Chemicals

From: Alan Golf, Human Resources Manager
To: The Managing Director
Date: Sept. 16, 2015
Subject: Proposed flexible scheme

Purpose

Mr. Rogers asked me to write this report on 12 September, 2015 to test the staff's opinion regarding the possible introduction of flexitime into Roche Chemicals.

Procedure

All of the staff was interviewed with their comments being recorded. The details were entered into two columns, one for comments in favor and the other for comments expressing concerns with flexitime.[11]

Findings

<u>Those in favor</u>

1. Flexibility was treated as a key benefit, allowing people to better plan their everyday activities around work, e.g. doctor's appointments.
2. Factors such as picking up children from school, and doing the shopping without any clashes with work, would lead to a happier workforce.
3. Time wasted in rush hours would also be saved.

<u>Comments against</u>

1. Some thought that the system would result in disappointment, especially with the issue of who would want to work on Saturdays.
2. People were also concerned that overtime could be affected and that a "key" person might be missing when decisions had to be made.
3. It was felt that workers with children might get the first choice of times ahead of those without children.[12]

Conclusions

Flexibility and convenience are the two key points in favor. Although there were a few objections articulated against the scheme, these can be overcome with the introduction of a detailed and fair system.

Recommendations

1. The flexitime scheme should go ahead for a trial period, e.g. 2 months; during this time it should be closely monitored to ascertain its effectiveness.
2. Essential services and operations should always be undertaken by qualified personnel, some of these may have to be exempt from the scheme.
3. Saturday work will still be allocated on a fair basis to avoid arguments, and the flexitime system will in essence only really operate from Monday to Friday.
4. In each department, managers and supervisors will be responsible for planning the hours of their small teams, and must ensure that the shift pattern is agreed on by their team and is fairly rotated.[13]

12.2 Analytical Reports and Feasibility Reports

12.2.1 Analytical Reports

Like informational reports, analytical reports collect and present data; but their emphasis is placed on analyzing, drawing conclusions, and proposing recommendations. The chief function of analytical reports is to persuade the readers to accept the conclusions and act on the recommendations. Therefore the facts presented for analysis should be reasonable enough and the analysis based on the facts should sound convincing and logical.

Writing principle:

- Present background information by either giving an introduction of something relating to the subject matter, or describing the main dimensions of a problem.
- Propose your solutions or action. Explain the benefits of your recommendation. Sometimes, pros and cons or costs can also be stated to provide a broader perspective for the audience to consider.
- Summarize your recommendation, the course of actions to be taken, and show how practical your actions or plans are.

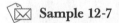**Sample 12-7**

To: Robert Herman, Vice President
From: Bill Reagan, Manager of Marketing Department
Date: December, 2015
Subject: Office in China

Introduction

In response to your request, my staff and I investigated the potential for establishing an office in China. After analyzing the behavior of our customers and major competitors and studying the cosmetic market and the overall development of China's economy, we have three recommendations:

1. We should establish an office in China.
2. We should engage in a firm that specializes in cosmetic advertisement to design and develop the image of our brand.
3. We must take care to make acquaintance with Chinese officials.

Reasons for Establishing an Office in China

First, establishing an office in China can make financial sense today. Studies suggest that our competitors are not currently generating significant revenue from Chinese market. Susenteng is the leader so far, but its sales haven't broken the $10 million mark. Moreover, at least half of our competitors' sales are from tariff-free stores in Hong Kong airports.

Second, we do need to establish an office in China now in order to make more profits in the future. It is difficult to predict the profits we may make from establishing an office in China in a quantitative way, but a qualitative view of strategy indicates that we should set up an office in China.[14]

As the size of middle class population in China becomes bigger and bigger and the purchasing power of affluent people increases, they will likely buy world top brand cosmetic products.

Setting up an office in China can erase geographical limits, and present more opportunities. Even though our customers in China can now get our products in tariff-free stores, we can target more customers in China who have no chance of purchasing items in tariff-free stores.

If the sales in China grow steadily, this will eventually be a viable market. Establishing an office in China now and working out any problem will prepare us for enlarging our market share in the years ahead.

We Should Engage a Firm to Design Brand Image

Designing a good brand image can help enlarge market shares. We have some expertise needed in brand building, but we have few people who are familiar with the local markets. I recommend that we engage an ad firm to help us with the design of a brand image acceptable in China.

We Must Make Acquaintance with Chinese Officials

The studies we reviewed showed that the most successful cosmetic products sellers are careful to make acquaintance with local officials. Companies that don't have sound relations with the governments find themselves with higher tax rates, high costs, and various inspections and fines. Before we establish an office in China, we should visit the various government agencies in Beijing. A sound relation with governments could pave a smooth way for our business in China, so it is vital that we do some work to communicate with local officials.

Summary

1. We need to establish an office in China now even though we may not make immediate profits, because we may lose the Chinese market if we don't have an office there in the near future.
2. Consult a well-known local ad firm to help design a good brand image since we are not familiar with the Chinese culture.
3. Make acquaintance with local officials particularly those who are in charge of registry, taxation and labor management.

12.2.2 Feasibility Reports

A feasibility report analyzes the available information to determine whether a project is worth doing and what is the chance of success. You should convince your readers that the project should be carried out and a particular plan is the best for doing it successfully.

Your report usually includes the following parts:

- Background in which you can describe the related information and brief on problems.
- Presentation of your problems or your plan for the project.
- Analysis of the problem or project on the basis of different related factors, such as costs, financial support, external factors, favorable resources, etc. or unfavorable factors.
- The feasibility for the problem to be resolved or for the project to be successfully carried out.
- The timetable for implementing the proposal.

In most cases, the feasibility report is rather long, and is sometimes undertaken by a consultancy to analyze the problem or conduct analysis of feasibility of a plan/project to be carried out.[15] It usually covers several big chapters; therefore here we will not present you a sample of this kind of report.

New Words and Expressions

subtopic	n.	副主题
compliance	n.	依从，顺从
periodic	a.	周期的，定期的
convention	n.	会议，传统
utensil	n.	器具
faucet	n.	水龙头
evacuate	v.	疏散，撤出
address	v.	解决（问题）
panel	n.	面板，嵌板，仪表板
hookup	n.	连接，转播，接线
outlet	n.	销路，市场
intranet	n.	企业内部局域网
marketable	a.	可销售的
monotony	n.	单调，无聊，千篇一律
piecework	n.	计件工作
overeating	a.	吃得过多
overtime	a.	超时，延长时间
ascertain	v.	确定，探知
personnel	n.	人员，职员
convincing	a.	令人信服的，有力的
dimension	n.	尺寸，角度，方面
quantitative	a.	定量的
geographical	a.	地理学的，地理的
viable	a.	可行的
expertise	n.	专家的意见，专门技术
consultancy	n.	咨询公司，顾问

investigative report	调查报告
electronic products	电子产品
fire extinguisher	灭火器
water hose	水龙带
progress report	进展报告
lease rate	租金

scouting plan	跟踪计划
flexitime scheme	弹性时间制
trial period	试验期，试用期
pros and cons	（正反两方面）争论，辩论，支持与反对
tariff-free stores	免税商店

1. The former focuses on facts and is generally organized around subtopics, while the latter includes analysis, interpretation, conclusions and recommendations, and is usually organized around logical arguments and conclusions. 前者侧重事实，大多围绕各种副主题来展开，而后者则包括分析、阐释、结论和建议，通常围绕逻辑推理和结论来进行。

2. ... the purpose of the trip was to learn of the problems associated with the establishment of a distribution network security program. ……本次出差是为了了解与建立安全销售网络相关的一些问题。

3. When I was in conversation with a number of other traders I met, I learnt that the company has come across some financial difficulties recently and is expected to close down in the fairly near future. 在和其他贸易商交流时，我了解到该公司最近财务上遇到了些问题，有可能不久就要倒闭了。

4. It has received a good deal of support from the Metro Bank in Santiago and is therefore in a strong financial position. 它得到了圣地亚哥商业银行的大力支持，因此财务状况非常好。

5. We were disappointed when we learned they were still working on the plan and had not established an effective system for dealing with emergencies. 我们发现他们仍然执行那个计划，并没有建立有效的突发事件处理体系，对此我们感到很失望。

6. Entrust one manager with the responsibility for implementing the plan. 我们已经委托一名经理负责执行该计划。

7. As of this date (Nov. 30), the installation of the GXP Information System is ahead of schedule and within the budget. 今日（11月30日）GXP信息系统已提前完成安装，而且没有超出预算。

8. In addition the individual video display terminals and the master printing station have been installed and are awaiting hookup and testing. 另外，个人影像显示终端和主打印站已经安装完成，正等待连接和调试。

9. I will contract CVBC Consultancy to conduct foot traffic counts at all three locations, and I may get those results in 7 days. 我将和CVBC咨询公司签订合同，对这三个地点的步行交通进行测量调查，我会在7天以后得到结果。

10. ... a brief description is necessarily made of the methods or procedures adopted to collect the information, for instance, questionnaires, personal interviews, or statistics consulted. ……有必要对信息搜集的方法和过程做简单的描述,譬如问卷、深访或者参考的数据。

11. The details were entered into two columns, one for comments in favor and the other for comments expressing concerns with flexitime. 详细信息分为两栏,一栏是支持弹性时间的评论,另一栏则是持怀疑态度的意见。

12. It was felt that workers with children might get the first choice of times ahead of those without children. 给人的感觉是有孩子的工人比那些没有孩子的工人在时间上有优先权。

13. ... must ensure that the shift pattern is agreed on by their team and is fairly rotated. ……必须保证部门人员都同意他们的轮班制度,而且确保该制度能公正地运行。

14. It is difficult to predict the profits we may make from establishing an office in China in a quantitative way, but a qualitative view of strategy indicates that we should set up an office in China. 很难从量上预测我们在中国设立办事处所带来的利益,但是从战略上的定性分析来看,我们应该在中国设立办事处。

15. In most cases, the feasibility report is rather long, and is sometimes undertaken by a consultancy to analyze the problem or conduct analysis of feasibility of a plan/project to be carried out. 在大多数情况下,可行性报告会很长,有时会委托咨询公司来分析问题或是对一个将执行的项目进行可行性研究。

Sentence Menu

(1) My purpose of the visit is to ...
(2) When I was in conversation with a number of other traders I met, I gathered that ...
(3) I therefore suggest ...
(4) Based on what I found when inspecting the two sites, I think ...
(5) When inspecting the factories, we did find ...
(6) In response to your request, my staff and I investigated the potential for ...
(7) The studies we reviewed showed that ...

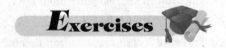

Writing practice.

Situational Writing 1

You are back from a business trip to Shanghai, Guangzhou, and Chengdu, looking into the causes of a fall in the market shares of your air conditioner, Chunlan, a well-established brand in China. You had investigated the wholesale channels, and found that rebates offered by other like brands were greater than yours, their promotional work more efficient, and..., whatever you found the possible causes (If possible, you can invent the causes). You are requested to write a trip report.

Situational Writing 2

You are one of the sales personnel from a trading company and are inspecting one of your suppliers to see the processing of the order placed by your clients. Your order involves two sorts of garments: they are being processed. Please write a progress report in which you need to describe the processing of the order and your forecast of how long it will be completed, and state the products being manufactured. If you have any good ideas to ensure the smooth fulfilling of your order in the rest of days, you can elaborate on them.

Situational Writing 3

Report on Improving the Campus Supermarket

Imagine that you are a consultant hired to improve the profits of your campus supermarket. Your task: visit the supermarket and look critically at its operations. Then draft a memo offering recommendations to the supermarket manager that would make the bookstore more profitable, perhaps suggesting products that the supermarket should carry, hours that the store should remain open, or added services that the store should make available to students. Be sure to support your recommendations.

Unit 13

Business Reports (III)
商务报告（三）

13.1 Proposal Reports

  Business proposal is a written description of how one organization can meet the needs of another. The goal of such report is to persuade the audience to accept a plan or to follow a recommendation, for instance, to solve a problem, or to provide services. Therefore, the proposal must be persuasive enough to let the readers understand the benefits they can get if they follow what are suggested in the report, and convince them of your credentials to accomplish the task that you have proposed.[1] In most cases, business proposals can be solicited or unsolicited. A solicited proposal is generated when a potential buyer submits exact specifications or needs in a request for proposal, commonly referred to as RFP. For instance, a government organization solicits proposals and place orders and contracts based on the most desirable proposals. A solicited proposal will describe a problem to be solved and invite respondents to describe their proposed solution. Unsolicited proposal is prepared by an individual or a firm who sees a problem to be solved and submits a proposal. That is, you decide on your own to submit even though no one has asked you to do so. For instance, a business consultant often goes to a retail store. On many occasions, he has attempted to buy an item that was out of stock. Recognizing that stock-outs decrease sales and profits, he prepares a proposal to assist the business in designing a computerized inventory management system. For the business to accept the proposal, the consultant will write to convince the retailer that the increase in sales and profits that result from the new system will more than compensate the cost of the computer system to be installed and the consulting fee that is to be offered.

  In most cases, business proposals can be classified into internal proposals and external proposals. Internal proposals are written to justify or recommend changes in the company, for instance, to install a new computer program or adopt flexible work schedules, etc. The internal proposal is usually in the format of memo. External proposals are crucial to the successful operation of many companies. They are typically longer than internal proposals and are taken as more formal manuscript reports, comprising many components of formal reports. The external proposal varies greatly in terms of length and format, which usually depends on the nature of the proposals. They are possibly written by one person or by several people or even written by a specialized consultancy to achieve business purposes such as seeking financial support from a foundation, to bid for a project from the World Bank or to win over a project from another company.[2]

13.1.1 Internal Business Proposal

1. Components of Internal Business Proposals

As is discussed above, the author is flexible enough in preparing proposals. When the author finds a particular pattern that seems to be successful, he or she will adopt it as their basic plan. Since most of internal business proposals are informal, the author will adopt a simpler form of proposals, which is in a memo format. They usually include three parts: introduction, body and conclusion.

1) **Introduction**

The introduction usually includes an account of purpose, theme or scope this proposal will involve. That is, in this part, the author needs to answer two questions: Why do you write the report? And what is the report about?

2) **Body**

The body of a proposal focuses on effective solutions to the problems, i. e. what kinds of approaches should be adopted, your timetable to complete the plan or project. Budget and cost of the program should also be detailed, if necessary. They can help increase the chance for your proposals to be approved.

3) **Conclusion**

In this part, you should be confident enough to summarize your solutions to the problem and your steps to carry out the plan. If necessary, you can offer to meet with the reader for further discussion or provide other information.

2. Samples

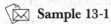 Sample 13-1

To: George Wang, Vice President
From: Paul Evan, Audio Manager
Subject: Acquiring CD Rich, Inc. as a new audio supplier
Date: July 8, 2015

Purpose

This report proposes a means of increasing the proficiency of the Audio Department through the reduction of costs while increasing service, expanding sales, and boosting profits.[3]

Problem

For the past 9 months, sales have been fluctuating sporadically with lows of $600 per month to highs of $1,000 per month, but never able to go beyond this peak. The reason for this erratic behavior in sales, and not a steady increase as predicted, can be attributed to the high costs and lack of service from our present supplier, David Enterprises, Inc.

Since becoming Audio Manager 9 months ago, I have seen sales increased by over 400% and would continue to increase if not for our present supplier. In ordering merchandise from David, it takes a minimum of 2 weeks to receive the shipment from Kansas City, whereas our competitors get theirs within 3 or 4 days. While we are waiting, they are selling out. And, when the shipment finally arrives, half of the order is not there, leaving us without many of the top sellers. This occurs frequently, especially when placing an order for advertised specials.

Though the lack of service is a major problem, it is not the only one, for the prices we are being charged are also ridiculous. This not only cuts gross profits, but also wastes store dollars.

Solution

To utilize the money designated to the Audio Department more efficiently, our company needs to take immediate action in replacing David Enterprises, Inc. as its main audio suppliers of CDs and accessories. CD Rich, Inc. would be a fine replacement. By switching to CD Rich, Inc., we would not only be able to offer better service to our customers, but also push sales to a new record high.

Benefits

The service offered by CD Rich, Inc. is above exceptional, for their next day service on all orders placed before 2:00 p.m. would put us well ahead of our competition in this department.[4] We would easily have our shipment the next day since they are practically at our backdoor.

Another plus is that CD Rich, Inc. is one of the largest suppliers of audio in the nation. They not only carry virtually every record label in stock, but also 40 lines of stereo and video equipment as well as a vast selection of blank tapes and accessories. This not only enables them to fill any order we will ever have with ease, but also gives us a head start in merchandising the new releases hot off the press and capture part of the market before many of our competitors receive their shipments.[5]

Cost Savings

Their service is not the only outstanding feature, for CD Rich, Inc. prices can not be beat. In comparing prices with those charged by David Enterprises, Inc., a noticeable price advantage can be seen, especially those with a suggested retail price of $8.98 (which constitutes about 75% of the total dollar sales in CD Rich, Inc.), as shown below:

David Prices vs. CD Rich, Inc. Prices

Suggested Retail Price	Cost from David Enterprises	Cost from CD Rich, Inc.	Savings Per Unit
7.98	5.65	5.16	.49
8.98	6.47	5.77	.70
9.98	7.19	6.47	.72
10.98	7.91	7.10	.81
11.98	8.63	7.70	.84

Though the savings per unit seems quite impressive, it can not truly be realized unless it is illustrated as a whole. Below is a list of the average sales for a month. It is broken down to show the quantity sold, cost and savings per item as well as the total costs, sales, savings, and profits for a month.[6]

An Average Month Comparing David and CD Rich, Inc.

Suggested Retail Price	Avg. No. Sold Per Month	Our Retail Price	Our Cost (David)	Our Cost (CD Rich, Inc.)	Total Sales
7.98	1	6.59	5.67	5.16	6.59
8.98	85	7.20	6.47	5.77	619.65
9.98	5	8.59	7.19	6.47	42.95
11.98	1	10.29	8.63	7.79	10.29

This clearly illustrates that by switching to CD Rich, Inc., the Audio Department can be very profitable. With the lower costs and better service from our supplier, we will be able to lower our prices, run more specials, and thus please more customers. By doing this, we will inevitably create greater sales and generate larger profits.

Conclusions

On the basis of these details, I firmly believe that by switching to CD Rich, Inc., it would mean only success for the company. Not only would it make our customers very happy when lowering prices, but it would also create greater sales while maintaining higher profits and thus making "the boss" very happy as well. I would like to meet with you on Friday to discuss this plan in detail and to answer any questions or gather any additional information, which you may desire. Please let me know if we can get together to discuss this proposed change. The quicker we can address this issue, the sooner we can better serve our customers, whom in turn will better serve us.

Sample 13-2

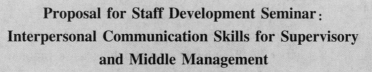

Proposal for Staff Development Seminar:
Interpersonal Communication Skills for Supervisory
and Middle Management

Larry Machoski, Staff Development Coordinator
September 11, 2015

The Problem

Management has perceived a need for improved communication performance on the part of supervisory and middle management personnel to strengthen relationships among them and their employees. The proposed training course is designed to help participants develop effective interpersonal communication skills.

Proposed Course of Instruction

Based on our experience, the following concepts should be effective in improving and understanding communication performance.

Teaching-learning Method

The acquisition of interpersonal skills result from an activity-oriented training program where participants apply theory through role playing, case discussion and feedback.

In this approach, the instructor is a learning facilitator rather than a lecturer. Frequent use of video feedback accompanied by instructor and group feedback reinforces learning.

Contents

The following topics constitute the content core of the program:

- Perception and self-control
- A positive communication climate
- Sending, receiving, and nonverbal skills
- Resolving conflict
- Interviewing
- Small-group communication

<u>**Staff Development Proposal**</u>

Learning Materials

Because participants seem to feel more comfortable when they have a textbook to guide them, we use the Verderber Book, Interact. Additionally, case problem handouts are provided for role playing and discussion.

Length of Course

This course consisted of 12 two-hour sessions over a six week period.

Number of Participants

Because of the activity orientation of the program, a maximum of 12 participants is desirable.

Cost

All teaching-learning materials will be provided by us which include textbooks, handouts, and video camera and recorder. Based on 12 sessions, 12-participant program, the total cost is $2,172. When two courses are offered on the same day, the total cost is reduced to $4,200. Exact charges:

Interact (12 copies at $25)	$300
Case Problem Handouts (12 copies at $6)	$72
Professional Fees (24 hours' instruction at 75/hr)	$1,800
Total	$2,172

13.1.2 External Business Proposal

The components of external business proposal include prefatory parts, body and conclusion.

1. Prefatory Parts

The prefatory parts include: the cover, title fly, title page, table of contents, and letter of transmittal, and executive summary, etc.

2. Body

This part is designed to describe what you can offer in the proposal. To convince the reader that your proposal has the merit, you should focus on the strength of your products or services to suit the needs of clients. Coupled with it, you need to spell out the details of your plan and what concrete steps to be taken and particularly the available resources that you can assemble for the project.[7] Surely credential of your company, expertise and qualification of the personnel who are going to undertake the project are equally helpful to adding the merits to your proposal. Of course, costs and budgets are sensitive issues to the clients, and should be included in the proposal, if any. They can be broken down in detail so that the reader can see them very clearly.

The text of a proposal is generally made up of introduction, body and summary or conclusion. The background of the problem, overview of approach, scope of the study and report organization are covered in the introduction section, while the proposed approach, work plan, statement of qualification and cost items fall into the body category.

3. Conclusion

Conclusion may serve as the last opportunity to persuade the reader to accept your proposal, therefore it is necessary to briefly restate the merits of the proposal, and stress your company's competitive edge. Since formal business proposal is rather long, only the table of contents of a proposal is presented here for your reference:

The table of contents of a business proposal is shown in Sample 13-3.

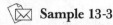 **Sample 13-3**

The Project Proposal of Designing Programs for Small and Medium Sized Enterprises in Wuhu

ACB Consultant Co., Ltd.

2015/03/06

Table of Contents

I. A letter

II. Our understanding of the project

III. Work program

IV. The approaches for the execution of the project program

V. The major projects accomplished by our company

VI. Specialists profile

VII. The work progress schedule

VIII. Our budget and quotation

13.2 Annual Report

An annual report is a yearly review of activities and is a document that outlines and analyzes the activities, especially the financial dealings, of a company or other organization over the past year. It is published in designated newspapers and filed at relevant government agencies. The audiences of the annual report include shareholders, bankers, and professional investment analysts, government agencies and various other readers as well.

The annual report is often used by senior executives as a showpiece reflecting the company's philosophy and character and plays an important role in building a good company image as what the Disney Company does in its 2004 annual report. Figure 13-1 is the cover of the Disney Company 2004 annual report.

Unit 13 Business Reports (III)

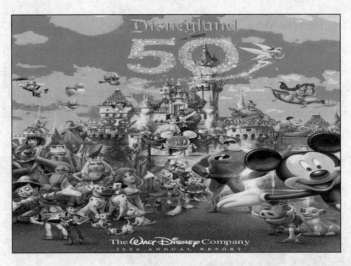

Figure 13-1   The cover of the Disney Company's 2004 annual report

An annual report is typically made up of six major sections: financial highlights, letter to share holders, chief executive's review, financial statements, auditor's report, and board of directors.

1. Financial Highlights

This part usually takes up the inside front cover and is the most read part of the annual report, for the figures provided can give the readers a general picture of the financial position and performance of the company. It presents the high points of the operations and finances, including the revenues and earnings of the company for the last two or three years. Figure 13-2 is a sample of Financial Highlights.

SUMMARY FINANCIAL HIGHLIGHTS
($ IN MILLIONS, EXCEPT PER SHARE AMOUNTS)

Fiscal year ended September 30	2000	2001	2002	2003	2004
Revenues					
Media Networks	$ 9,836	$ 9,569	$ 9,733	$10,941	$11,778
Parks and Resorts	6,809	7,004	6,465	6,412	7,750
Studio Entertainment	5,918	6,009	6,691	7,364	8,713
Consumer Products	2,762	2,590	2,440	2,344	2,511
	$25,325	$25,172	$25,329	$27,061	$30,752
Segment Operating Income					
Media Networks	$ 1,985	$ 1,758	$ 986	$ 1,213	$ 2,169
Parks and Resorts	1,615	1,586	1,169	957	1,123
Studio Entertainment	126	260	273	620	662
Consumer Products	386	401	394	384	534
	$ 4,112	$ 4,005	$ 2,822	$ 3,174	$ 4,488
Diluted earnings per share before the cumulative effect of accounting change	$ 0.57	$ 0.11	$ 0.60	$ 0.65	$ 1.12
Cash provided by operations	$ 3,755	$ 3,048	$ 2,286	$ 2,901	$ 4,370
Free cash flow[1]	$ 1,742	$ 1,253	$ 1,200	$ 1,852	$ 2,943

Figure 13-2   A sample of Financial Highlights

2. Letter to the Shareholders

This letter is a direct statement from the chairman or CEO of the company to the shareholders, giving an in-depth review of the company's performance during the past year. The major change to the board of directors is reported in this letter and the dividend is usually formally announced if there is any. It often follows immediately the Financial Highlights. Figure 13-3 is a part of a sample letter to the shareholders.

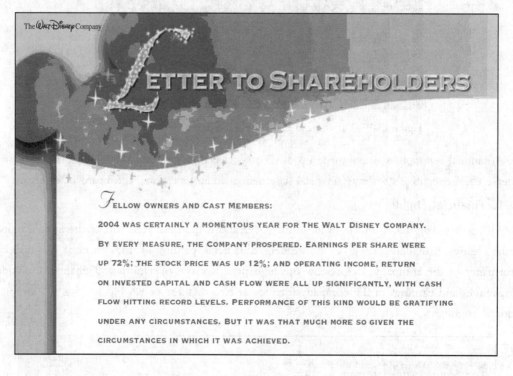

Figure 13-3　A part of of a sample letter to the shareholders

Manuscript of Figure 13-3 is presented as follows:

> *Fellow Owners and Cast Members*:
>
> *2004 was certainly a momentous year for the Walt Disney Company. By every measure, the Company prospered. Earnings per share were up 72%; the stock price was up 12%; and operating income, return on invested capital and cash flow were all up significantly, with cash flow hitting record levels.*[8] *Performance of this kind would be gratifying under any circumstances. But it was that much more so given the circumstances in which it was achieved.*

3. Chief Executive's Review

This part involves a wide range of topics concerning the company's operations. Sometimes the components of this part are just listed separately. In the Walt Disney Company 2004 annual report, this part is divided into Financial Review and Company Review as shown in Figure 13-4 and

Figure 13-5.

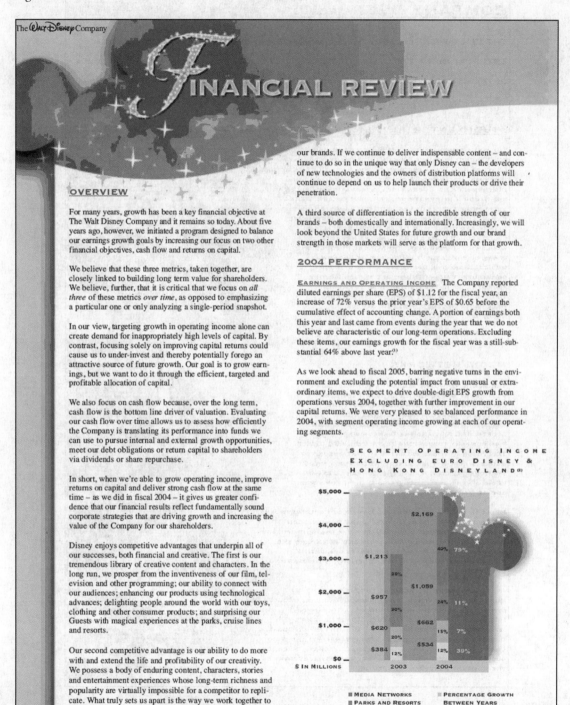

Figure 13-4　A sample of Financial Review

COMPANY OVERVIEW

THE WALT DISNEY COMPANY IS COMMITTED TO PRODUCING UNPARALLELED ENTERTAINMENT EXPERIENCES FOR THE WHOLE FAMILY BASED ON ITS RICH LEGA OF QUALITY CREATIVE CONTENT AND EXCEPTIONAL STORYTELLING.

STUDIO ENTERTAINMENT

THE WALT DISNEY STUDIOS DISTRIBUTES MOTION PICTURES UNDER WALT DISNEY PICTURES – WHICH INCLUDES WALT DISNEY FEATURE ANIMATION AND DISNEYTOON STUDIOS – TOUCHSTONE PICTURES, HOLLYWOOD PICTURES, MIRAMAX FILMS AND DIMENSION FILMS. BUENA VISTA INTERNATIONAL SERVES AS THE STUDIOS' INTERNATIONAL DISTRIBUTION ARM. BUENA VISTA HOME ENTERTAINMENT AND BUENA VISTA HOME ENTERTAINMENT INTERNATIONAL TOGETHER DISTRIBUTE DISNEY AND OTHER FILM TITLES TO THE RENTAL AND SELL-THROUGH HOME ENTERTAINMENT MARKETS WORLDWIDE. BUENA VISTA THEATRICAL PRODUCTIONS IS ONE OF THE LARGEST PRODUCERS OF BROADWAY MUSICALS, AND THE BUENA VISTA MUSIC GROUP DISTRIBUTES ORIGINAL MUSIC AND MOTION PICTURE SOUNDTRACKS UNDER ITS FOUR RECORD LABELS: WALT DISNEY RECORDS, BUENA VISTA RECORDS, HOLLYWOOD RECORDS AND LYRIC STREET RECORDS.

MEDIA NETWORKS

THE MEDIA NETWORKS SEGMENT ENCOMPASSES A VAST ARRAY OF PROPERTIES ON THE TELEVISION, CABLE, RADIO AND INTERNET LANDSCAPE. THE ABC TELEVISION NETWORK INCLUDES ABC ENTERTAINMENT, ABC DAYTIME, ABC NEWS, ABC SPORTS, ABC KIDS AND THE DISNEY-OWNED PRODUCTION COMPANY TOUCHSTONE TELEVISION. ABC OWNED TELEVISION STATIONS OPERATES 10 STATIONS IN TOP MARKETS ACROSS THE COUNTRY, ABC RADIO OWNS 71 STATIONS NATIONWIDE, AND THE COMPANY'S EXPANSIVE RADIO OFFERINGS INCLUDE RADIO DISNEY, ESPN RADIO AND ABC NEWS RADIO.

MEDIA NETWORKS INCORPORATES A SUITE OF CABLE NETWORKS, INCLUDING ESPN, DISNEY CHANNEL, ABC FAMILY, TOON DISNEY, AND SOAPNET. ADDITIONALLY, THE SEGMENT OPERATES WALT DISNEY TELEVISION ANIMATION AND JETIX, AND THE COMPANY ALSO HOLDS EQUITY INTERESTS IN LIFETIME ENTERTAINMENT SERVICES, A&E TELEVISION NETWORKS AND E! NETWORKS.

ALSO INCLUDED IN THE MEDIA NETWORKS SEGMENT ARE BUENA VISTA TELEVISION, WHICH PRODUCES AND DISTRIBUTES SYNDICATED PROGRAMMING; BUENA VISTA TELEVISION INTERNATIONAL, WHICH DISTRIBUTES DISNEY'S SERIES AND MOVIES FOR TELEVISION OUTSIDE THE U.S.; HYPERION BOOKS, DISNEY'S GENERAL INTEREST PUBLISHING IMPRINT; AND WALT DISNEY INTERNET GROUP, WHICH LEADS CORPORATE INTERNET BUSINESS AND TECHNOLOGY STRATEGY AND MANAGES MANY OF THE COMPANY'S INTERNET PROPERTIES.

Figure 13-5　A sample of Company Overview

The manuscript of Figure 13-4 is presented as follows:

FINANCIAL REVIEW

OVERVIEW

For many years, growth has been a key financial objective at the Walt Disney Company and it remains so today. About five years ago, however, we initiated a program designed to balance our earnings growth goals by increasing our focus on two other financial objectives, cash flow and returns on capital.

We believe that these three metrics, taken together, are closely linked to building long term value for shareholders. We believe, further, that it is critical that we focus on all three of these metrics over time, as opposed to emphasizing a particular one or only analyzing a single-period snapshot.[9]

In our view, targeting growth in operating income alone can create demand for inappropriately high levels of capital. By contrast, focusing solely on improving capital returns could cause us to under-invest and thereby potentially forego an attractive source of future growth.[10] Our goal is to grow earnings, but we want to do it through the efficient, targeted and profitable allocation of capital.

We also focus on cash flow because, over the long term, cash flow is the bottom line driver of valuation. Evaluating our cash flow over time allows us to assess how efficiently the Company is translating its performance into funds we can use to pursue internal and external growth opportunities, meet our debt obligations or return capital to shareholders via dividends or share repurchase.

In short, when we're able to grow operating income, improve returns on capital and deliver strong cash flow at the same time — as we did in fiscal 2004 — it gives us greater confidence that our financial results reflect fundamentally sound corporate strategies that are driving growth and increasing the value of the Company for our shareholders.[11]

Disney enjoys competitive advantages that underpin all of our successes, both financial and creative. The first is our tremendous library of creative content and characters. In the long run, we prosper from the inventiveness of our film, television and other programming; our ability to connect with our audiences; enhancing our products using technological advances; delighting people around the world with our toys, clothing and other consumer products; and surprising our Guests with magical experiences at the parks, cruise lines and resorts.

Our second competitive advantage is our ability to do more with and extend the life and profitability of our creativity. We possess a body of enduring content, characters, stories and entertainment experiences whose long-term richness and popularity are virtually impossible for a competitor to replicate. What truly sets us apart is the way we work together to amplify our creative properties across multiple lines of business, with each consumer experience further strengthening our brands. If we continue to deliver indispensable content — and continue to do so in the unique way that only Disney can — the developers of new technologies and the *owners of distribution platforms will continue to depend on us to help launch their products or drive their penetration.*

A third source of differentiation is the incredible strength of our brands — both domestically and internationally. Increasingly, we will look beyond the United States for future growth and our brand strength in those markets will serve as the platform for that growth.

The manuscript of Figure 13-5 is indicated as follows:

COMPANY OVERVIEW

The Walt Disney Company is committed to producing unparalleled entertainment experiences for the whole family based on its rich legacy of quality creative content and exceptional storytelling.

STUDIO ENTERTAINMENT

The Walt Disney Studios distributes motion pictures under Walt Disney Pictures-which includes Walt Disney Feature Animation and DisneyToon Studios — Touchstone Pictures, Hollywood Pictures, Miramax Films and Dimension Films. Buena Vista International serves as the Studios' international distribution arm. Buena Vista Home Entertainment and Buena Vista Home Entertainment International together distribute Disney and other film titles to the rental and sell-through home entertainment markets worldwide. Buena Vista Theatrical Productions is one of the largest producers of Broadway musicals, and the Buena Vista Music Group distributes original music and motion picture soundtracks under its four record labels: Walt Disney Records, Buena Vista Records, Hollywood Records and Lyric Street Records.

MEDIA NETWORKS

The Media Networks segment encompasses a vast array of properties on the television, cable, radio and Internet landscape. The ABC Television Network includes ABC Entertainment, ABC Daytime, ABC News, ABC Sports, ABC Kids and the Disney-owned production company Touchstone Television. ABC Owned Television Stations operates 10 stations in top markets across the country, ABC Radio owns 71 stations nationwide, and the Company's expansive radio offerings include Radio Disney, ESPN Radio and ABC News Radio.

Media Networks incorporates a suite of cable networks, including ESPN, Disney Channel, ABC Family, Toon Disney, and SOAPnet. Additionally, the segment operates Walt Disney Television Animation and JETIX, and the Company also holds equity interests in Lifetime Entertainment Services, A&E Television Networks and E! Networks.

Also included in the Media Networks segment are Buena Vista Television, which produces and distributes syndicated programming; Buena Vista Television International, which distributes Disney's series and movies *for television outside the U.S.; Hyperion Books, Disney's general interest publishing imprint; and Walt Disney Internet Group, which leads corporate Internet business and technology strategy and manages many of the Company's Internet properties.*

4. Financial Statements

This part usually consists of an income statement, a balance sheet, a cash flow statement and a statement of total recognized gains and losses, together with supporting notes and tables for at least two years. Consolidated statements are often provided to save time for the readers if they just want to have a rough idea of the information they need. Figure 13-6 is a sample of consolidated income statement.

CONSOLIDATED STATEMENTS OF INCOME

(in millions, except per share data)	Year Ended September 30,		
	2004	2003	2002
Revenues	$ 30,752	$ 27,061	$ 25,329
Costs and expenses	(26,704)	(24,348)	(22,945)
Gain on sale of business	—	16	34
Net interest expense	(617)	(793)	(453)
Equity in the income of investees	372	334	225
Restructuring and impairment charges	(64)	(16)	—
Income before income taxes, minority interests and the cumulative effect of accounting change	3,739	2,254	2,190
Income taxes	(1,197)	(789)	(853)
Minority interests	(197)	(127)	(101)
Income before the cumulative effect of accounting change	2,345	1,338	1,236
Cumulative effect of accounting change	—	(71)	—
Net income	$ 2,345	$ 1,267	$ 1,236
Earnings per share before the cumulative effect of accounting change:			
Diluted	$ 1.12	$ 0.65	$ 0.60
Basic	$ 1.14	$ 0.65	$ 0.61
Cumulative effect of accounting change per share	$ —	$ (0.03)	$ —
Earnings per share:			
Diluted	$ 1.12	$ 0.62	$ 0.60
Basic	$ 1.14	$ 0.62	$ 0.61
Average number of common and common equivalent shares outstanding:			
Diluted	2,106	2,067	2,044
Basic	2,049	2,043	2,040

Figure 13-6 A sample of consolidated income statement

5. Auditor's Report

This section, also called independent audit report, states whether the Financial Statements are prepared in accordance with relevant requirements and regulations governing its production. The following is a sample of auditor's report:

Report of Independent Registered Public Accounting Firm

To the Board of Directors and Shareholders of The Walt Disney Company:

In our opinion, the accompanying consolidated balance sheets and the related consolidated statements of income, shareholders' equity, and cash flows present fairly, in all material respects, the financial position of The Walt Disney Company and its subsidiaries (the Company) at September 30, 2004 and 2003, and the results of their operations and their cash flows for each of the three years in the period ended September 30, 2004, in conformity with accounting principles generally accepted in the United States of America. Also in our opinion, management's assessment, included in the accompanying Management's Report on Internal Control Over Financial Reporting, that the Company maintained effective internal control over financial reporting as of September 30, 2004 based on criteria established in Internal Control — Integrated Framework issued by the Committee of Sponsoring Organizations of the Treadway Commission (COSO), is fairly stated, in all material respects, based on those criteria. Furthermore, in our opinion, the Company maintained, in all material respects, effective internal control over financial reporting as of September 30, 2004, based on criteria established in Internal Control — Integrated Framework issued by the COSO. The Company's management is responsible for these financial statements, for maintaining effective internal control over financial reporting, and for its assessment of the effectiveness of internal control over financial reporting. Our responsibility is to express opinions on (i) these financial statements; (ii) management's assessment; and (iii) the effectiveness of the Company's internal control over financial reporting based on our audits.

We conducted our audits in accordance with the standards of the Public Company Accounting Oversight Board (United States). Those standards require that we plan and perform the audits to obtain reasonable assurance about whether the financial statements are free of material misstatement and whether effective internal control over financial reporting was maintained in all material respects. Our audit of financial statements included examining, on a test basis, evidence supporting the amounts and disclosures in the financial statements, assessing the accounting principles used and significant estimates made by management, and evaluating the overall financial statement presentation. Our audit of internal control over financial reporting included obtaining an understanding of internal control over financial reporting, evaluating management's assessment, testing and evaluating the design and operating effectiveness of internal control, and performing such other procedures as we considered necessary in the circumstances. We believe that our audits provide a reasonable basis for our opinions.

A company's internal control over financial reporting is a process designed to provide reasonable assurance regarding the reliability of financial reporting and the preparation of financial statements for external purposes in accordance with generally accepted accounting *principles. A company's internal control over financial reporting includes those policies and procedures that (i) pertain to the maintenance of records that, in reasonable detail, accurately and fairly reflect the transactions and dispositions of the assets of the company; (ii) provide reasonable assurance that transactions are recorded as necessary to permit preparation of financial statements in accordance with generally accepted accounting principles, and that receipts and expenditures of the company are being made only in accordance with authorizations of management and directors of the company; and (iii) provide reasonable assurance regarding prevention or timely detection of unauthorized acquisition, use, or disposition of the company's assets that could have a material effect on the financial statements.*

Because of its inherent limitations, internal control over financial reporting may not prevent or detect misstatements. Also, projections of any evaluation of effectiveness to future periods are subject to the risk that controls may become inadequate because of changes in conditions, or that the degree of compliance with the policies or procedures may deteriorate.

As discussed in Note 2 to the Consolidated Financial Statements, the Company adopted FASB Interpretation 46R, Consolidation of Variable Interest Entities and, accordingly, began consolidating Euro Disney and Hong Kong Disneyland as of March 31, 2004. Additionally, the Company adopted EITF No. 00-21, Revenue Arrangements with Multiple Deliverables as of October 1, 2002, changing the timing of revenue from certain contracts.

Los Angeles, California
December 9, 2004

6. Board of Directors

This section gives a profile of the board of directors, with their biographic data and their responsibilities covered.

New Words and Expressions

solicit	v.	恳求，请求
credential	n.	（常用复数）（学历、资历、资格或成就等）背景，证件
stock-out	n.	脱销
proficiency	n.	熟练，精通

sporadically	ad.	偶发地，零星地
erratic	a.	不稳定的，奇怪的
ridiculous	a.	荒谬的，可笑的
accessory	n.	（常用复数）附件
virtually	ad.	事实上，实质上
constitute	v.	构成
oriented	a.	导向的
feedback	n.	反馈，反应
resolve	v.	处理，解决
showpiece	n.	展示，展出品
highlight	n.	精彩场面，最显著（重要）部分
in-depth	a.	深入的
momentous	a.	重大的，重要的
gratifying	a.	悦人的，令人满足的
metric	a.	公制的，标准的
snapshot	n.	快照，简单印象
valuation	n.	估价，评价，计算
forego	v.	走在……之前，居先
fiscal	a.	财政的，会计的
cash flow	n.	现金流
underpin	v.	加强……的基础，巩固，支撑
cruise	v.	游览，航行
enduring	a.	持久的，不朽的
replicate	v.	复制
amplify	v.	放大，增强
property	n.	特性，（小）道具，财产
legacy	n.	遗赠（物），遗产
studio	n.	影视工作室
array	n.	排列，编队
incorporate	v.	合并，使组成公司
consolidated	a.	整理过的，统一的
subsidiary	n.	子公司
assessment	n.	估价，被估定的金额
criteria	n.	标准
audit	v.	审计
disclosure	n.	披露，揭发
reliability	n.	可靠性
disposition	n.	处理

Unit 13 Business Reports (III)

detection	n.	察觉，发觉，侦查
be attributed to		归因于
blank tape		空白磁带
specials		特别的东西
facilitator		推动者，帮助者
competitive edge		竞争优势
annual report		年报
financial dealings		财务交易
senior executives		高级主管
front cover		封面
earnings per share		每股收益
financial objective		财务目标
returns on capital		资本回报
share repurchase		股票回购
competitive advantages		竞争优势
technological advances		技术进步
indispensable		不可缺少的，绝对必要的
motion pictures		电影
soundtrack		声道，音带，声迹
media networks		媒体网络
a suite of		一套，一组
income statement		损益表
balance sheet		资产负债表
cash flow statement		现金流量表
in conformity with		和……一致，符合
accounting principles generally accepted		公认会计准则
pertain to		属于，关于，附属
financial statements		财务报表
receipts and expenditures		收支

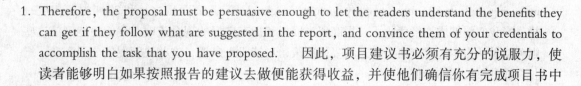

1. Therefore, the proposal must be persuasive enough to let the readers understand the benefits they can get if they follow what are suggested in the report, and convince them of your credentials to accomplish the task that you have proposed.　　因此，项目建议书必须有充分的说服力，使读者能够明白如果按照报告的建议去做便能获得收益，并使他们确信你有完成项目书中

任务的资质。

2. They are possibly written by one person or by several people or even written by a specialized consultancy to achieve business purposes such as seeking financial support from a foundation, to bid for a project from the World Bank or to win over a project from another company. 项目建议书通常由一人或几人,甚至由专门的咨询公司来完成,以实现一系列商业目标,如获取基金、向世界银行投标及从其他公司赢得项目等。

3. This report proposes a means of increasing the proficiency of the Audio Department through the reduction of costs while increasing service, expanding sales, and boosting profits. 本报告提出了一种提高音频器材部门效率的途径:降低成本、提高服务、扩大销售、增加利润。

4. The service offered by CD Rich, Inc, is above exceptional, for their next day service on all orders placed before 2:00 p.m. would put us well ahead of our competition in this department. 锐启唱片公司的服务非常完美,每天2点以前所有的订单都将在第二天得到处理,这会使我们在该领域具有很强的竞争力。

5. ... gives us a head start in merchandising the new releases hot off the press and capture part of the market before many of our competitors receive their shipments. ……这样,我们便在销售热门唱片方面领先,在竞争对手尚未收到唱片之前就抢占了部分市场。

6. It is broken down to show the quantity sold, cost and savings per item as well as the total costs, sales, savings, and profits for a month. 我们对销量、单位产品的成本和节省余额,以及月成本、销售额、节省余额和利润都进行了单列。

7. Coupled with it, you need to spell out the details of your plan and what concrete steps to be taken and particularly the available resources that you can assemble for the project. 同时你要详细说明具体的计划、拟采取的措施,特别是你为该项目所能筹集到的资源。

8. Earnings per share were up 72%; the stock price was up 12%; and operating income, return on invested capital and cash flow were all up significantly, with cash flow hitting record levels. 每股收益增长72%,股价上升12%,经营收入、投资回报、现金流量也都大幅攀升,特别是现金流量达到了创纪录的新高。

9. ... it is critical that we focus on all three of these metrics over time, as opposed to emphasizing a particular one or only analyzing a single-period snapshot. ……关键是长时间内对这三个标准都要侧重,而不只是强调一点或仅仅分析一段时间的情况。

10. By contrast, focusing solely on improving capital returns could cause us to under-invest and thereby potentially forego an attractive source of future growth. 通过对比发现,如果仅仅注重提高资本回报,将会导致投资不足,进而使未来增长的丰厚资源流失。

11. In short, when we're able to grow operating income, improve returns on capital and deliver strong cash flow at the same time — as we did in fiscal 2004 — it gives us greater confidence that our financial results reflect fundamentally sound corporate strategies that are driving growth and increasing the value of the Company for our shareholders. 简而言之,和2004财务年度一样,当我们能够增加经营收入、提高资产回报和拥有良好的现金流时,我们便能确信这些财务结果从根本上反应出了公司稳妥的决策,对持股人来说,这些决策促使公司实现了增长,提升了公司的价值。

Unit 13 Business Reports (Ⅲ)

Sentence Menu

(1) This report proposes a means of ... through ...
(2) To utilize the money designated to the ... department more efficiently, our company needs to take immediate action in ...
(3) Another plus is that ...
(4) This clearly illustrates that by ..., ... can be very profitable.
(5) On the basis of these details, I firmly believe that ...
(6) I would like to meet with you on ... to discuss this plan in detail and to answer any questions or gather any additional information which you may desire.
(7) Performance of this kind would be gratifying under any circumstances.
(8) For many years, growth has been a key financial objective at ... Company and it remains so today.
(9) We also focus on cash flow because, over the long term, cash flow is the bottom line driver of valuation.
(10) Our second competitive advantage is our ability to do more with and extend the life and profitability of our creativity.

Exercises

Writing practice.

Situational Writing 1

Nowadays, the theft on campus has become a headache to the school authority, can you write a proposal to the school to solve this problem?

Situational Writing 2

Suppose you were working in a medical apparatus company. Now the company is experiencing the downward trend of its sales volume for two quarters. The investigation shows that there are many factors, but the biggest one is that some personnel of the sales team are not technically qualified.

Now you are going to write a business proposal for sponsoring a training course for those personnel.

Situational Writing 3

Assume you were a manufacturer of outdoor shoes and tried to get a local supermarket to sell them. Write a sales proposal to the manager of the store, proposing that the shoes be stocked. Tell the costs and services your company provides (return of unsold items, free replacement of unsatisfactory items, necessary repairs and the like).

Situational Writing 4

Write a proposal to the owners of a business you are familiar with. Convince them that they need a workshop for employees on improving their communication skills. Include a statement of the problem, purpose (benefits), scope (areas in which your workshop will help the business), methods and procedures, work plan and schedule, your qualifications, projected costs, and any other pertinent information.

Unit 14

Contracts

合 同

In a broad sense, a contract is an agreement that defines a relationship between one or more parties, and the essence of a contract is the mutual understanding reached by two parties who hold adverse positions against each other. Once signed, a contract is enforceable by law. Any party that fails to fulfill its contract obligations may be ordered to make compensation.

Contract can be formal and informal. For an informal contract, writing is not always necessary. A spoken word will do. But formal contracts require certain formalities. They are mostly made for large or important details. They should be detailed and specific, stating all terms and conditions agreed upon by the parties and listing the rights and obligations of the two parties and all matters concerning the transaction

14.1 Types of Business Contracts

14.1.1 Form-style Contract and Clause-style Contract

The form-style contract is generally the standard contract, which is printed in advance with some blanks left for future signature. Compared with the form-style contract, the clause-style contract is more complex and detailed. The terms and conditions are concretely stated with substantial sub-clauses.

14.1.2 In Terms of Function and Contents

1. Sales Contract and Purchase Contract

The sales contract is an agreement between the seller and the buyer. When the contract is made by the seller, it is called a sales contract, when made by the buyer, a purchase contract. A sales or purchase confirmation is less detailed than a contract, covering only the essential terms of the transaction. It is usually used for smaller deals or between familiar trade partners. A sales contract usually contains:

(1) information about the offeror;
(2) name and address of offeree;
(3) information on the goods to be sold or bought, such as specification, quantity, and price, etc.;
(4) payment conditions;
(5) transport conditions;
(6) customs clearance;
(7) insurance conditions;
(8) time and place of delivery;
(9) inspection, force majeure;
(10) the law applicable to the contract;
(11) means for arbitration or settlement of any disputes;
(12) any other points the offeror considers relevant to the proposed contract.

Under a sales contract, the seller must deliver the goods, hand over relevant documents, such as the bill of lading, commercial invoice, certificate of origins and etc as required by the contract. As for the buyer, he must make payments of the goods and take delivery of them as stipulated in the contract.

2. Counter-trade Contract

Counter-trade contracts include barter, switch, and offset, etc. A barter contract is a contract covering the simple exchange of goods. A switch contract covers the purchase of goods in a non-convertible currency and their sales in a convertible currency. But offset contract means that an exporter buys goods from a market and makes a counter-balancing sale to the market.

3. Leasing Contract

Under a leasing contract, the owner of a property, or leaser, gives the exclusive right of the use of that property to someone else, the lessee.

4. Engineering Contract

Engineering contracts generally include construction contract and contracts for delivery. Construction contracts cover the construction of buildings or other high-rise structures, roads, bridges, tunnels and other civil works. Contracts for delivery refer to the engineering contracts that provide for the delivery of either mechanical or electronic equipment or both.

5. Foreign Investment and Joint Venture Agreement

Agreements covering foreign investments usually consist of several inter-related contracts. The main contract may be a joint venture agreement. The other agreements may cover such matters as the set-up of a new company, transfer of technology and other areas essential to the implementation of the main contract.

6. Transfer of Technology Agreement

It is generally called licensing agreement. Under the agreement, the owner of a trademark or a patent allows someone to use it. A licensing agreement often forms part of a joint venture agreement and sometimes of an engineering agreement.

14.2 Components of a Business Contract

A contract should contain the following items in the order of the following: the title, contract proper, the signature and attached schedules, if there is any.

1. The Title

The type of the contract is indicated in the title such as Sales Contract, Purchase Contract, Consignment Contract, etc. The number of the contract and the date are given below the title to the right side.

2. The Contract Proper

This part includes:

(1) The full name address of the buyer and the seller;

(2) The commodities involved including quantity, quality, specifications, packing, etc.;

(3) All the terms and conditions agreed upon such as the price, total amount, terms of payment, transportation, insurance, etc.;

(4) Indication of the number of original copies of the contract, the languages used, the term of validity and possible extension of the contract.

3. The Signature

The signature of the contracting parties indicating their status as the seller or the buyer.

4. The Stipulations on the Back of the Contract

They are constituent parts of the contract and are equally binding upon the contracting parties. These may include the shipping documents required, force majeure, arbitration, claims, etc.

14.3 Language and Stylistics Features

The formal international sales contract, strictly speaking, is one of the legal documents. It has many features of the legal English.

14.3.1 Lexical Features

1. Employment of Archaic Words and Phrases

In order to render the contract formal and dignified, composers, usually lawyers, often employ words and phrases that are unique to this variety. In our daily trade practice, we often come across archaic words like *thereafter*, *thereby*, *heretofore*, *hereinabove* and etc. These all present a degree of formality.

2. Preference for Lexical Repetition to Pronoun Reference

In order to achieve exactness of reference, leaving no loopholes whatsoever, contract composers tend to use lexical repetition as the formal device to link their long and self-contained sentences. Repetition of the same exact word or phrase not only occurs between sentences, but also between different parts within the same sentences. Or the other way around, preference for pronoun is rare. Actually in legal documents, almost no pronoun is used unless it is unmistakably clear. Repetition within the same sentence is remarkably unique in this variety. Look at the following example:

> Having examined the conditions of contract specifications, drawings and bill of quantities for the execution of the above mentioned works, we, the undersigned, offer to execute and complete such works in conformity with the conditions of contract, specification, drawings and bill of quantities.

3. Special Use of Common Words

Like all other specialists who have built a technical vocabulary for themselves, the professional composers of contracts, who are profound in law and business, also have a set of technical words at their disposal.

Common words used in such a special ways and the technical terms help to mark out that the contract is belonging to the field of both legal and business English. This also shows the composers' effort to guard against any disputable man-in-street understanding of the respective meanings and avoid any possible misinterpretation.[1]

4. Heavy Use of "and", "or" and "and/or"

So when the composer prepares a contract, he tries to cover everything and take every detail and condition into account. The clause, with the use of *and/or*, can clearly cover every circumstance that may happen, which helps to avoid any disputes beforehand. Look at the special use of *and/or* in Clause 11 in Sample 14-2.

> The prices mentioned herein are all based upon the current rate freight and/or war and marine insurance premium.
>
> Any increase in freight and/or insurance premium rate at the time of shipment shall be for BUYERS' risk and account.

The clause, with the use of *and/or*, clearly covers every circumstance that may happen, which helps to avoid any disputes beforehand and has guaranteed the SELLERS' interests.

14.3.2 Grammatical Features

1. Wide Use of Statement-type Sentences

As is the nature of legal documents, most of the sentences of a contract are in the form of statements with no questions. Occasionally a command tone is used at the beginning or the end of the contract. A large number of sentences are of the structure **SPOC** or **ASPO**. We may tell this from the following insurance clause.

S   SELLERS
P   shall arrange
O   marine insurance covering WA plus TPND and war risk for 110% of the invoice value
P   and provide for
C   if any
O   claim, payable in New York in US currency

In this sentence, there's an adverbial introduced by "*if any*".
The claim clause, however, is different from the above one.

A   in any event
S   SELLERS
P   shall be responsible for
O   damages that may result from the use of the goods or for consequential or special damages, or for any amount in excess of the invoice value of the defective goods

Conditional clauses introduced by *if*, *provided that*, *in the event*, etc. are many in this variety. Attention should be paid to the unusual positioning of adverbials in this variety of English. Normally adverbials are not placed between a transitive verb and its objects, but adverbials often come before the object in legal English. In formal contracts, we often come across sentences as follows:

> To pay on behalf of ... all sums
> A proposal to effect with the society an assurance ... [2]

No doubt the idea is given emphasis to the adverbials or to avoid any possible ambiguity.

2. Simple Present Tense

The composer uses the simple present tense when he makes a contract. The past consideration is not consideration. The consideration (called conditions in the Civil Law System) and the obligation of both parties are realized at present or in the future, therefore using the simple present tense is the general rule for making contracts.

3. Use of Simpler Verbal Groups

Compared with nominal groups, verbal groups in legal documents are structured simple. Quite a number of verbs are of the type "modal auxiliary (often *shall*) + be + participle" or "modal auxiliary (often *shall* or *may*) + be or do". "*shall*" is invariably used to express obligation or certainty.

4. Long Sentences

The composer of a formal contract tends to employ complex sentences with an array of subordinating devices for it is believed that each legal sentence is a self-contained unit and conveys all the sense that has to be conveyed. The front page of Sample 14-2 is of only one sentence but contains 72 words and a sentence under the FORCE MAJEURE clause has as many as 70 words.

14.3.3 Stylistic Features

1. Being Concise and Straightforward

Contracts are to be scrutinized not only by the parties concerned but also by lawyers when necessary, so whoever draws up a contract is constantly and inescapably concerned with the special kind of meaning that he or she is called upon to produce. He or she must meet the demands to be precise and exact, to avoid ambiguity and the possibilities of misinterpretation so as to conform to the linguistic dictates of the law. Therefore, meticulous way of expression is adopted to achieve exactness of reference lest there arise anything disputable concerning the stipulations on the rights and obligations. Still let's look at the Clause 15 in Sample 14-2:

> Any disputes, controversies or difference which may arise between the parties, out of, or in relation to, or in connection with the contract... [3]

By such wording, every circumstance that may cause disputes, controversies, or differences has been taken into consideration and placed under stipulation.

2. Clarity

The sales letter is closely organized and full of specific details. The composer identifies exactly what the problem is and what he would like to do. There is also no ambiguous phrase; the message is clear on the first brief reading. All these make the reader never have to puzzle out his meaning and have no unanswered questions after reading the letter.

14.4 Layout

1. Use of Different Types

The purpose of this kind of arrangement is to make the main points be caught easily, because the use of different types is a weapon of drawing the reader's attention to the particular important places in a contract.

2. Particular Arrangement of Blocks

The blocks of print are clear with white space between them and with indentations and/or numbers (or letters) at the beginning of paragraphs or clauses that are subordinate to the foregoing paragraph. All these are evidently efforts to give the content a good organization and make its internal relations clear. Some of the long sentence are broken up by spaces to mark out certain important points.

3. Limited Range of Punctuation

The most characteristic phenomenon of some old forms of legal documents is perhaps the dearth of punctuation. Many of them are either unpunctuated or punctuated only with a final period or a colon. The idea is to avoid any possible forgery — either addition or deletion.

Today, however, the tendency is to employ a limited range of punctuation marks as a useful guide to grammatical structure. The most frequently used are commas and periods, but we also find many colons and semicolons appear in documents. Together with numbers (letters) and block arrangement, they make the clauses of the contract much easier to refer to. Let us look at the following example:

> Any disputes, controversies or difference which may arise between the parties, out of, or in relation to, or in connection with the contract.

14.5 Writing Steps

1. Step 1: Ascertaining Basic Documents

Many documents are expected to be drafted before a contract is finally completed, and these basic documents generally include the letters of inquiry, offer and counteroffer, acceptance, minutes of talks and memorandums.

2. Step 2: Familiarizing Contract Formats

Business contracts can be classified into various categories, and the parties should choose the right one and the right format. The following are some examples employed often in international business: contracts for international sale of goods, contracts for international technology transfer, contracts for international engineering projects, contracts for foreign labor services, contracts for international leasing affairs, contracts for credits and loans, and contracts for international build-operate-transfer (BOT).

3. Step 3: Standardizing the Structure

A standardized contract is usually made up of a preamble, main body and a section of final clauses. The preamble displays the corporate or personal names of the parties, their nationalities, principal places of business or residential addresses and the date and place for signing of the contract. The main body covers the various rights and obligations of the parties concerned, while languages in which the contract is to be written, validity of the contract, and signature are put in the section of the final clauses.

4. Step 4: Clarifying the Specific Conditions and Terms

Conditions in a contract are designed to specify a requirement or prerequisite, namely, to state a requirement that must be fulfilled, or to make something dependent on a requirement, while terms are the particular requirements laid down formally in an agreement or contract, or proposed by one side when negotiating an agreement.

To clarify the specific conditions and terms, the producer of a contract may study some sample forms first and these sample forms are expected to be similar to the situation. The study of such samples can help alert the producer to issues not considered. In addition, these samples provide good samples of language for the preparation of the contract.

However, the form chosen may not be applicable to the situation or it is drafted for the benefit of the wrong side, so the drafter has to revise the specific conditions and terms, and create new articles to guarantee the interests of his organization.

5. Step 5: Referring to International Conventions and Practices

Various international conventions and practices were established in international trade in the last decades and these conventions and practices can greatly facilitate transactions across different countries and therefore are followed by many individuals and organizations. The drafter should make sure if our country has signed or approved those conventions, and then refer to those conventions and practices to avoid cheats and risks. The most popular international conventions and practices in foreign trade are the United Nations Convention on International Sales of Goods (CISG) and Incoterms 2000.

6. Step 6: Standardizing the Language

The last step is to review the draft contract, focusing on the language. The drafter should review every word to polish any expression that is ambiguous or that may incur unnecessary disputes. When standardizing the language, the drafter can also refer to relevant sample forms and borrow their words, phrases, and structures.

14.6 Samples

 Sample 14-1（A Sales Confirmation）

SHANGHAI TEXTILES TRADING CO., LTD.

H. Woods & Co., Ltd.   September 6, 2015
Nesson House, Newell Street
Birmingham B15 3EL
United Kingdom

SALES CONFIRMATION

We confirm having sold to you the following merchandise on terms and conditions set forth below:

Article: Printed Cotton Sheeting
Specification: #2015
        30's ×30's, 68 ×60, 35/3G" in width
        abt. 40 yds, per piece
Quality: As per our sample submitted on August 25, 2015
Quantity: 50,000 yds.
Price: US$0.76 per yd. CIF Birmingham
Amount: US$38,000.00
Packing: In export standard bales packing
Shipment: During November/December, 2015
        Partial shipment to be allowed
Destination: Birmingham, United Kingdom
Payment: Draft at sight under an irrevocable letter of credit to be opened by the end of
        October, 2015
Insurance: Against W. P. A. plus War Risk for 110% of Invoice Value.
Remarks: (1) Your commission 3% on FOB value has been included in the above price.
        (2) Please open L/C advising through Bank of China.
Accepted by:
(Buyer)   SHANGHAI TEXTILES TRADING CO., LTD.

Sample 14-2（A Sales Contract）

CONTRACT

This contract is made this 15th day of July, 2015 by ABC Corporation （hereinafter referred to as "SELLERS"）, a corporation having their principal office at 200 Central Boulevard, Pudong, Shanghai, PRC _____ who agree to sell, and XYZ Corporation （hereinafter referred to as "BUYERS"）, a New York corporation having their principal office at 30, Wall St., New York, N. Y., USA, who agree to buy the following goods on the terms and conditions as below[4]:

1. **COMMODITY**: Ladies double folding umbrellas.

2. **QUALITIES**: 2 section shaft, iron and chrome plated shaft, unichrome plated ribs, silicone coated water-proof plain nylon cover with same nylon cloth sack as per sample submitted to BUYERs on July 2, 2015

3. **QUANTITY**: 10,000（Ten thousand）dozen only.

4. **UNIT PRICE**: US$14 per dozen CIF New York
Total amount US$140,000（Say US Dollars one hundred forty thousand only）CIF New York

5. **PACKING**: One dozen to a box, 10 boxes to a carton.

6. **SHIPPING MARK**:

XYZ
NEW YORK
NO. 1 & up

7. **SHIPMENT**: To be shipped on or before December 31, 2015 subject to acceptable L/C reached SELLERS before the end of October 2015, and partial shipments allowed, transshipment allowed.

8. **PAYMENT**: By a prime banker's irrevocable sight L/C in seller's favor, for 100% value of goods.

9. **INSURANCE**: SELLERES shall arrange marine insurance covering WA plus TPND

and war risk for 110% of the invoice value and provide for claim, if any, payable in New York in US currency.

10. INSPECTION: Goods are to be inspected by an independent inspector and whose inspection certificate of quality and quantity is to be final.

11. FLUCTUATION OF FREIGHT, INSURANCE PREMIUM, CURRENCY, ETC.:
(i) It is agreed that the prices mentioned herein are all based upon the present IMF parity rate of . . . to one US dollar. In case there is any change in such rate at the time of negotiating drafts, the prices shall be adjusted and settled according to the corresponding change so as not to decrease SELLERS' proceeds in . . . dollars.

(ii) The prices mentioned herein are all based upon the current rate of freight and/or war and marine insurance premium. Any increase in freight and/or insurance premium rate at the time of shipment shall be for BUYERS' risks and account.

(iii) SELLERS reserve the right to adjust the price mentioned herein, if prior to delivery there is any substantial increase in the cost of raw material or component parts.[5]

12. TAXES AND DUTIES, ETC.:
Any duties, taxes or levies imposed upon the goods, or any packages, material or activities involved in the performance of the contract shall be for account of origin and for account of BUYERS if imposed by the country of destination.

13. CLAIMS:
In the event of any claim arising in respect of any shipment, notice of intention to claim should be given in writing to SELLERS promptly after arrival of the goods at the port of discharge and opportunity must be given to SELLERS for investigation. Failing to give such prior written notification and opportunity of investigation within twenty-one (21) days after the arrival of the carrying vessel at the port of discharge, no claim shall be entertained. In any event, SELLERS shall not be responsible for damages that may result from the use of goods or for consequential or special damages, or for any amount in excess of the invoice of defective goods.

14. FORCE MAJEURE:
Non-delivery of all or any part of the merchandise caused by war, blockage, revolution, insurrection, civil commotions, riots, mobilization, strikes, lockouts, act of God, severe weather, plague or other epidemic, destruction of goods by fire or flood, obstruction

of loading by storm or typhoon at the port of delivery, or any other cause beyond SELLERS control before shipment shall operate as a cancellation of the sale to the extent of such non-delivery. However, in case the merchandise has been prepared and ready for shipment before shipment deadline but the shipment could not be effected due to any of the above-mentioned causes, BUYERS shall extend the shipping deadline by means of amending relevant L/C or otherwise, upon the request of SELLERS.[6]

15. ARBITRATION:

Any disputes, controversies or differences which may arise between the parties, out of, or in relation to or in connection with this contract may be referred to arbitration. Such arbitration shall take place in _____ and shall be held and shall proceed in accordance with the Chinese government arbitration regulations.

16. PROPER LAW:

The formation, validity, construction and the performance of this contract are governed by the laws of the People's Republic of China.

IN WITNESS WHEREOF, the parties have executed this contract in duplicate by their duly authorized representative as on the date first above written.[7]

BUYERS	SELLERS
XYZ CORPORATION	ABC CORPORATION
Manager	Manager

Sample 14-3 (A Service Contract)

Cooperation Agreement
for
Customer Service Under
ABC _____
— hereinafter referred to as "Agreement" —
Between

DEF
— hereinafter referred to as "Service Partner" —
and
ABC _____
— hereinafter referred to as "**ABC**" —
— hereinafter individually referred to a "Party" and collectively as the "Parties"—

WHEREAS, XYZ has appointed ABC as the agent in providing the after-sales services in the People's Republic of China (PRC) to the _____ Equipment produced by XYZ (hereinafter "Equipment"); and WHEREAS, XYZ has granted ABC as the representative with exclusive right to coordinate the after-sales services in the PRC for the Equipment produced by XYZ; and

WHEREAS, ABC intends to authorize the Service Partner to provide after-sales service in the PRC for the Equipment.

NOW THEREFORE, the Parties hereto have entered into the following agreement after friendly discussion:

Subject of Agreement
ABC hereby authorizes the Service Partner on a non-exclusive basis as a service provider for clearly specified Equipment produced by ABC. The details of service to be provided and equipment covered by such service (hereinafter "Contractual Products") shall be defined in Attachment I. The Service Partner will provide after-sales services, including site inspection, installation, handing over, maintenance and application training, and warranty and modifications, during the warranty and after-warranty periods upon request of ABC within the defined territory.[8] The service can only be performed by the service engineers of the Service Partner, who have authorization according to the official certification.

For the purpose of this Agreement, Warranty Period refers to specific warranty period as defined in respective sales contract of Equipment to the end user.

In order to assure the proper performance of the contracted commitments, the Service Partner shall submit a performance bond to ABC in the amount of RMB300,000 (hereinafter "Performance Bond"). In case any amount is deducted by ABC according to the provisions contained in this Agreement, the Service Partner shall pay to ABC within [ ] days so as to keep the Performance Bond up to RMB300,000.[9]

Service Activities

The Service Partner shall use its best efforts to serve the end-user of Equipment and shall maintain the organization necessary to ensure optimum service activities.

The Service Partner shall provide qualified personnel to answer customer service calls in a prompt and efficient manner.

The Service Partner shall provide the installation services and the after-sales services during the warranty period and the after-warranty period (On Call Service).

ABC will provide technical documentation in English on the functionality, service and repair of the Contractual Products.

Quality of Services

The Service Partner shall perform its services with care, skill, and diligence, up to the professional standards recognized by such profession, and shall be responsible for the professional quality, technical accuracy, completeness, and coordination of all services furnished under the Agreement.

Invoice and Payment

For services provided by the Service Partner during warranty period of Contractual Products, ABC shall pay to the Service Partner a fix amount of RMB [   ] upon receiving formal tax invoice issued by the Service Partner of the said amount.

Service Process/Call Handling/Service Request Form

ABC will collect all service calls from customers/end-users in the ABC Uptime Service Center and forward the service request to the Service Partner accordingly within 1 hour. Working hour in the ABC Uptime Service Center will be [   ] (see Attachment II: "Service Request Form").

Response Time

The response time for the Service Partner to make phone call to the customers/end-users should be within [   ] hours from receiving the "Service Request Form" of ABC.

The Service Partner shall inform the ABC in written form immediately after completing the work.

Handing Over Protocol and Reporting

The Service Partner will provide ABC with the "Handing Over Protocol", signed by the

Service Partner and the customers/end-users, for each of the Contractual Products installed by the Service Partner. Only after ABC SPM has received the Handing Over protocol, the Service Partner may provide its after-sales services to the Customers/end-users.

Training
Basic Training for specified equipment: The Service Partner shall send maximum two (2) of its service engineers to a basic training program, which is to be performed in the PRC. The service engineers shall have qualifications with a university degree for technical engineering. ABC will define the training contents, provide training facilities, training materials and trainers once for each Service Partner free of charge. Service Partner will bear cost for accommodation and travel expenses.

Nevertheless, ABC has no obligation to provide training to the Service Partner or its staff under any circumstance.

Intellectual Property Right
All copyrights and other intellectual property rights existing prior to the Effective Date shall belong to the party that owned such rights immediately prior to the Effective Date.

Confidentiality
The Service Partner shall not disclose to any other parties any technical or marketing information (e.g. drawings, internal interfaces, software) of a confidential nature which it may acquire in the course of its cooperation with ABC, and shall also prevent the afore mentioned information from being disclosed to or used by unauthorized persons or parties.[10]

These confidentiality obligations shall survive the termination of this Agreement for any reasons.

Third Party Claims
The Service Partner shall indemnify and hold ABC harmless from any claims, fines, punishment and other requests for compensation made against ABC by any patient, customer, hospital, governmental authorities, courts or any other third party pertaining to service provided by the Service Partner under this Agreement, provided that such claims, fines, punishment and other requests for compensation made against ABC are due to the Service Partner or its employees or agency. The Service Partner shall use its best efforts to assist ABC in defending the same.

Breach of Agreement

Without prejudice to any other remedies available to ABC as provided in other Articles of this Agreement, where the Service Partner fails to perform any of its obligations under this Agreement[11], ABC may terminate this Agreement immediately with a writing notice and seek for compensation of any losses incurred due to the said failure.

Duration of Agreement, Termination

This Agreement shall remain in force for one (1) year after taking effect. It will be extended automatically for another one (1) year if neither Party terminates the agreement in writing with three (3) months prior notice before the expiration date.

Notwithstanding the provisions of Subsection 17.1, either Party is entitled to terminate this Agreement in advance and with immediate effect for important reasons.

Arbitration

All disputes arising out of or in connection with this Agreement, including any question regarding its existence, validity or termination, shall be submitted to China International Economic and Trade Arbitration Commission (CIETAC) for arbitration by three (3) arbitrators in accordance with its arbitration rules.

The arbitration venue shall be in Beijing. The procedural law of the PRC shall be applicable where the arbitration rules are silent. The language to be used in the arbitration proceedings shall be English.

The award of the arbitration tribunal shall be final and binding upon the disputing Parties, and the winning Party may, at the cost and expenses of the losing Party, apply to any court of competent jurisdiction for enforcement of such award.[12]

Compliance with Law

This agreement shall be governed by the substantive law of the PRC without reference to its rules of conflict.

The Service Partner shall strictly comply with all local laws and regulations, which are applicable to the Service Partner as a service provider in the PRC.

Amendment

No amendments of this Agreement shall be valid unless made in writing and signed by the Parties.

Severability

If individual provisions of this Agreement are or become ineffective, this shall not affect other provisions. The Parties shall amicably attempt to agree on new provisions of equal economic effect to the ineffective provisions they replace.

Assignment

This Agreement shall not be assigned without the prior written consent of the Parties.

Appendices

The Appendices and/or Attachments attached hereto are integral part of this Agreement. If there is any discrepancy between the Appendices and/or Attachments and any terms and conditions in this Agreement, the terms and conditions in this Agreement shall prevail.[13]

Duplicates

This Agreement is written in both Chinese and English and each Party will hold one (1) set of original. In case of any discrepancies between English and Chinese version, the English version shall prevail.

Effective Date

This Agreement shall be effective as of the date on which the Parties hereto have caused this Agreement to be executed by their duly authorized representatives.[14]

IN WITNESS WHEREOF, the Parties have executed this Agreement on the dates specified below.

DEF _____   **ABC** _____

Name: _____   Name: _____

Signature: _____   Signature: _____

Date: _____   Date: _____

Attachment No. ... (omitted)

New Words and Expressions

archaic	a.	古老的，古代的，陈旧的
thereafter	ad.	其后，从那时以后
thereby	ad.	因此，从而
heretofore	ad.	直到此时，迄今
hereinabove	ad.	在上文
herein	ad.	于此，在这里
subordinating	a.	连接主句和从句的
complex	a.	复杂的，合成的
adverbial	n.	状语
ambiguity	n.	含糊，不明确
blockage	n.	封锁，妨碍
scrutinize	v.	细察
dictate	v.	规定，指示
lexical	a.	词汇的
loophole	n.	漏洞
whatsoever	pron.	无论什么
unmistakably	ad.	明白地
specification	n.	详述，规格
undersign	v.	在……的下面签名，签名于末尾
meticulous	a.	小心翼翼的
indentation	n.	缩排，呈锯齿状，缺口
foregoing	a.	在前的，前述的
dearth	n.	缺乏
forgery	n.	伪造物，伪造
preamble	n.	导言
principal	a.	主要的，首要的
validity	n.	有效性，合法性
prerequisite	n.	先决条件
incur	v.	招致
shaft	n.	轴，杆状物
chrome	n.	铬，铬合金
unichrome	n.	单层铬
plate	n.	镀（金、银等），电镀

rib	n.	肋骨
silicone	n.	硅树脂
coat	v.	涂上，包上
entertain	v.	满足（要求），接受
invoice	n.	发票，发票额
bond	n.	合同，抵押
provision	n.	规定，条款
optimum	a.	最适宜的
functionality	n.	功能性
furnish	v.	供应，提供
uptime	n.	正常运行时间
confidentially	ad.	秘密地，机密地
interface	n.	分界面，接触面
indemnify	v.	赔偿，偿付，付还
notwithstanding	prep.	虽然，尽管
tribunal	n.	法庭
severability	n.	中止
amicably	ad.	友善地
prevail	v.	胜过，占优势或统治地位

China International Economic and Trade Arbitration Commission	中国国际经济贸易仲裁委员会
contracting parties	签约方
provided that	假如，设若
modal auxiliary	情态动词
bill of quantities	数量清单
technology transfer	技术转让
foreign labor service	国外劳务服务
international leasing affairs	国际租赁业务
credits and loans	信用和贷款
IMF	国际货币基金组织
parity rate	平价率
in excess of	超过，超出
force majeure	不可抗力
exclusive right	专有权
contractual products	合同产品
end user	终端用户
warranty period	保用期，保修期

intellectual property right	知识产权
third party claim	第三方索赔
breach of agreement	违约
substantive law	实体法
integral part	不可分割的部分

Notes

1. This also shows the composers' effort to guard against any disputable man-in-the-street understanding of the respective meanings and avoid any possible misinterpretation. 这也表明，合同撰写人努力避免任何可能产生争议的大众化理解，以及任何可能的曲解。

2. A proposal to effect with the society an assurance... 一个向社会保证……的建议

3. Any disputes, controversies or difference which may arise between the parties, out of, or in relation to, or in connection with the contract... 双方因合同或与合同相关而产生的争议、矛盾或分歧……

   "in connection with" 为"与……有关"的意思。

4. This contract is made this 15th day of July, 2015 by ABC Corporation (hereinafter referred to as "SELLERS"), a corporation having their principal office at 200 Central Boulevard, Pudong, Shanghai, PRC _____ who agree to sell, and XYZ Corporation (hereinafter referred to as "BUYERS"), a New York corporation having their principal office at 30, Wall St., New York, N.Y., USA, who agree to buy the following goods on the terms and conditions as below.　ABC公司（以下简称卖方），主要办公地址在中国上海浦东中央大道200号，同意销售，XYZ公司（以下简称买方），主要办公地址在美国纽约华尔街30号，同意按以下条款购买以下货物。本合同由ABC公司和XYZ公司于2015年7月15日签订。

5. SELLERS reserve the right to adjust the price mentioned herein, if prior to delivery there is any substantial increase in the cost of raw material or component parts.　交货前，如果原材料或零部件价格有任何实质性的增长，卖方保留调整价格的权利。

6. However, in case the merchandise has been prepared and ready for shipment before shipment deadline but the shipment could not be effected due to any of the above-mentioned causes, BUYERS shall extend the shipping deadline by means of amending relevant L/C or otherwise, upon the request of SELLERS.　然而，如果在装运截止日期前货物已备好，但因上述任何原因而无法启运，买方应该，或应卖方请求，通过修改相关信用证延长装运日期。

7. IN WITNESS WHEREOF, the parties have executed this contract in duplicate by their duly authorized representative as on the date first above written.　本合同由双方充分授权的代表于上述日期履行生效，一式两份，以资证明。

8. The Service Partner will provide after-sales services, including site inspection, installation, handing

over, maintenance and application training, and warranty and modifications, during the warranty and after-warranty periods upon request of ABC within the defined territory.　在规定区域内，应 ABC 公司请求，服务合作商在保修期和保修期后提供各种售后服务，包括现场勘查、安装、转交、维护、应用培训、保修和维修等。

9. In case any amount is deducted by ABC according to the provisions contained in this Agreement, the Service Partner shall pay to ABC within 〔　〕days so as to keep the Performance Bond up to RMB300,000.　如果 ABC 公司根据本合同规定扣除一定金额，服务合作商应该在〔　〕日内支付相应金额，以使运营保证金保持在 30 万元人民币。

10. The Service Partner shall not disclose to any other parties any technical or marketing information (e.g. drawings, internal interfaces, software) of a confidential nature which it may acquire in the course of its cooperation with ABC, and shall also prevent the afore mentioned information from being disclosed to or used by unauthorized persons or parties.　因保密原因，服务合作商不可向其他任何方披露在与 ABC 公司合作中可能获得的任何技术或营销信息（如图纸、内部界面和软件），同时应该防止未经授权的任何人或组织了解或使用上述信息。

11. Without prejudice to any other remedies available to ABC as provided in other Articles of this Agreement, where the Service Partner fails to perform any of its obligations under this Agreement...　在服务合作商没有履行本合同的任何义务时，应毫无区别地使用本合同其他条款提供的 ABC 公司可以获取的任何救济方式……

12. The award of the arbitration tribunal shall be final and binding upon the disputing Parties, and the winning Party may, at the cost and expenses of the losing Party, apply to any court of competent jurisdiction for enforcement of such award.　仲裁结果为最终裁决，对争议双方具有约束力，胜方在败方负担费用的情况下，可向任何有效法院申请执行仲裁裁决。

13. If there is any discrepancy between the Appendices and/or Attachments and any terms and conditions in this Agreement, the terms and conditions in this Agreement shall prevail.　如果附件或附录和本合同条款有任何冲突，以合同条款为准。

14. This Agreement shall be effective as of the date on which the Parties hereto have caused this Agreement to be executed by their duly authorized representatives.　本合同于经充分授权的代表签署之日起生效。

Sentence Menu

(1) We confirm having sold to you the following merchandise on terms and conditions set forth below.

(2) This agreement is made between Party A and Party B in respect of...

(3) This contract is made this 15th day of... by A (hereinafter referred to as "SELLERS"), a corporation having their principal office at..., who agree to sell, and B (hereinafter referred to as "BUYERS"), a... corporation having their principal office at..., who agree to buy

the following goods on the terms and conditions as below:

(4) To be shipped on or before … subject to acceptable L/C reached SELLERS before …, and partial shipments allowed, transshipment allowed.

(5) SELLERES shall arrange marine insurance covering … for 110% of the invoice value and provide for claim, if any, payable in … in … currency.

(6) In the event of any claim arising in respect of any shipment, notice of intention to claim should be given in writing to …

(7) IN WITNESS WHEREOF, the parties have executed this contract in duplicate by their duly authorized representative as on the date first above written.

(8) WHEREAS, A has appointed B as the agent in …

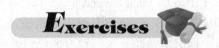

1 The following is the main body of a draft of a sales contract. You are required to standardize its structure and format, and make it complete. You may invent any information necessary.

---

1. Names of Commodity(ies) and Specification(s)
2. Quantity
3. Unit Price
4. Amount Total: _____% more or less allowed
5. Packing:
6. Port of Loading:
7. Port of Destination:
8. Shipping Marks:
9. Time of Shipment: Within _____ days after receipt of L/C, allowing transhipment and partial shipment.
10. Terms of Payment: By 100% Confirmed, Irrevocable and Sight Letter of Credit to remain valid for negotiation in China until the 15th day after shipment.
11. Insurance: Covers all risks and war risks only as per the Clauses of the People's Insurance Company of China for 110% of the invoice value. To be effected by the Buyer.
12. The Buyer shall establish the covering Letter of Credit before _____; failing which, the Seller reserves the right to rescind this Sales Contract without further notice, or to accept whole or any part of this Sales Contract, non-fulfilled by the Buyer of ____ to lodge claim for direct losses sustained, if any.
13. Documents: The Sellers shall present to the negotiating bank, Clean On Board Bill of Lading, Invoice, Quality Certificate issued by the China Commodity Inspection Bureau or the

Manufacturers, Survey Report on Quantity/Weight issued by the China Commodity Inspection Bureau, and Transferable Insurance policy or Insurance Certificate when this contract is made on CIF basis.

14. For this contract signed on CIF basis, the premium should be 110% of invoicevalue. All risks insured should be included within this contract. If the Buyer asks to increase the insurance premium or scope of risks, he should get the permission of the Seller before time of loading, and all the charges thus incurred should be borne by the Buyer.

15. Quality/Quantity Discrepancy: In case of quality discrepancy, claim should be filed by the Buyer within 30 days after the arrival of the goods at port of destination; while for quantity discrepancy, claim should be filed by the Buyer within 15 days after the arrival of the goods at port of destination. It is understood that the Seller shall not be liable for any discrepancy of the goods shipped due to causes for which the Insurance Company, Shipping Company, other transportation organizations and/or Post Office are liable.

16. The Seller shall not be held liable for failure or delay in delivery of the entire lot or a portion of the goods under this Sales Contract in consequence of any Force Majeure incidents.

17. Arbitration: All disputes in connection with this contract or the execution thereof shall be settled friendly through negotiations. In case no settlement can be reached, the case may then be submitted for arbitration to China International Economic and Trade Arbitration Commission in accordance with the provisional Rules of Procedures promulgated by the said Arbitration Commission. The arbitration shall take place in Beijing and the decision of the Arbitration Commission shall be final and binding upon both parties; neither party shall seek recourse to a law court nor other authorities to appeal for revision of the decision. Arbitration fee shall be borne by the losing party. Or arbitration may be settled in the third country mutually agreed upon by both parties.

II Fill in the contract form in English with the particulars given in the following letter.

2015 年 11 月 5 日中国化工进出口总公司与新加坡 Smith & Son's Co., Ltd. 在北京签订了第 CE113 号合同。中国化工进出口总公司向 Smith 公司出售 50 公吨锌钡白（Lithophone），其中硫化锌（ZnS）含量不得低于 28%。要求用内衬纸袋的玻璃纤维（glass-fibre）袋装。货物于 2016 年 1 月自天津新港装船运往新加坡，允许分批装运和转船。合同其他主要内容如下：买方允许卖方 5% 的溢短装，价格仍按单价计算；单价为 CIF 新加坡每公吨人民币 1,000 元含佣金 3%；支付条件为由买方通过卖方接受的银行于装运前 30 天开立并送达卖方不可撤销的即期信用证，至装运后 15 天在中国议付有效；保险由卖方根据中国人民保险公司海洋货物运输条款并按发票总值 110% 投保一切险和战争险，如买方欲增加其他险别或超过上述保额时，须于装船前征得卖方同意，所增加的保险费由买方负担。

SELLERS：
BUYERS：

This Contract is made by and between the Buyers and the Sellers agree to sell the undermentioned commodity according to the terms and conditions stipulated below：

Commodity：
Specifications：
Quantity：
Unit Price：
Total Value：
Packing：
Shipping Mark：
Insurance：
Time of Shipment：

III Translate the following sales contract into English.

正本　　　　　　　　　合　同

卖方：
地址：
买方：
地址：

双方同意按下列条款由卖方出售，买方买进下列货物：

（1）货物名称、规格、包装及唛头	（2）数量	（3）单价	（4）总值
检验：以中国商品检验局出具的品质重量证书作为付款依据	卖方有权在____% 内多装或少装		

（5）装运期限：
（6）装运口岸：
（7）目的口岸：
（8）保险：由卖方按发票金额 110% 投保。
（9）付款条件：凭保兑的、不可撤销的、可转让的、可分割的即期信用证在中国见单付款。信用证以卖方为受益人，并允许分批装运和转船，该信用证必须在装运月____天前开到卖方，并在装船后在上述转船港继续有效 15 天。否则卖方无需通知即可有权取消本销售合同，并向买方索赔因此而发生的一切损失。

（10）单据：卖方应向议付银行提供已装船清洁提单、发票、中国商品检验局或工厂出具的品质证明、中国商品检验局出具的数/重量鉴定书；如果本合同按 CIF 条件，应再提供可转让的保险单或保险凭证。

（11）装运条件：

① 装运船只由卖方安排，允许分批装运并允许转船。

② 卖方于货物装船后，应将合同号码、品名、数量、船名、装船日期以电报通知对方。

（12）品质与数量、重量的异议与索赔：货到目的口岸后，买方如发现货物品质及/或数量/重量与合同规定不符，除属于保险公司及/或船公司的责任外，买方可以凭双方同意的检验机构出具的检验证书向卖方提出异议。品质异议须于货到目的口岸之日起 30 天内提出，数量/重量异议须于货到目的口岸之日起 15 天内提出。卖方应于收到异议后 30 天内答复买方。

（13）不可抗力：由于人力不可抗拒事故，使卖方不能在本合同规定期限内交货或者不能交货，卖方不负责任。但卖方必须立即以电报通知买方。如买方提出要求，卖方应以挂号函向买方提供由中国国际贸易促进会或有关机构出具的发生事故的证明文件。

（14）仲裁：凡因执行本合同或与本合同有关事项所发生的一切争执，应由双方通过友好的方式协商解决。如果不能取得协议时，则在被告国家根据被告仲裁机构的仲裁程序规则进行仲裁。仲裁决定是终局的，对双方具有同等的约束力。仲裁费用除非仲裁机构另有决定外，均由败诉一方负担。

（15）备注：

卖方： 买方：

IV Translate the following Articles into Chinese.

Part II Formation of the Contract

Article 14

(1) A proposal for concluding a contract addressed to one or more specific persons constitutes an offer if it is sufficiently definite and indicates the intention of the offeror to be bound in case of acceptance. A proposal is sufficiently definite if it indicates the goods and expressly or implicitly fixes or makes provision for determining the quantity and the price.

(2) A proposal other than one addressed to one or more specific person is to be considered merely as an invitation to make offers, unless the contrary is clearly indicated by the person making the proposal.

Article 15

(1) An offer becomes effective when it reaches the offeree.

(2) An offer, even if it is irrevocable, may be withdrawn if the withdrawal reaches the offer before or at the same time as the offer.

Article 16

(1) Until a contract is concluded an offer may be revoked if the revocation reaches the offeree before he has dispatched an acceptance.

(2) However, an offer cannot be revoked.

    (i) if it indicates, whether by stating a fixed time for acceptance or otherwise, that it is irrevocable; or

    (ii) if it was reasonable for the offeree to rely on the offer as being irrevocable and the offeree has acted in reliance on the offer.

Article 17

An offer, even if it is irrevocable, is terminated when a rejection reaches the offeror.

Article 18

(1) A statement made by or other conduct of the offeree indicating assent to an offer is an acceptance. Silence or inactivity does not in itself amount to acceptance.

(2) An acceptance of an offer becomes effective at the moment the indication of assent reaches the offeror. An acceptance is not effective if the indication of assent does not reach the offeror within the time he has fixed or, if no time is fixed, within a reasonable time, due account being taken of the circumstances of the transaction, including the rapidity of the means of communication employed by the offeror. An oral offer must be accepted immediately unless the circumstances indicate otherwise.

(3) However, if, by virtue of the offer or as a result of practices which the parties have established between themselves or of usage, the offeree may indicate assent by performing an act, such as one relating to the dispatch of the goods or payment of the price, without notice to the offeror, the acceptance is effective at the moment the act is performed, provided that the act is performed within the period of time laid down in the preceding paragraph.

Unit 15

Questionnaires

调查问卷

15.1　Introduction

A questionnaire is a list of question used to gather information in a survey, or printed paper that contains questions. It is often produced in business to ask people for their opinions or comments, or suggestions on a topic or a group of topics. The questionnaire is an important step in formulating a research design since the information gathered is then turned into questionnaire results and analyzed carefully for decision-making or preparation of a report.

The questionnaire may take the form of schedule, interview or measuring instrument. No matter what form it is, a standardized questionnaire will help ensure comparability of the data, increase speed and accuracy of recording, and facilitate data processing.

15.2　Types of Questionnaire

There are three types of questionnaires frequently used in practice: mail questionnaire, telephone questionnaire and in-person administered questionnaire. This classification is conducted on the basis of interviewing method and different interviewing methods should be accommodated with different questionnaire designs.[1]

1. Mail Questionnaire

When designing a mail questionnaire, the researcher must always keep in mind the trade-off between data quantity and data quality. Since mail questionnaires are self administered, the researcher should make the questions simple and provide detailed instructions. If the researcher attempts to obtain too much information in a mail survey, the percentage of people responding will drop. If so, the responses obtained in the survey will be less representative and the survey costs will increase for more questionnaires are likely to be mailed to obtain an adequate number of responses.

The importance of the questionnaire subject to the respondent determines the questionnaire length.[2] Most mail questionnaires are designed with one or two pages, and some may need four or more pages.

2. Telephone Questionnaire

A telephone survey is done over the phone. It may include both open and closed-ended questions.

Compared with mail surveys, telephone surveys are faster, better for open-ended questions, and can achieve higher response rates. In addition, they are less costly than personal surveys and permit probing to some extent.

3. In-person Administered Questionnaire

Surveys may be designed as questionnaires and administered to groups of people. The questionnaires are completed by individuals on their own and can guarantee privacy in completing the survey. Since large number of responses can be obtained, this method is more cost-effective. However this method does have some disadvantages. Sometimes questions may not be answered completely or understood properly and there is no chance to elicit opinion or probe for greater clarity. Besides, it is hard to get groups of people together and requires the respondents of good reading and writing skills.

15.3 Layout of a Questionnaire

There is no definitive layout for a questionnaire, but four parts are typically included: introduction, questions, demographic information, and thank-you note. Certainly, an appropriate title can tell the reader what the questionnaire is about and make it more professional.

1. Introduction

A questionnaire begins with an introduction. It is a statement, or an explanation why the questionnaire is important for the respondents to complete the form, and/or a section of instructions on how to complete the questionnaire.

2. Questions

This section is a set of questions for the readers to answer, and/or some space where you invite them to make comments or suggestions. The questions just constitute the central part of the questionnaire and can be designed in different ways.

3. Demographic Information

This section, sometimes called footnote, leaves space for demographic information such as the name, title, department, gender, age, education, or occupation of the respondents. For example:

Unit 15 Questionnaires

Respondent Information
Name: _____ Position: _____
Home Tel #: _____ Office Tel #: _____
Address: _____

If the demographic information is very important for the interviewer, and he may want detailed information, then he can design some relevant questions to ask them. Look at the following examples:

"Thank you for agreeing to participate in this survey. To start with, I'd like to ask you a few questions about yourself."

SQ1　Do you or any of your family members work in any of the following industries?
　　　[**Read list. Circle all mentions**.]

1　Market research or consulting firm
2　Journalism/Mass media/Advertising or PR agency
3　Company that manufactures mobile communications devices
4　Company that distributes mobile communication devices ➡ *Close Interview*
5　Telecommunication company or mobile service provider
6　None of the above

SQ2　Have you participated in any form of consumer research or focus group discussions in the past 6 months?
1　Yes　　➡ *Close Interview*
2　No

SQ3　Gender (Record)
1　Male　　➡ *Check Quota*
2　Female　➡ *Check Quota*

4. Close

　　The close, also called a thank-you note, is given at the end to thank the respondents for filling the questionnaire, and tell them what to do with the completed form.

　　Besides the above four parts, some other parts may also be added to the questionnaire in an optional way. One of them is the interviewer information, which is designed to encourage the respondents' confidence on the organizer. For example:

Interviewer Information				
Interview 2015 _____ / _____	Date:	1st Attempt	2nd Attempt	3rd Attempt

Interview Start: _____   Interview End: _____

I certify that I will conduct the interview in the manner instructed by ABCMAR code of conduct, and that the information will be correct and complete.

Interviewer Number: _____   Interviewer Name: _____

Interviewer: Record all your attempts in the Contact Diary.

15.4 Preparing a Questionnaire

To prepare an effective questionnaire, we may follow the following steps.

1. Step 1: Specify the Information Needed

Since the questionnaire is produced to draw information from respondents, it is of great importance to define the goals of the questionnaire, that is, the information needed.

2. Step 2: Determine the Content of Individual Questions

Each question in a questionnaire should contribute to serving some specific purpose. If any of them fails to get information needed, that question should be eliminated. However, it is appropriate to ask some neutral questions at the beginning of the questionnaire to obtain trust from the respondents when the questionnaire is sensitive, or ask some filter questions to disguise the purpose of the survey.

The producer has to make sure each question is sufficient to get the desired information. Sometimes to obtain the required information, the producer needs to design several questions, while sometimes complete information can only be obtained by asking several separate questions instead of one, particularly for those why questions.

3. Step 3: Design the Questions to Overcome the Respondent's Inability and Unwillingness to Answer

Certain factors limit the respondents' ability to provide the desired information for they may not be informed, may not remember, or may be unable to phrase their answers, so the producer of a questionnaire is required to overcome the respondents' inability to answer.

The respondents may be unwilling to answer a particular question either because too much effort is required, the situation may not seem appropriate for disclosure, no legitimate purpose or the information requested is sensitive.[3] Such ways as placing sensitive topics at the end of the questionnaire and prefacing the question with a statement that the behavior of interest is common can help resolve this problem.

4. Step 4: Choose the Question Structure

A question may be structured or unstructured. Structured questions include multiple-choice, dichotomous and scales, while unstructured questions refer to the open-ended questions. A dichotomous question has only two response alternatives, often supplemented by a neutral alternative. The first question of the following examples is a dichotomous question and the second is a scale sample.

> **In comparison with other art disciplines, do you think "Interdisciplinary Arts" is especially meaningful to Hong Kong arts and cultural development?** (1 option only)
> ☐ Yes ☐ No ☐ Not sure
> 3.1 **If yes, how meaningful is "Interdisciplinary Arts" especially?**
> (1 = the least; 10 = the most; 1 option only)
> ☐ 1 ☐ 2 ☐ 3 ☐ 4 ☐ 5 ☐ 6 ☐ 7 ☐ 8 ☐ 9 ☐ 10

When deciding on the question structure, ask open questions as well as closed questions. As regards open questions, the reader has maximum freedom to present his view and offer things unknown. On the contrary, closed questions involve specific questions and can give precise information.

5. Step 5: Determine the Wording

To obtain accurate and honest information, the questions should be easy for the readers to understand. The producer of a questionnaire is recommended to use ordinary and unambiguous words, positive and negative statements, and avoid using jargon, estimates, generalization, implicit alternatives, or pompous language.

15.5 Interpreting the Findings

Once the questionnaires are returned, the researcher is required to compute the answers, tabulate and prepare the data, do the analysis, and then produce a report or prepare a presentation.

When preparing the data, the researcher is recommended to follow the established data preparation process. If there are any unsatisfactory responses, the researcher may return to the field, assign missing values and discard unsatisfactory responses. He also needs to be familiar with the methods used to treat missing responses and methods of statistically adjusting data.

When analyzing the data, the researcher has to select an efficient and appropriate analysis strategy and know clearly the factors influencing the process. Besides, the researcher should understand the intracultural, pan-cultural, and cross-cultural approaches to data analysis if the marketing research involves different countries and cultures.

When the researcher finally arrives at the stage of interpreting the results, he needs to know that those people who have strong opinions on a subject are more likely to respond to the questionnaire thus to make the results skewed. He may discard those unsatisfactory responses, and those that violate the assumptions underlying the data analysis techniques, and evaluate and interpret the results cautiously.

15.6 Samples

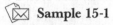 **Sample 15-1**

A Survey about a Beverage

Introduction

Good morning/afternoon/evening.

My name is _____ from ABC Company, a market research company. Today I am conducting a survey about a beverage and we would like to include your opinions. Would you help me by answering some questions please?

SQ1. Do you or any members of your household or close friends work for:
      A beverage company ················· 1 ⎫
      In the beverage trade ················· 2 ⎬ → **Terminate**
      An advertising agency ················ 3 ⎪
      A market research agency ············ 4 ⎭
      A media company ···················· 5
      A management consulting firm ······· 6
      Others ································ 7 → **Continue**

SQ2. Have you participated in any kind of research survey in the past 6 months?
      Yes ···································· 1 → **Terminate**
      No ····································· 2 → **Continue**

SQ3. How old are you?
      Under 15 years ······················· 1 → **Terminate**
      15 – 19 years ························· 2 ⎫ → **Check**
      20 – 24 years ························· 3 ⎭
      Quota
      25 – 29 years ························· 4
      30 years or over ····················· 5 → **Terminate**

SQ4.   Did you purchase and drink any JUICE or READY-TO-DRINK TEA in the past month?

    Yes ....,.. 1
    No .... 2 → **Terminate**

QG11.   Thinking of the advertisement for [**ADVERTISED BRAND**], did you get the feeling that people like yourself would like to watch this advertisement?

    Yes   1
    No   2
    Don't know 3

QG12.   Would you yourself like to see this advertisement for [**ADVERTISED BRAND**] again some time?

    Yes   1
    No   2
    Don't know 3

QG13.   Did this advertisement increase your interest in using [**ADVERTISED BRAND**]?

    Yes   1
    No   2
    No — already use 3
    Don't know   4

SECTION H — Demographics

DQ1.   What is your occupation?

    Professional/Administrator/Office Worker 1
    Sales/Technician/Service 2
    Self-employed 3
    Student 4
    Housewife 5
    Unemployed/Retired 6
    Others (specify:) 7

DQ2.   What is your educational background?

    High school graduate or under 1
    2 year college graduate 2
    4 year college graduate 3
    Graduate school graduate or over 4

DQ3.　Are you married?
　　　　Married ·· 1
　　　　Not married ·· 2
　　　　Refuse ··· 3

Thank you for filling this questionnaire. Data collected is for research purpose only and your personal data will be kept confidential and be destroyed after the completion of the research project.[4]

Sample 15-2

Annual Customer Survey

Thank you for being an ADB customer over the past year. We would appreciate your feedback so we can continue to improve our products and better serve you. Please take 5 minutes to fill out this questionnaire and return it by February 1st in the enclosed postage-paid envelope, or Fax it (408) ×××××××.

What products did you order last year?
☐ CX492 4-dr Legal file cabinet　　☐ BZ800 Desk hutch　　☐ QQ201 Delux lit. rack
☐ CX357 4-dr Letter file cabinet　☐ CZ902 Copier Stand　☐ KL300 Ergonomic chair
☐ CX268 2-dr Letter file cabinet　☐ QQ200 Literature rack　☐ DF309 Monitor stand
☐ Others: _____

Would you like to see any change in the above products? (Attach pages as needed)
_____
_____

Please rate the following items, both on their importance to you, and on our performance over the past year.

	Very Important	Somewhat Important	Little Important	Not Needed	Performance			
					Excellent	Good	Fair	Poor
Credit Policy	☐	☐	☐	☐	☐	☐	☐	☐
Delivery Time	☐	☐	☐	☐	☐	☐	☐	☐
Customer Service	☐	☐	☐	☐	☐	☐	☐	☐
Price	☐	☐	☐	☐	☐	☐	☐	☐
Product Quality	☐	☐	☐	☐	☐	☐	☐	☐
Product Features	☐	☐	☐	☐	☐	☐	☐	☐
Special Order	☐	☐	☐	☐	☐	☐	☐	☐
Repair Service	☐	☐	☐	☐	☐	☐	☐	☐

Unit 15 Questionnaires

Please explain any performance ratings of Fair or Poor. (Attach pages as needed)
_____
_____

Approximately how much was your average monthly order last year?
☐ $0–90   ☐ $100–199   ☐ $200–399   ☐ $400–599   ☐ $600–799   ☐ $800+

What size is your business?
☐ Small (under 100 employees)   ☐ Medium (100–1,000 employees)
☐ Large (over 1000 employees)

Optional information:
Name: _____   Company: _____

Thank you for your time!

New Words and Expressions

formulate	v.	制作，表达
schedule	n.	目录，一览表，清单，预定日期（计划）
comparability	n.	相似性，可比较性
probe	v.	探查，查明
demographic	a.	人口统计学的
footnote	n.	脚注
legitimate	a.	合法的
terminate	v.	终止
administrator	n.	管理人，行政官
technician	n.	技术人员
dichotomous	a.	分成两个的，叉状分枝的
scales	n.	级别，等级（表）；量表
discipline	n.	学科，领域
jargon	n.	行话

implicit	a.	含蓄的，固有的
pompous	a.	华而不实的
tabulate	v.	把……制成表格
intracultural	a.	局域文化的
pan-cultural	a.	泛文化的
skew	a.	歪斜的，扭曲的
underlying	a.	根本的，潜在的
mail questionnaire		邮寄问卷
in person administered questionnaire		人员组织问卷
personal survey		深访
PR agency		公共关系部门
code of conduct		行为准则
office worker		办公室职员
cross cultural		跨文化

Notes

1. This classification is conducted on the basis of interviewing method and different interviewing methods should be accommodated with different questionnaire designs.　该分类是依据访问方法来进行的，不同的访问方法采用不同的问卷设计。

2. The importance of the questionnaire subject to the respondent determines the questionnaire length.　问卷长度应以问卷对受访者的重要程度而定。

3. The respondents may be unwilling to answer a particular question either because too much effort is required, the situation may not seem appropriate for disclosure, no legitimate purpose or the information requested is sensitive.　受访者可能会嫌过于麻烦、不符场合或不合法及所问信息比较敏感等因素而不愿回答某个具体问题。

4. Data collected is for research purpose only and your personal data will be kept confidential and be destroyed after the completion of the research project.　所收集信息仅用于研究目的，您的个人资料将会保密并在项目完成后予以销毁。

Sentence Menu

(1) I certify that I will conduct the interview in the manner instructed by ... code of conduct, and that the information will be correct and complete.

(2) Today I am conducting a survey about a beverage and we would like to include your opinions.

(3) Thank you for filling out this questionnaire. Data collected is for research purpose only and your personal data will be kept confidential and be destroyed after the completion of the research project.

(4) Thank you for answering the following questions. Please tick or circle the answers with 2B pencil attached and return this questionnaire in the enclosed self-addressed stamped envelop by November.

(5) This questionnaire is designed to collect some information about ... Please don't put your name on it. It is confidential. Please fill in the box or circle the relevant number.

(6) In order to provide better service to people who have bought our products, we designed this paper to ask for your opinion. Please return this paper to the person who gives this questionnaire after you have finished completing it.

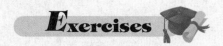

Exercises

I Please revise the following inappropriate questions in questionnaires and tell why.

1. In a typical month, how often do you shop in department store?

    ____ Never
    ____ Occasionally
    ____ Sometimes
    ____ Often
    ____ Regularly

2. Do you think that patriotic Chinese should buy imported autos when that would put Chinese labor out of work?

    ____ Yes
    ____ No
    ____ Don't know

3. Do you think it is the last straw?
4. Do you think the distribution of soft drinks is adequate?
5. Don't you think the result is satisfying?
6. Do you like to fly when you are traveling short distances?

II. Translate the following parts of a questionnaire from Chinese into English.

银行账户服务市场研究

_____女士/先生：您好！我叫_____，是 ABC 市场研究股份有限公司的访问员，我们是一家专门从事市场研究的公司。现在，我们正在本市进行一项有关银行服务的研究，希望能够听取您家里对银行账户服务选择有决定权的家庭成员的意见。请问他/她在家吗？

被访者姓名：_____ 问卷编号：_____
家庭详细地址：_____
联系电话（家庭电话/工作单位电话/BP 机/手机）：_____
访问员姓名：_____ 访问员编号：_____
访问日期：_____ 访问开始时间：_____ 访问结束时间：_____

过滤问卷

SQ1. 请问您是本地居民吗？
　　　是 ·· 1 → 继续
　　　不是 ·· × → 终止

SQ2. （出示卡片）请问您或您的家人有没有在以下行业工作的？
　　　广告/市场研究/公共关系公司或相关部门 ·············· ×
　　　媒体/出版社/新闻机构 ·· ×
　　　银行/保险/信托/证券基金等金融服务部门 ·············· ×
　　　以上皆无 ·· × → 继续

SQ3. 请问在过去 6 个月内，您有没有参加过任何形式的市场研究活动？
　　　有 ·· × → 终止
　　　没有 ·· 1

SQ4. （出示卡片）请问这张卡片上的哪个说法最适合描述您的年龄？
　　　25 岁以下 ·· × → 终止访问
　　　25～30 岁 ·· 1 → 检查配额
　　　31～35 岁 ·· 2 → 检查配额
　　　36～40 岁 ·· 3 → 检查配额
　　　40 岁以上 ·· × → 终止访问

SQ5. 记录性别：
　　　男 ·· 1 → 检查配额
　　　女 ·· 1 → 检查配额

SQ6. 您家里目前总共拥有几家银行的银行账户？
　　　只有1家 ……………………………………… 1→ 终止访问
　　　2家或以上 ……………………………………… 2

C1. （出示产品概念卡片）请问在您看过这个银行账户信息服务的介绍后，您对这项服务的感兴趣程度如何呢？（单选）
　　　非常感兴趣……………………………………… 1
　　　比较感兴趣……………………………………… 2
　　　感兴趣程度一般………………………………… 3
　　　不太感兴趣……………………………………… 4
　　　一点也不感兴趣………………………………… 5

C2. 请问您对"账户信息即时通"<u>感兴趣</u>的地方有哪些呢？还有呢？

C3. 请问您对"账户信息即时通"<u>不感兴趣</u>的地方有哪些呢？还有呢？

访问结束时间：　　　　　使用24小时制
　　　　　　　　　小时　　　分　　　　　年　月　日
（空格中不许有空白）　□□　　□□　日期 □□□□□□

　　非常感谢您的配合！再次介绍一下，我的名字是_____，ABC 市场研究股份有限公司的访问员。假如您对这次访问有什么疑问的话，请给我的公司打电话。垂询电话是：010-639××××。

III Writing practice.

Situational Writing 1

　　You are hired by the marketing research department of a shampoo company, and asked to prepare a questionnaire to determine household preference for shampoo products and to obtain information for a report on sales promotion of products of your company. You are required to use the principles of questionnaire design discussed in this chapter.
　　Draft an appropriate questionnaire.

Situational Writing 2

　　Several of your colleagues have fallen sick in recent months and the management want to know the reasons and take some measures to improve the staff's health. You are required to design a questionnaire to obtain information for them.

You want to find out: How many people work overtime; how people spend their free time; the diet pattern of the staff; what pressure people feel; if people would use physical exercise facilities if offered by the company; if people would be happy to pay for the exercises and how much they would like to pay.

Unit 16

Business Summary
商务概要

16.1 Introduction

Nowadays, businesspeople have to deal with masses of information, particularly after the popularization of computer and Internet, and sometimes they can only rely on someone else's summary of a situation, publication, or document to save time. They may be bored with a long report, and a fixed summary sheet before the text may help them see at a glance what the report is about and catch the main points.

Summary is defined as short version containing gist of something, and it is a shortened version of something that has been said or written, containing only the main points. Generally speaking, the summary is written in the producer's own words. To write a summary, the writer has to gather information, organize that information, and then present it in his own words.

16.2 Features of a Well-written Summary

(1) The content is accurate.

One of the basic purposes of business communication is to convey information. It is no exception with summarizing. Make sure the information is presented without error. First check the references and then check for typing errors.

(2) The summary is comprehensive and balanced.

The summary is usually used to help colleagues and supervisors make a decision, so all the information necessary should be covered. Although a summary is intended to be as brief as possible, the readers need a minimum amount of information to understand the situation or the issue.

(3) The sentence structure is clear, with good transitions.

When the sentence structure is clear and transitions are properly employed, the readers can easily understand the summary and move from one point to another.

16.3 Writing a Summary

1. **Step 1: Understand the Material to Be Summarized**

We must understand the material to be summarized to achieve accuracy. On first reading, it is difficult to extract the essentials and summarize them, so just read the material for the second or third time and sift out what you consider to be the main points.

2. **Step 2: Remove and Retain**

Summarizing requires the producer to select and retain the essential messages and remove unimportant details. The main points must be retained and some supporting materials can be taken away. In General, the supporting materials of examples, definitions, rephrasing and additions can be removed. Table 16-1 shows some clues of the above four categories.

Table 16-1 The clues for supporting materials

Category	Clues
Examples	For example...; For instance; e.g.; such as
Definitions	Be defined as...; This is...; This means...
Rephrasing	In other words; That is...; ...i.e....
Additions	Especially...; ...particularly...

The rules mentioned above can be further illustrated by the following examples (The words in bold type should be retained and the italicized words can be removed):

(1) **The central government needs to coordinate efforts by various departments**, *such as finance, taxation, poverty alleviation, education and even the police,*" **said Li.**
(**The italicized parts are examples of various departments and can be removed. The clue is "***such as***".**)

(2) **He says that since the reform and opening policy was introduced, China's regional income gap has not been enlarged, but narrowed.** *Take East China's Zhejiang province for example. In the past, local people refused to venture outside their own provinces to make money because they could not earn very much. But now they are rushing to other provinces, even to those in the west.*
(**The italicized part is an example and can be removed. The clue is "***take... for example***".**)

(3) **Fill out the application and obtain any necessary supporting documents**, *i.e. transcript, certification of student status letter, processing fees, etc.*
(**The italicized part is a rephrasing expression and can be removed. The clue is "***i.e.***".**)

(4) Now, Americans are waiting to see what direction the Supreme Court will take. Justices serve as long as they wish. *This means that the presidents who appoint them may leave a long-lasting influence on the court, and on American life.*
(**The italicized part is a definition and can be removed. The clue is "*this means*".**)

(5) Soil conservation, he pointed out, would require reductions in certain crops[1], *particularly the intertilled and consequently soil-depleting crops such as corn, soybeans, and dry peas.*
(**The italicized part is an addition. The clue is "*particularly*".**)

3. Step 3: Simplify or Shorten the Expressions

One feature of summarizing is to say the same thing in a simple way with fewer words. The retained parts then can be reorganized after the work of retaining and removing has been completed. Those long-winded phrases and sentences may be replaced with one or a few words without affecting the meaning and information conveyed.

The above rule can be further illustrated by the following sentences. The sentences have been rewritten in a simpler and shorter way but there is no change in meaning.

Original: At last his clients arrived at the restaurant, but they only choose small parts of the dishes to eat with neither interest nor enjoyment and then left early.
Rewritten: His clients finally arrived at the restaurant, only to pick at her food and leave early.

Original: In order to get this task finished this week, we must keep working hard all the time.
Rewritten: We must make a sustained effort to get this task finished this week.

Original: Some private business owners try every means to make friends with government officials in the hope that they could be given some privilege in doing business.[2]
Rewritten: To get more privilege in business, some private business owners try to make friends with government officials.

4. Step 4: Organize the Contents and Present a Logic and Coherent Summary

The producer does not need to include all the relevant information retained, and they also can condense two or more points into one sentence by reorganizing the materials.

The preparation of a business summary can be illustrated by the following example. The article is an introduction of people's life in Beijing.

✉ Sample 16-1

The life in China's capital has undergone remarkable **changes** since the founding of China in 1949 and nowadays **Beijingers have begun living "well-to-do" lives**, as shown in a decline in the Engel's coefficient.

The Engel's coefficient (proportion of income that goes into food) in Beijing **has dropped to 31.7 percent**, indicating that the lifestyle of residents in both urban and rural areas of the China's capital has **changed from being merely sufficiently fed and clothed, to comfortable**[3], Han Nuansheng, spokesman of the Beijing Bureau of Statistics, said recently.

The Engel's coefficient is a major indicator of the people's living standard.

According to the measure set by the Food and Agricultural Organization of the United Nations, an Engel's coefficient above 59 percent represents absolutely poverty; 50–59 percent, barely enough food and clothing; 40–50 percent, a "moderately well-off" standard of living; 30–40 percent, a "well-to-do" standard of living; and below 30 percent, a "wealthy" life.

The lowered Engel's coefficient explained why the traditional greeting used by Beijingers — "Have you eaten yet?" — is being heard less and less now. Eating is taking up a smaller and smaller proportion of Beijing residents' awareness.

Statistics show that **from 1978**, when China initiated its reform and opening-up drive, to 2003, **the per-capita disposable income of Beijing's urbanites increased from 365.4 yuan (44.02 US dollars) to 13,882.6 yuan (1,672.6 US dollars)**, 500 percent allowing for price fluctuations.[4] **Last year, farmers in the city's suburban area saw their per-capita pure income rise to 6,496.3 yuan (782.7 US dollars)**, up 800 percent from the 1978 level. The Engel's coefficient for farmers has plunged from 62.9 percent in 1978 to 31.7 percent in 2003.

Another symbol for the improved living standard of Beijingers is the **shift from a "kingdom of bicycles" to "a society of motor vehicle**," Han Nuansheng said.

Last year, Beijing's population of private vehicles topped one million for the first time, including 656,000 private cars. Since the start of 2004, Beijing has sold 38,000 motor vehicles per month on average, including 27,000 new vehicles.

There are, of course, also low-income earners in Beijing, Han said. **A social welfare system for low-income people was introduced in Beijing in 1997**. Last year it benefited 161,000 people in the urban area, involving 340 million yuan (40.96 million US dollars) and 67,000 people in the suburban area, involving 36 million yuan (4.3 million US dollars).

First we sift out the main points (they have been underlined as shown above), then we may list these points clearly, and finally we rearrange the essential points and rewrite the material to produce a clean copy. Though the original article does not have a title, we may give a title to the summary for the convenience of the reader. The following is the summary of the above article we make for reference.

Sample 16-2 (Improved Business Summary)

Beijingers Enjoy a Well-to-do Life

The life in Beijing has undergone remarkable changes and Beijingers have begun living "well-to-do" lives. The Engel's coefficient in Beijing has dropped to 31.7 percent, indicating that the lifestyle has changed from being merely sufficiently fed and clothed, to comfortable. According to the measure set by the Food and Agricultural Organization of the United Nations, an Engel's coefficient between 30–40 percent represents a "well-to-do" standard of living. Statistics show that from 1978 to 2003, the per-capita disposable income of Beijing's urbanites increased from 365.4 yuan (44.02 US dollars) to 13,882.6 yuan (1,672.6 US dollars). Another symbol for the improved living standard of Beijingers is the shift from a "kingdom of bicycles" to "a society of motor vehicle". Last year, Beijing's population of private vehicles topped one million, including 656,000 private cars. A social welfare system was also introduced for low-income people in 1997.

16.4 Checklist and List for Speech

Checklist and notes for speech are the results of the development of business communication and they are two realistic summaries designed to suit specific purposes.

1. Checklist

Checklist, sometimes known as code of practice, is a list of names, items, or points for consideration or action. Enumeration is required in such a summary. When preparing a checklist, we should bear in mind the consistency of expression, and it is recommended that verbs be used at the start of each point. As regards a formal code of practice, an introduction is usually added.

The following is a sample checklist produced by a survey organization and can serve as a model.

 Sample 16-3

Risk Survey Checklist

Policy

Does the company have a health and safety policy?
Is a copy of the signed and dated statement of intent displayed?
Is the policy reviewed annually?

Risk Assessment

Have risk assessments been carried out?
Have the findings of the assessments been passed onto employees?
Have adequate control measures been implemented?

Audits

Are internal safety audits carried out?
Are details of these audits recorded?
Are external safety audits carried out?

Signage

Is a copy of the health & safety abstract law poster displayed?
Is health and safety signage on the premises adequate?
Are the premises registered with the local enforcing authority?
Is a copy of a your Employers Liability Insurance displayed?

Accident History

Is an accident book held?
Are F2508 Forms available?

2. List for Speech

When a businessman is expected to make a speech at a meeting, it is necessary for him to prepare a summary of the report in advance to avoid the possible embarrassment of forgetting some points, and such a summary is called a list or notes for speech. The rules for the production of a list for speech are similar to that of a checklist. The following is a list of points for the president of a company to make a speech at a meeting to introduce his firm to prospective investors.

 Sample 16-4

Brief Introduction of the Business

1. Introduction

- The world's largest motorcycle rental and touring company.
- Marketing the "American Dream" to destination minded vacationers, businessmen and motorcyclists.

- A recreation and tourist organization that is pioneering a new industry, motorcycle tourism.
- A fleet of well over 2000 Harley-Davidson motorcycles out of its 35 worldwide rental facilities.

2. Executive Management

- The executive management team conceived the business as a natural extension of their own personal interests and marketing expertise.
- They invested more than ten years in the research of market potential, demographics, structure, and distribution.

3. Marketing and Demographics

- The Company has developed an extensive marketing network of international and domestic tour operators, wholesalers, and business partners in the travel, entertainment and vacation service industry.
- Business partners are contractually committed to promote and market the rental and tour programs.

4. Company Growth Plans

- The expansion of corporate and franchise rental locations around the world.
- The business segment expansion includes recreational rental vehicles.
- To become the most recognized adventure and recreational rental and motorcycle tour company in the world.

New Words and Expressions

gist	n.	要点，要旨，依据
comprehensive	a.	全面的，广泛的
transition	n.	转变，转换，过渡
transcript	n.	誊本，抄本，副本
intertill	v.	中耕，间作
soybean	n.	大豆
peanut	n.	花生

pea	n.	豌豆
privilege	n.	特权，特别待遇
checklist	n.	清单
signage	n.	信号，标志
vacationer	n.	度假者，休假者
franchise	n.	特权，授权，专营权
segment	n.	部分，部门
at a glance		一瞥，一眼
poverty alleviation		扶贫
soil depleting		土壤耗竭
the Engel's Coefficient		恩格尔系数
prospective investors		潜在投资者
motorcycle rental and touring company		摩托车租赁和旅游公司

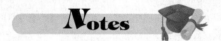

Notes

1. Soil conservation, he pointed out, would require reductions in certain crops... 他指出，土壤保护需要降低某些作物的产量……

2. Some private business owners try every means to make friends with government officials in the hope that they could be given some privilege in doing business. 一些私营企业主利用各种方式和政府官员交往，希望能够在生意上得到某些优惠待遇。

3. The Engel's coefficient (proportion of income that goes into food) in Beijing has dropped to 31.7 percent, indicating that the lifestyle of residents in both urban and rural areas of the China's capital has changed from being merely sufficiently fed and clothed, to comfortable... 北京的恩格尔系数（食品占收入的比重）下降了31.7%，意味着中国首都城乡居民的生活已经实现了从温饱到小康的转变……

4. Statistics show that from 1978, when China initiated its reform and opening-up drive, to 2003, the per-capita disposable income of Beijing's urbanites increased from 365.4 yuan (44.02 US dollars) to 13,882.6 yuan (1,672.6 US dollars), 500 percent allowing for price fluctuations. 统计显示，从1978年中国开始改革开放到2003年，北京城市居民的人均可支配收入从365.4元（44.02美元）增加到了13,882.6元（1,672.6美元），扣除价格因素增长了500%。

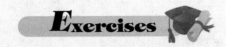

1. Summarize the following article with one paragraph.

China's growing income gap is likely to trigger social instability after 2010 if the government finds no effective solutions to end the disparity.

An expert team at the Ministry of Labour and Social Security recently delivered the warning in a newly designed system detailing the populous country's statistics for income distribution.

Calling upon the government to keep alert over growing income disparities, the team found that the income gap in China has been expanding since 2003, despite some measures in place to increase income among those in poverty.

The team, headed by Su Hainan, president of the Ministry's Income Research Institute, has used "blue-, green-, yellow- and red-lights" to predict income disparity trends. The yellow light warns the government to be alert and the red one means the disparity is totally unacceptable.

"Income disparity in China is in the yellow-light area now," the team warned. We are going to hit the red-light scenario after 2010 if there are no effective solutions in the next few years.

Su's team found little reason to be optimistic about bridging the urban-rural income gap. Incomes in cities are growing at 8-9 per cent annually, while the rate in rural regions has averaged a year-on-year growth of 4-5 per cent.

The National Bureau of Statistics forecasted over the weekend that per capita urban income this year is likely to surpass 10,000 yuan (US$ 1,234).

Last year, the average annual income for rural residents reached 2,936 yuan (US$ 355), far behind that of urban residents, whose average annual income was 9,422 yuan (US$ 1,139) in 2004.

The team found that income disparity in rural areas is very close to the "red light". Average farmers earned 3.39 times as much as officially-designated poor farmers in 2004. In 1992, the disparity was only 2.45 times as much.

"The government's top priority is to make those farmers still in poverty earn more," the team concludes in a report.

A gap also exists among the urban residents. "And the gap is growing," added Xu Fengxian, a researcher with the Chinese Academy of Social Sciences.

He said incomes of laid-off workers are decreasing while the wallets of private business owners have been fattening at incredible rates.

The government has already become concerned by the growing income disparity.

II **Please summarize the following passages into one passage within the length of 60 words.**

A department store is a very large shop which is divided up into a number of different departments, each one specializing in its own products. It is from this division into departments that it gets its name.

You would expect to find in such stores a separate department for food, clothing, shoes, furniture and so on. Usually a department store is housed in its own building which may be several storeys high.

The range of goods offered to the shopping public is very large indeed, and runs into several thousand different items. Such stores, however, are only found in towns and cities where there is a large buying public to support them.

They employ many staff and are very expensive to run. To pay for all these expenses they need to have a very high sales turnover. To achieve this they have to attract many shoppers to buy from them. You can readily see that a village or small town just doesn't have enough shoppers to support a department store.

Needing a large sales turnover, does not necessarily mean that high prices have to be charged. In fact, with department stores the reserve is often the case. They are usually very competitive in their pricing, relying on these competitive prices, goods display, pleasant shopping conditions and efficient service to attract plenty of customers. In this way they achieve a high sales turnover.

III **Translate the following code of practice into English.**

1. 与客户及潜在客户的关系
   (1) 为客户及潜在客户间提供最优的服务。
   (2) 除非授权，绝不透露客户及潜在客户的姓名。
   (3) 始终保守客户及潜在客户的秘密。

2. 管理者与队伍成员的关系
   (1) 始终相信应给予有能力的同事及队伍成员以合适的报酬。
   (2) 创造专业的、有益的工作氛围。
   (3) 强调合作工作和相互尊重。
   (4) 保证给予员工公平报酬。
   (5) 坚持机会均等的原则。

3. 我们成员的责任
   (1) 遵守香港及他们工作、居住地区的法律。
   (2) 遵守第一部分所列关于与客户及潜在客户间关系的行为标准。
   (3) 负责，合作，保持客户的信任。

IV Prepare a list for the following speech.

Good morning. As families across the country enjoy the summer, Americans can be optimistic about our economic future. In the past four years, our economy has been through a lot: we faced a stock market decline, a recession, corporate scandals, an attack on our homeland, and the demands of an ongoing war on terror.

To grow the economy and help American families, we acted by passing the largest tax relief in a generation. And today, thanks to the tax relief and the efforts of America's workers and entrepreneurs, our economy is strong and growing stronger.

This past week, we learned that America added over 200,000 new jobs in July. Since May of 2003, we've added nearly 4 million new jobs. The unemployment rate is down to 5 percent, below the average of the 1970s, 1980s and 1990s. And more Americans are working today than ever before in our nation's history.

Recent economic reports show that our economy is growing faster than any other major industrialized nation. Small businesses are flourishing. Workers are taking home more of what they earn. Real disposable personal income has grown by over 12 percent since the end of 2000. Inflation is low and mortgage rates are low. And over the past year, the home ownership rate in America has reached record levels.

The tax relief stimulated economic vitality and growth and it has helped increase revenues to the Treasury. The increased revenues and our spending restraint have led to good progress in reducing the federal deficit. Last month we learned that the deficit is now projected to be US$ 94 billion less than previously expected. I set a goal of cutting the deficit in half by 2009, and we are ahead of pace to meet that goal.

To continue creating jobs and to ensure that our prosperity reaches every corner of America, we're opening markets abroad for our goods and services. This past week, I was proud to sign the Central American-Dominican Republic Free Trade Agreement. This historic agreement will level the playing field for America's workers and farmers, and open up a market of 44 million customers for products made in the United States.

To keep our economy growing we also need affordable, reliable supplies of energy. Next week in New Mexico, I'll sign a bipartisan energy bill that encourages conservation, expands domestic production in environmentally sensitive ways, diversifies our energy supply, modernizes our electricity grid and makes America less dependent on foreign sources of energy. And next Wednesday in Illinois, I'll sign a highway bill that will improve the safety of our roads, strengthen our transportation infrastructure and create good jobs.

Our economy is strong, yet I will not be satisfied until every American who wants to work can find a job. So this coming Tuesday I will meet with my economic team in Texas to discuss our agenda to keep the economy moving forward. As Congress considers appropriations bills this fall, we will work with the House and the Senate to ensure that taxpayer dollars are spent wisely, or not at all.

We need to make the tax relief permanent, end the death tax forever, and make our tax code simpler, fairer and more pro-growth. We'll continue working on Social Security reform. Social Security is sound for today's seniors, but there's a hole in the safety net for our younger workers, so I'll work with the Congress to strengthen Social Security for our children and grandchildren. I'll continue to press for legal reform to protect small businesses, doctors and hospitals from junk lawsuits. And we will work to make health care more affordable and accessible for all Americans.

The American economy is the envy of the world and we will keep it that way. We will continue to unleash the entrepreneurial spirit of America, so more of our citizens can realize the American Dream. Thank you for listening.

Unit 17

Employment Writing
就业写作

To find the right people, the various company recruiters make many advertisements and conduct tens of thousands of interviews every year. Before conducting the interviews, the recruiters usually publicize the job descriptions and ask for resumes of the interested candidates. To find the opportunities for advancement, good pay, and excellent benefits, people might apply to these positions and send out their CVs. Those who look the best on paper may be invited to attend the interviews.

In this chapter, we will focus on the writing involved in the employment process, and it includes the writing of a job description for the employer, and the preparation of an application letter and a resume.

17.1 Job Description

The job description is designed to tell the prospective candidates the tasks and requirements for the position and it often covers the description of the mission, the specific tasks, requirements on education, experience, various skills needed, and additional information. The employer often puts a brief introduction of the company at the beginning of the job description to attract the job seekers or as an effort to build a sound image.[1] The above features can be illustrated by the following samples.

 Sample 17-1

ABC is one of the world's leading providers of microprocessor cards, and a major supplier of point-of-sale terminals. The company has 25 years' experience in smart card innovation and leads its industry in security technology and open operating systems.

Receptionist/Secretary (Beijing)

Primary Responsibilities:

— Provide receptionist service to Beijing Office.
— Pick up phone calls, make appointment, receive visitors, record and file documents.
— Travel arrangement including administration and purchase of tickets, hotel reservations, preparation and calculation of travel orders and the corresponding payments.[2]
— Post service including local express service, EMS, DHL handling.
— Provide secretarial support to related teams (HR, Sales, Marketing). Coordinate the operation of different departments independently by taking initiative.
— Meeting arrangement upon requirement.
— Prepare presentation materials.
— Organize customer event.
— Consolidate data and help administration dept to coordinate schedule.

Education/Skill Requirements:

— University degree or equivalent, major in English is preferred.
— At least 1 year's experience as a secretary.
— Self-motivated, could work under pressure and independently.
— Strong in telecommunication skill and interpersonal communication skill.
— Good team spirit, quick learner.
— Result oriented, self-discipline.

 Sample 17-2

Career in Motion   Job Opportunities

At General Motors, opportunities for talented people exist all over the world. From the design and engineering of new state-of-the-art assembly plants in Singapore and China, to developing new marketing programs for all of Europe, you can go as far as your hard work and determination will take you.

Job Posting for Senior Buyer
Apply for this position
GENERAL INFORMATION

Requisition ID: CYS-904004   **Date Posted**: 15/11/06
Job Family: Purchasing   **Location**: Southeast Michigan

JOB SUMMARY

Responsible for purchase of all or a specific portion of production/nonproductive materials, suppliers, machinery and services. Work is of a difficult nature involving considerable amount of initiative and a high level of independent judgment. Instruct, train and assign work to a group of employees.

JOB RESPONSIBILITIES

Analyze purchase orders to determine most appropriate source; Negotiate prices and terms with supplier; Negotiate settlements on rejected and defective materials; Ensure timely delivery of materials and services purchased. Adhere to corporate purchasing and accounting policies and procedures; establish a course of action to accomplish projects. Keep abreast of current product developments; Coordinate input from customers to better understand customer needs. Respond to changing market price trends...

JOB REQUIREMENTS

Knowledge of basic math; Oral and written communication skills; Mechanical background; Relatively high level of analytical ability; Demonstrated technical and professional skills in job related areas; Knowledge of computer software; Appropriate interpersonal styles.

EDUCATION REQUIREMENTS

Bachelor degree or equivalent training.

17.2 Job Application Letter

17.2.1 Introduction

The job application letter is a form of advertising and the writer needs to stimulate the reader's interest before showing how he can satisfy the organization's needs. The writer is suggested to organize the letter like a sales one and emphasize the reader benefits. Make sure the style projects confidence; a person cannot hope to sell a potential employer on his merits unless he truly believes in them himself.[3] Of course, the writer needs to adjust the tone when seeking jobs abroad because blatant self-promotion is considered bad form in some cultures.

In the application letter, the writer should show that he knows something about the organization. By showing some homework that has been done, the writer can capture the reader's attention and convey his desire to join the organization. The more the writer can learn about the organization, the better he will be able to write about how his qualifications fit its needs.

During the preparation, the writer had better find out the name, title, and department of the person he is writing to. Reaching and addressing the right person is the most effective way to gain attention.

17.2.2 Preparation of an Application Letter

1. Write the Opening Paragraph

In response to an announced job opening, no special attention-getting effort is needed since the writer is invited to apply. While as to the letter to an organization that has not announced a job opening, it should start by capturing the reader's interest. In some respects, the latter one stands a better chance of receiving attention.

To get the attention, the writer may describe his understanding of the job's requirements and then show how well his qualifications fit the job. He may also mention the name of a person known to and highly regarded by the reader, or refer to publicized activities, achievements or changes.

Besides, the applicant is expected to state his reason for writing and identify the desired job area.

2. Summarize the Key Selling Points

The body section presents the applicant's strongest selling points in terms of their potential benefit to the organization. The applicant may spell out his key qualifications, together with supporting evidence. Evidence of such job-related qualities as to be diligent, learn quickly and get along well with people should also be presented.

However, the applicant is recommended to mention only the qualifications that indicate he can do the job, and not to repeat the facts presented in his resume.

3. Write the Closing Paragraph

This section is designed to ask the reader for a specific action and to make a reply easy. The applicant may state his phone number and the best time to reach him to make convenience for the reader. He also can refer again to his strongest selling point in this part.

In brief, the most effective application letter is the one that can help the reader create interest in the applicant and a desire to interview him.

The above tips can further be illustrated by the following samples.

Sample 17-3

February 14th, 2016

Ms. Alice Green, Store Manager
Carefour
Building 8, Red Star Street
Dongcheng District, Beijing

Dear Ms. Green,

You want retail clerks and managers who are accurate, enthusiastic, and experienced. You want someone who cares about customer service, who understands merchandising, and who can work with others to get the job done. When you are ready to hire a manager trainee or a clerk who is willing to work toward promotion, please consider me for the job.

Working as clerk and then as assistant department manager in a large department store has taught me how challenging a career in retailing can be. Moreover, my AA degree in retailing (including work in such courses as retailing, marketing, and business information system) will provide your store with a well-rounded associate. Most important, I can offer Carefour Dongcheng Store more than my two years' of study and field experience: You will find that I am interested in every facet of retailing, eager to take on responsibility, and willing to continue learning throughout my career. Please look over my resume to see how my skills can benefit your store.

I understand that Carefour prefers to promote its managers from within the company[4], and I would be pleased to start out with an entry-level position until I gain the necessary experience. Do you have any associate positions opening up soon? Could we discuss my qualifications? Please phone me any afternoon at about 5 p.m. at (010) 82206139 to let me know the day and time most convenient for you.

Sincerely yours

Lenard Dong

Sample 17-4

Dear Mr. Wood,

Your advertisement in this morning's paper for a manager of pubic relations appeals to me, and I found that your advertisement emphasizes such qualifications of an applicant as being cooperative, innovative and aggressive. And my experience and qualifications show that I am the right person you are looking for.

The enclosed résumé indicates my experience in the area of public relations and management communications. It seems to me that this experience, together with my education, well equips me with ideal preparation to assume the role of the manager of pubic relations in firms as yours. Most recently, I was manager of ABT Chemical Corporation, manufacturing products closely allied to your own, so I am quite familiar with the kinds of issues and problems that your public relations people have to deal with.

I would like to call your attention to page 2 of my résumé, on which I describe my concept of public relations. And I am most eager to carry out my concept to prove it to you.

Although I am satisfied with my job and colleagues, I still see no opportunity in the near future to direct a full-scale public relations program. I hope to join your company where I can assume this broader responsibility.

May I have a privilege of an interview? If it is possible, Please contact me at 622 ××××.

Sincerely yours

17.3 Curriculum Vitae

A curriculum vitae (CV), also known as résumé in American English, is a summary of a person's education, employment, and job qualifications. A good CV can convey the specific qualities that employers seek and the purpose of it is to get you an interview.

17.3.1 Format of CV

In terms of layout, the objective is to make the information easy to grasp, so the applicant may employ the following techniques.

- Break up the text by using headings that call attention to various aspects of the background.
- Underline or capitalize key points.
- Set them off in the left margin.
- Use indented lists to itemize the most important qualifications.

Generally, there are two main formats: the chronological résumé and the functional one. A chronological résumé is to start from the present and go back in time or begin at the start of one's career and go forward in time, while a functional CV stresses the applicant's attributes and skills and uses headings that appropriately demonstrate the individual's qualifications. The chronological CV is the most familiar layout, and it is typically grouped under several headings. Before moving on to each specific section, we would like to show the following sample.

 Sample 17-5

Curriculum Vitae

Objective

Accounting management position in businesses specializing in foreign trade.

Personal Data

Name: Ronnie Cheng   Gender: female   Height: 163 cm
Marital Status: single   Date of Birth: Sep. 20, 1975   Tel: 010 – 89099738
MP: 13336789421   E-mail: ronniecheng@yahoo.com

Education

1997.9 – 1999.6   Master of Economics, Minnesota State University
1995.3 – 1997.7   BBA, Accounting, Nanjing University

Working Experiences

2001.3 – present   Beijing Horizon Import and Export Co., Ltd.
 ★ Prepare accounting reports for the company
 ★ Audit financial transactions with suppliers in Beijing
 ★ Negotiated joint-venture agreements with suppliers in Hebei
2000.10 – 2001.2   Merchandise Support Team of Oriental Home (Beijing)

Highlights of Qualifications

- Excellent oral and writing skills, namely, be able to negotiate with foreign counterparts without difficulties and can write business letters appropriately and free of errors.
- Conversant with such office softwares as Word, Excel, Powerpoint, etc.
- Familiar with economics and international trade theories and practices. Be able to design a well structured and complete trade contract on the basis of the related laws and terms.
- Capable of strict accounting and budget control, with the certificate of a public accountant.

Intercultural Qualifications

- Born in China, and studied in US
- Fluent in Chinese and English
- Traveled extensively in China and US

17.3.2 Preparation of a Résumé

With the help of the above example, we may see a CV generally includes the following parts.

1. Personal Data

This part is made up of the applicant's address and telephone number, date of birth, marital status and other necessary personal data. The first thing an employer needs to know is who the applicant is and where he can be reached. Many résumé headings are just the name and address centered at the top of the page as shown in the following sample. The applicant needs not to include the work résumé or CV but if he has a specific job in mind, he can do this as shown in the above sample. No matter what headings employed, the applicant has to make sure the reader can tell easily who he is and how to communicate with him

2. Career Objective

Some experts argue that the applicant need not state the objective since it is obvious from his qualifications, while others point out that doing so may help the reader categorize the applicant. If the applicant decides to state his job objective, he had better make his objective as specific as possible and avoid leaving the reader any impression that he will soon move on to another organization or try for the boss's job. If the applicant has two or more types of qualifications, he had better prepare two or more separate résumé, each with a different job objective.

3. Education

If the applicant is still in school or has just graduated, education is probably the strongest selling point. The educational background should be presented in depth. This section can be given a heading as "Education", "Professional College Training" or "Academic Preparation". The applicant may begin with the school he most recently attended, list for each school the name and location, the term of enrollment, the major and minor fields of study, significant skills and abilities that have been developed, and the degrees or certificates. Besides, this part also includes off-campus training sponsored by business, industry or government.

4. Work Experience

In this section, the applicant lists his jobs in chronological order, with the current one first. This part may include any part-time, summer, or intern positions even if the jobs have no relation to the present career objective because the employer will see that you have the ability to get and hold a job.[5] However, the applicant must highlight the relationship between the previous responsibilities and the target field to serve the overall goal of getting that job.[6] When preparing this part, the following tips can be followed:

- Each listing includes the name and location of the employer;
- State the functional title before or after each job listing;
- Be honest about the positions, the companies and dates of employment;
- Devote the most space to the jobs that relate to the target position.

5. Relevant Skills

This section describes other aspects of the applicant's background that pertain to his career objective. The applicant may mention his command of another language, the ability to operate a computer, or other equipment. The applicant can even title a special section "Language Skills" or "Computer Skills" and place it near the "Education" or "Work Experience" section.

6. Additional Information

The academic transcripts, samples of work, or letters of recommendation might increase the applicant's chances of getting the job, so the applicant may offer to supply these on request at the end of the résumé.

The following is another sample curriculum vitae.

Sample 17-6

Leonard Tang

Gender: Male, Date of Birth: Mar 27, 1975, Degree: MA

PO Box 1887
No. 620 Gubei Rd
Shanghai, 200336
E-mail: timetide@yahoo.net
Tel: 021-633311××   MP: 13339××××××

Job Objective

I hope to work as legal assistant in a foreign-funded law firm. Willing to travel or relocate.

Summary of Qualifications

- Familiar with various laws, passed the National Bar Exam and qualified as a lawyer.
- Sound knowledge of laws related to international trade. Be able to compose trade contracts professionally.
- Able to work efficiently with information systems like Windows, Office (Word, Excel, Powerpoint, etc.), Photoshop, etc.
- Passed TEM 8, 1997. Be able to well translate Chinese legal documents into English.
- Good command of Japanese: can negotiate with Japanese counterparts fluently.

Working Experiences

2000.2 – present   **Shanghai Sino-star Imp. & Exp. Co., Ltd.**
Worked as a lawyer. Successfully settling two trade disputes.

1999.9 – 1999.12   **Shanghai Atlas Tiger Medical Imaging Systems Co., Ltd.**
Worked as a translator and a trade personnel involved in settling a claim case and in other importing activities; Assisted CEO of the company in setting up a JV with a local company.

1997 – 1999   Worked as a part-time interpreter or translator for Two Shanghai Foreign Investment and Trade Fairs.

Education

1997-2000   Shanghai Institute of Foreign Trade (SIFT)
                   MA degree in International Business English

Awards

- Won the "Bing Zhu Prize" and People's Scholarship (three times, SIFT, 1997-1999)
- Won the championship in the 1998 Winter Cross-country Race of SIFT (SIFT, 1998)
- Won the First Prize of "English Speaking Contest among Shanghai Universities" (1998)

College Activities

Sports: A key basketball team member of the SIFT graduates.
                   Champion of the '98 SIFT Cross-country Match.
Social activities: Organizer of Volunteers of SIFT.
                   Sponsor English Training for Personnel of the State-owned Enterprises in Shanghai.

Interests

Sports, Public Speaking, Reading, Travelling.
Related academic transcripts, and letters of recommendation are provided on request.

17.4 Job Offer and Acceptance

Job offer is a formal written document provided by an employer to a candidate selected for employment. It is designed to offer employment, and gives the job applicant an idea of what to expect. Usually, it contains information concerning the employment terms, such as the date employment is to start, the position the individual is being hired to perform, the agreed upon salary, benefits to be provided, etc.

The employer often requires the candidate to sign and return the letter as a formal acceptance, thus to get ready for a contract. However, an acceptance does not mean that a contract has been entered. The employer and the candidate still need to sign an employment contract to confirm the terms mentioned in the offer. Mostly, the acceptance part is prepared in advance by the employer, and sent together with the offer for the candidate to sign.

The following is a job offer and acceptance sample.

Sample 17-7

Sharon Associates
Expert Advisers to the Business of Medicine

Dear Adam,

We are very pleased to invite you to join Sharon Associates as a consultant in our Beijing Office. Every one agrees that you will be an excellent addition to the firm.

As a consultant, your responsibilities include working on assigned projects to gather information from secondary sources; designing, setting up, and conducting telephone interviews; preparing quantitative analyses; defining issues and solutions in the course of projects; writing presentation documents; presenting findings to fellow team members and clients; supporting and mentoring junior staff, and generally being an integral member of a team striving to meet client expectations.

The following is a revised outline of the terms of our intended offer.

Title: Consultant

Start date: April 22, 2015

Contract duration: two years, with the first two months being a trial period. Contract can be extended or made permanent at the end of two years.

Annual salary: RMB 20,000 per calendar month (based on 12 monthly payments per year)

Performance bonus: up to 15% of annual salary, depending on firm and employee performance

Full benefits totaling approximately 40% of annual salary will be provided additionally by Sharon Associates; these benefits include pension insurance, medical insurance, housing fund, heating subsidies, etc.

Paid holidays: 10 days each year, specific schedule to be finalized according to both Chinese and U.S. holiday schedules.

Paid personal vacation days: 12 days each year, flexible schedule. However, you must notify the Chief Representative at least 2 weeks ahead of time. If all of your vacation days are not used, up to 5 vacation days can be transferred to the following year. With each additional year of service, an extra day of vacation is added to a maximum of 20 days.

Annual reviews are conducted for all employees at the end of August, at which time salary and bonus may be adjusted and promotion may be awarded if warranted by your performance.

As a full time employee, you are prohibited from providing services to any other employer.

According to Chinese Law, the official contract needs to be validated and handled by a registered employment agent (such as FESCO). This agent may adjust certain language/terms to ensure compliance with Chinese law, and will also provide any additional employment documents that are required.

Adam, we are continuing to build Sharon Associates by bringing together the highest caliber of people to create superior value for our clients, and we are all convinced that you will be a superb addition to our firm. You mad a terrific impression on everyone in our Beijing office, and we are looking forward to having you join the SA family.

If you have any further questions, please do not hesitate to call or e-mail me. I can be reached at 212-789-7865 or roberthr@sharonassociates.com. To officially accept this offer, please endorse this letter in the space provided and mail a copy to us at the address listed on the previous page.

Very truly yours,

Tylon R. Robert
Director of Human Resources

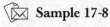

Sample 17-8

Acceptance

In accepting our revised offer of employment dated March 27, 2015, you certify your understanding that your employment will be based on an at-will basis and that neither you nor Sharon Associates has entered into a contract regarding the terms or the duration of your employment.

In Agreement by:

_____

Adam Yang

17.5 Reference Check

It is many companies' policy to conduct a reference check to complete a prospective employee's application and start providing him/her with job opportunities. Most companies write a letter and provide a reference check form for the former employer to fill in, and some just ask questions directly in the letter. From the perspective of the employee, he/she may know what the employers are concerned about, and then improve his/her performance. Below are two samples of reference check letters.

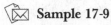 **Sample 17-9**

Dear Mr. Leonard,

Sorry to bother you. Please complete the following questions so DaliasTeam can complete Liara's application and start providing her with job opportunities.

What was the professional relationship with the candidate?

What job did the candidate perform?

Why did the candidate leave this position?

What can you tell me about his/her knowledge of the job?

What can you tell me about the candidate's work: (1) Ethic? (2) Initiative? (3) Attendance & Punctuality? (4) Communication Skills?

What can you tell me about the candidate's technical knowledge on the job?

What were the candidate's professional/technical weak points?

How did the candidate react to pressure and/or deadlines?

Why and how was the candidate hired and/or promoted into this role?

Were there any specific successes or projects the candidate was responsible for or was engaged in?

How did the candidate get along with peers, supervisors and subordinates?

Is he/she eligible for rehire?

Please let me know if you have additional questions. Thanks!

Yours Truly,

Rachael Gourley
Staffing Manager

 Sample 17-10

Dear Mr. Robin,

Greetings from Kelly Services! My apologies to bother you on a busy Monday but I do require some assistance from you. We have considered JackRasin for a vacancy with the company. It is our policy that we conduct a reference check of the employee and Jack has listed you as a former manager that he reported to. I would be grateful if you could spare me some of your time by completing the attached reference check form and emailing it back to me.

Best Regards,

Derrick Dass

The following is the attached reference check form.

	Name of Candidate:		Jack Rasin
	Date:		21-Mar.-15
	Referee:		Mr. Robin
	Company Name:		League International
	E-mail:		robintime@gmail.com
	Ref Check Done by:		Derrick Dass
	Reference Check Form		
		Ö	Comments
Dates of Employment	Checks		
	Doesn't Check		

Position Held/Duties	Checks		
	Doesn't Check		
Last Drawn Salary	Checks		
	Doesn't Check		
Attendance/Punctuality	Excellent		
	Acceptable		
	Below Average		
Work Habits	Industrious		
	Acceptable		
	Below Average		
Level of Supervision needed	Self Motivated		
	Occasional		
	Regular		
Learning Ability	Excellent		
	Good		
	Slow Learner		
Ability to Get along with Others	Excellent		
	Good		
	Needs Improvement		
Overall Quality of Work Performed	Checks		
	Doesn't Check		
Strengths			
Areas Needing Improvement			
Reason for Leaving	Checks		
	Doesn't Check		
Would You Rehire This Person?	Yes		
	No		
Comments			

Unit 17 Employment Writing

New Words and Expressions

recruiter	n.	招聘人员
microprocessor	n.	微处理器
file	v.	归档
initiative	n.	主动性，创造性
self-discipline	n.	自律
blatant	a.	公然的，明目张胆的
attribute(s)	n.	属性，品质，特征
major	n.	专业，主修
minor	n	辅修
smart card		智能卡
interpersonal communication		人际交往
team spirit		团队精神
selling points		卖点，亮点
well-rounded		全面的
chronological		按年代顺序排列的
marital status		婚姻状况
term of enrollment		入学年限
off-campus training		校外培训
quantitative analysis		定量分析
contract duration		合同期限
annual salary		年薪
performance bonus		业绩奖
annual review		年度测评
reference check		背景审查

Notes

1. The employer often puts a brief introduction of the company at the beginning of the job description to attract the job seekers or as an effort to build a sound image.　雇主经常在招聘信息开头对公司做简单介绍，以吸引求职者或用来树立良好的公司形象。
2. Travel arrangement including administration and purchase of tickets, hotel reservations,

preparation and calculation of travel orders and the corresponding payments. 差旅事务安排包括管理和买票、预订房间、差旅单据的准备和计算，以及相应的支出。

3. Make sure the style projects confidence; a person cannot hope to sell a potential employer on his merits unless he truly believes in them himself. 请记住你的举止要给人以自信的感觉；如果一个人不自信，他是不可能把自己的优势推销给他未来雇主的。

4. I understand that Carefour prefers to promote its managers from within the company... 我知道家乐福倾向于从本公司内部提拔经理……

5. This part may include any part-time, summer, or intern positions even if the jobs have no relation to the present career objective because the employer will see that you have the ability to get and hold a job. 本部分包括任何业余、暑期或实习职位，虽然这些工作和现在的求职目标没有关系，但雇主会发现你有能力找到并拥有一份工作。

6. However, the applicant must highlight the relationship between the previous responsibilities and the target field to serve the overall goal of getting that job. 但是，申请人必须突出以往的工作责任和现在目标职位的关系，以便获得那份工作。

Sentence Menu

1. **Job description**

   (1) The nation's leading manufacturer of household appliances requires the best people to join progressive team.

   (2) A well-established auto maker is seeking applications for position as: chief engineer.

   (3) Our company specializing in advertisement is seeking candidates with background in finance to join our highly professional team.

   (4) Priority will be given to individuals with the following qualifications.

   (5) Minimum of two years' experience in HR management field is required.

   (6) Please send your resume and relevant references to...

   (7) We will offer you excellent salary and benefits.

   (8) All your materials sent us will be treated confidential.

2. **Application letters**

   (1) Your advertisement in the latest issue of *Job Hunting* offers a most tempting job to a young man just out of college.

   (2) I learn from Mr. Smith that there is an opening for a journalist on the staff of the China Daily.

   (3) I am now referring to your advertisement for an accountant in the May 20th edition of China Times, and I am writing to apply for the position of... Please see my attached résumé and

relevant references.

(4) The attached résumé details my qualifications and experience in the business, which give me confidence to apply for this desirable job.

(5) It seems to me that this experience, together with my education, has given me ideal preparation to assume the role of the director of pubic relations in a firm such as yours.

(6) I have consistently built up and developed business relationship with many corporations, which helps me increase the sales volume.

(7) You want ... who are accurate, enthusiastic, and experienced and now I am the right person for the job.

(8) When you are ready to hire a ... who is ..., please consider me for the job.

(9) May I have the privilege of an interview? If you will let me know when it is convenient for you to see me, I will arrange my schedule accordingly.

(10) I hope you will give me an interview at your convenience.

(11) Please contact me at the address I give in my résumé.

3. Résumé

(1) Worked as ... in ...
(2) Majored in business and marketing management.
(3) Able to work efficiently/effectively with ...
(4) Conversant with/ adept at/proficient at ...
(5) Capable of ...
(6) Have gained rich experience of ...
(7) I am awarded ...
(8) I am well recognized for my outstanding academic achievements.
(9) I am interested in/good at ...
(10) Reference will be available on your request.
(11) Any needed references or a transcript will be submitted upon request.

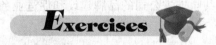

I **Fill in the blanks in the following application letter with the words given, and change the form where necessary.**

> qualify, note, each, interest, while, available, start, apply, position

Dear Sir or Madam:

I have noticed with _____ your ad for an English editor in June 6th China Daily. Because writing and publication work have long been interests of mine. I wish to _____ for this position.

I believe both my education and work experience _____ me for the job. In 2005 I earned my BA degree with a major in English and a major in journalism. _____ in school, I was the news editor of English Newsletter of Campus. Since graduation, I have written and edited business news in an English magazine.

Your ad _____ that applicants should be able to _____ immediately and be willing to relocate. I am in a _____ to do both of them.

I am currently _____ for an interview any weekday. I can be _____ at the phone call: 656-8865.

I am looking forward to hearing from you soon.

Yours faithfully

Ⅱ Translate the following job description into English.

某世界知名跨国制药公司招聘项目经理

工作职责：

- 对公司的战略项目进行可行性分析、计划、执行及评估；
- 建立并维护与卫生部、政府机构及医院重点客户的合作关系；
- 与公司其他部门沟通，共同推进公司的品牌建设和促进业务发展。

任职条件：

- MBA学历；
- 具有大型项目管理经验，有咨询公司工作经验者优先考虑；
- 良好的信息收集及分析、计划制订和项目执行能力；
- 出色的沟通、协调和人际技能；
- 出色的英文沟通能力；
- 良好的电脑操作技巧；
- 能适应频繁的出差。

III Writing practice.

Assume you had come across a job advertisement in a newspaper as follows:

Fortune 500 International Communication Networks Company Controlling Manager

Tasks:

- Planning
- Cost controlling
- Reporting to headquarter
- Coordinating internal audits
- Analyzing and commenting business development competencies
- Accounting (expert level)
- Audit (advanced)

Experience:

- Professional experience: controlling in international company or auditing
- Leadership

You are required to prepare a letter of application to this position.

IV Prepare a résumé for yourself and pay attention to the rules discussed in this chapter.

References
参考文献

[1] GEFFNER A B. Business English. Barrion's Educational Series, Inc., 2003.

[2] LEHMAN M C, HISMSTREET C A, BATY M W. Business communications. 11th ed. Dalian: Dongbei University of Finance & Economics Press, 1998.

[3] BOVEE L C, THILL V J. Business communication today. 5th ed. Upper Saddle River, NJ: Prentice Hall, 2006.

[4] BILBOW T G. Write for modern business. Beijing: Foreign Language Teaching and Research Press, 2001.

[5] FRAILEY L E. Handbook of business letters. Englewood Cliffs, NJ: Prentice Hall, 2010.

[6] LESIKAR V R. Basic business communication. 12th ed. Homewood, IL: Irwin, 2010.

[7] 陈苏东. 商务英语写作. 北京: 高等教育出版社, 2007.

[8] 陈永生, 赵金仲, 陈晓鹏, 等. 国际商务与合同. 北京: 华语教学出版社, 1999.

[9] 陈富强. 英文商业效用短信99篇. 香港: 香港商贸出版社, 1991.

[10] 曹菱. 商务英语信函. 北京: 外语教学与研究出版社, 2002.

[11] 范红. 英文商务写作教程. 北京: 清华大学出版社, 2004.

[12] 付美榕. 现代商务英语写作. 北京: 北京理工大学出版社, 2002.

[13] 高恩光, 戴建东. 英语写作新论. 上海: 上海外语教育出版社, 2004.

[14] 龚嵘, 徐迎捷. 商务文案与实务宝典. 上海: 华东理工大学出版社, 2007.

[15] 胡英坤, 车丽娟. 商务英语写作. 北京: 外语教学与研究出版社, 2013.

[16] 霍尔特, 桑普森. 国际商业书信. 北京: 外语教学与研究出版社, 1999.

[17] 普拉斯. 怎样写英文商业文书. 北京: 商务印书馆, 1998.

[18] 戚云方. 新编外经贸英语函电与谈判. 杭州: 浙江大学出版社, 2007.

[19] 王兴孙, 邬孝煜, 张春锟, 等. 新编进出口英语函电. 上海: 上海交通大学出版社, 2002.

[20] 松尾裕一. 轻松掌握英语商务书信110. 大连: 大连理工大学出版社, 2006.

[21] 王素清. 国际商务写作教程. 北京: 对外经济贸易大学出版社, 1995.

[22] 王关富, 蒋显璟. 实用商务英语写作. 北京: 对外经济贸易大学出版社, 2008.

[23] 边毅. 商务英语写作. 修订本. 北京: 北京交通大学出版社, 2006.

[24] 杨翠萍. 实用文秘英语文函. 西安: 西安交通大学出版社, 1999.

[25] 易露霞, 陈原. 实用英文商业信函. 广州: 广东经济出版社, 2004.

[26] 张春柏. 新编商务英语写作. 北京: 高等教育出版社, 2006.